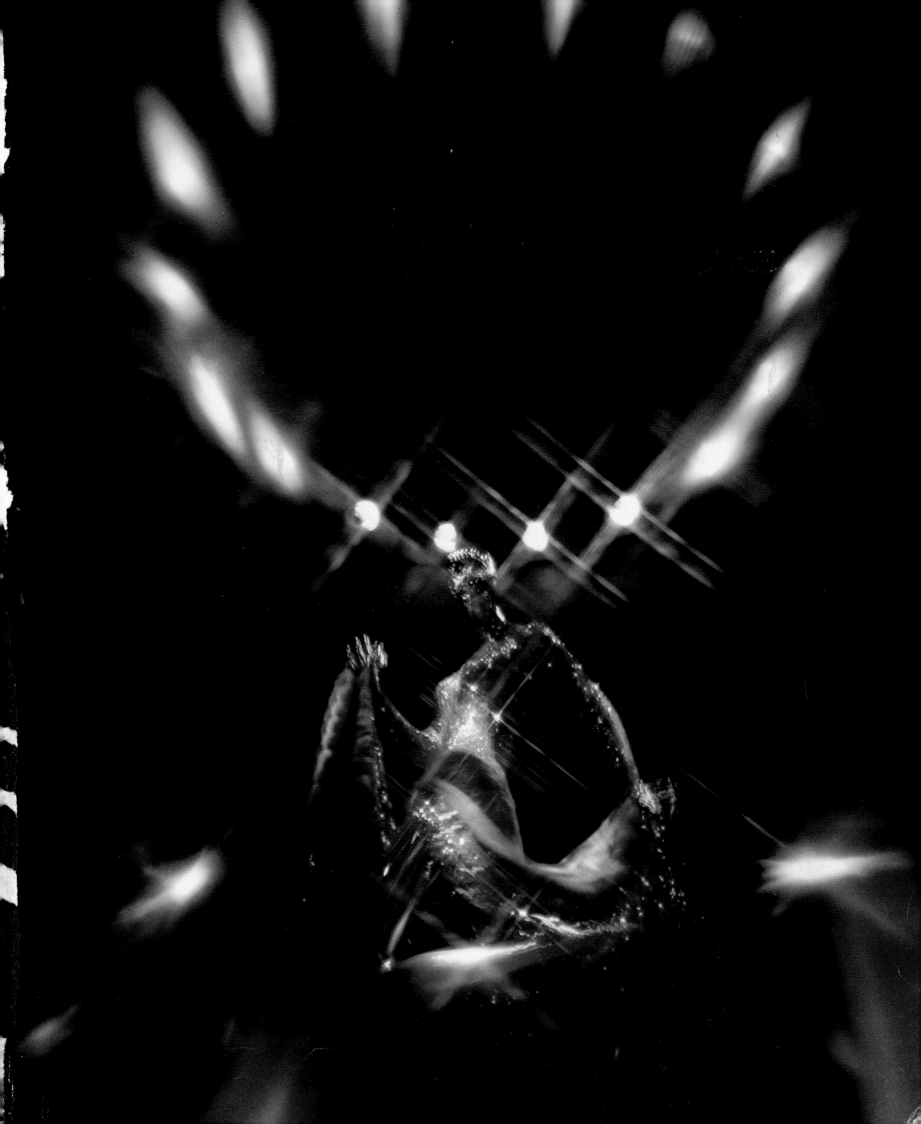

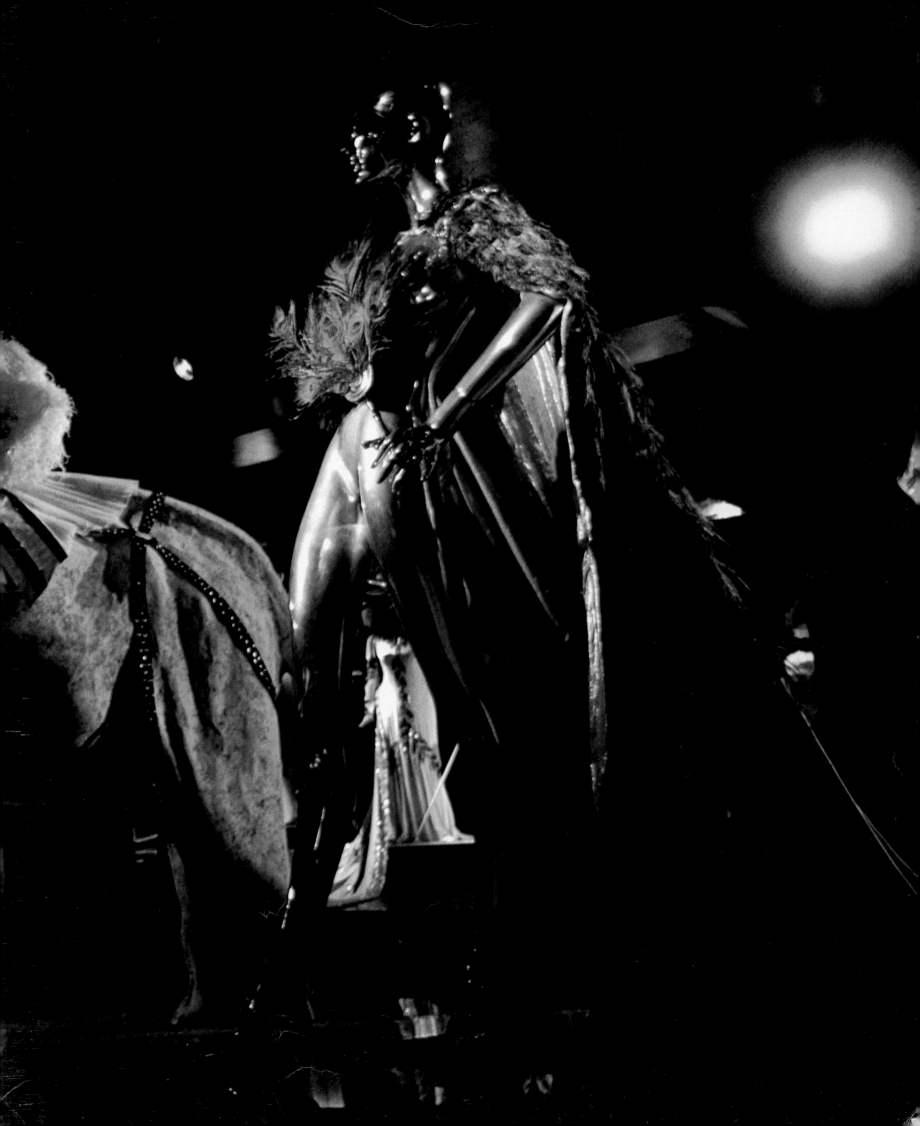

by Dale McConathy

with Diana Vreeland

Standard Book Number: 8109-1050-0
Library of Congress Catalogue Card Number: 76-12128
Published 1976 by Harry N. Abrams, Incorporated, New York,
in cooperation with the Metropolitan Museum of Art, New York
A Balance House Book

directed and produced by Marshall Lee

costume photographs by Keith Trumbo

A BALANCE HOUSE BOOK

Harry N. Abrams, Inc., Publishers, New York

with the cooperation of The Metropolitan Museum of Art, New York

Contents

Make it big!
DIANA VREELAND

What we remember most about Hollywood is the glamour and the romance they gave us. How they glorified their heroes and worshiped their heroines. Those beautiful women, those handsome men. For Hollywood, everything was larger than life, bigger than anything before or since. The diamonds were bigger, the furs were thicker; the silks, velvets, satins, chiffons were richer and silkier. There were miles of ostrich feathers, maribou, white fox, and sable; miles of bugle beads, diamante, and sequins. Hollywood was paved with glitter, shine, and glory. Everything was an exaggeration of history, fiction, and the whole wide extraordinary world. After all, nothing was too good for Hollywood, and for Hollywood nothing was too good for the people.

Hollywood was the world's back porch. At Hollywood's height, people didn't travel as much as they do now. But they were still curious about what was going on in the rest of the world. And they had a fantasy about what happened in history. Whoever you were, a secretary in Bavaria, a housewife in South Dakota, you went to the movies—and it was the biggest, most important thing that ever happened in your life. You paid ten or twenty-five cents and you related to Salome, Cleopatra, Camille, or Catherine, Empress of all the Russias. To hell with relating to the lady next door. That was the essence of the movies: the magic wrought by Hollywood design.

Can you imagine the excitement of settling down in your seat in one of those mystical city movie palaces—the dazzle of chandeliers, the carpets you waded through to get to your seat, those enormous organs that pumped out the music, and the flashy stage shows that came on before the movies? And then up there on the screen was Rudolph Valentino or Gloria Swanson. What a guy! What a girl! What could be more fantastic! You forgot yourself. You forgot where you were. You dreamed. Your fantasies came to life.

And those big dramatic moments in the movies that we all remember! Who could be more romantic than Greta Garbo playing Queen Christina? Garbo was unbelievably beautiful no matter what she wore. For Queen Christina, she dressed as a man. By tradition, only men could inherit the throne of Sweden, so Christina rode through the snow-bound countryside like some wonderful cavalier. Or when Mae Murray waltzed with John Gilbert in *The Merry Widow* and they took that famous dip and her bird of Paradise plumes almost swept the floor. That was the most dashing and exciting dance sequence in the history of film. At least, I remember it that way.

Or when Scarlett creates from sheer will *that* dress out of the dining room curtains—the dress in which she says, "Never, never again will I be hungry." The dress in which she walks away and survives, survives, survives. That is the real spirit of the American Woman. That's drama. That's triumph. That's *Gone with the Wind*.

"Make it big. Do it right. Give it class"—MGM's motto—was the motto of Hollywood. Nothing was too good for the beautiful women who played those extraordinary roles. Nothing but the best —the best lighting man, the best makeup man, the best hairdresser, the best dressmaker, all backed up by the producer and director, who also backed up the stars. It was all an extraordinary game of doing everything to utmost perfection. Those people demanded the top and they got it. That's why the costumes in the pages that follow are not just a lot of old clothes. The fact is that they were magnificently designed from the beginning and beautifully made of superb materials and that's why they are still perfection today. Hollywood overflowed with great designers—Adrian, Plunkett, Banton, Irene Sharaff, Helen Rose, Jean Louis, and many, many others—who made exquisite clothes for a Milky Way of gorgeous stars.

These costumes made the movies thick with excitement, filled them with a dizzying, heady atmosphere that meant both danger and desire, and sometimes total charm.

What could be more perfect than the costumes Adrian designed for *Marie Antoinette,* starring Norma Shearer? They have the most beautiful lamé and lace and tulle, with scrolls and festoons— designed of total wonderment. Norma Shearer wore panniers six feet across and skyscraping court wigs that were draped with pearls and massed with roses and diamond stars! Nothing was too good for Adrian. He demanded the most luxurious fabrics and the most sumptuous embroidery.

Much of the money the studios brought in at the box office was spent on the costumes—thousands of yards of silk velvet, forests of bolts of chiffon, cartons of glittering lamé. The fabrics they used simply aren't available any more. And they lavished those extraordinary fabrics not just on stars but on whole production numbers. They heaped hand embroidery, beading, and appliqué on the dresses as if they were nothing. And who has seen such finishing, such attention to detail?

When I think of detail, I think of Travis Banton's marvelous beaded dress for Marlene Dietrich in *Angel*—like a million grains of golden caviar. That is one of the most beautiful dresses ever. Banton, who was Paramount's big designer, had a great feeling for workmanship. It showed in his designs for Marlene Dietrich and others and certainly in the dresses he did for Mae West—dresses on which the embroidery is like a hard crust with the most wonderful detail.

Mae West definitely stood for "Them's that has 'em, wears 'em." She loved the big time, she loved big guys with big muscles—lots of white fox, lots of ostrich feathers, lots of diamonds, lots of everything. She still does. The world loves her for being what she is. There's nothing wrong with Mae West.

I don't think you can really understand the effect those designs had on the actresses until you've seen the costumes. Can you imagine how they felt surrounded by real chinchilla and satin and how it must have felt to touch the embroidery so much like jewels? Why, they must have felt like the most important women on earth. And in a way they were.

I can remember the photographic sitting for *Vogue* that Dick Avedon and I did with Plisetskaya, the Russian dancer. She came to the studio straight from the ballet. It was the middle of the night, but it was the only time she could be photographed. She arrived and she looked so tired. All the beauty had gone out of her face. But when she saw the furs we'd brought in and the champagne and the white lilacs, she was another creature. She was transformed. She stretched out her beautiful arms to touch the furs and to caress them. She put the sables to her cheek and made a delighted sound —like some small Russian bird, a dove perhaps. She didn't speak English and I didn't speak Russian. I pointed to the lipsticks in beautiful order on the dressing table and said, "For you. For you." She was like a hungry child—feeding herself with our attention. What she gave to the camera that night!

I think it must have been that way for Garbo. What a lot Adrian poured into his clothes for her! Garbo and Adrian were an extraordinary combination. He dressed her as the great heroines of history and fiction. She never ceased to inspire him, and I don't think you could find more beautiful costumes than those.

Once, long after Adrian had left Hollywood, I had lunch with him. He never mentioned those days at MGM. I think it had broken his heart to leave there. Somehow the subject of Garbo came up and I asked him what gave her that special quality. He thought for a long time and then answered me in a voice I shall always remember. "She has a very erotic atmosphere," Adrian said. And no more. How much was contained in that one sentence.

That was glamorous, romantic Hollywood.

The ruby slippers, the trenchcoat, and the lion's suit

When James T. Aubrey, Jr., became president of MGM in 1969, he needed money and he needed it fast. For his next board meeting, Aubrey had to raise $1,500,000 from one day to the next. He got the cash overnight by selling off some of MGM's assets to a West Coast auctioneer—warehouses of costumes, furniture, *objets,* carriages, vintage cars, military tanks, and even a landlocked showboat, *Cotton Blossom.* As certainly as the year of auctions at Versailles after the Revolution had ended the *ancien régime* in France, the ten days of auctions at Culver City, California, and the private sales that followed them, marked the end of the old Hollywood. That year MGM, the former giant of the American studios, lost $8,288,000 at the box office. Aubrey turned the forty-six-year-old studio from film-making to real estate. And he covered the deficit by selling most of the assets, land, cameras, and equipment, as well as costumes and props, for a total of $9,801,000.

Six years later—largely as a result of the *Romantic and Glamorous Hollywood Design* exhibition, organized by Diana Vreeland for the Costume Institute of New York's Metropolitan Museum of Art—Hollywood crafts, most notably the splendid and extravagant costumes, again were coming into their own. The exhibit of 146 spectacular costumes captured the magical fascination of the world that was Hollywood at its height. At the core of the exhibition were the MGM costumes, ferreted out by Diana Vreeland and her staff after almost a year's research. Within a year after the opening of the Metropolitan exhibition, Hollywood costume had become the subject of a series of shows across the United States, and in Paris and Teheran.

The 800,000 people who attended the New York exhibition had moved through the crowded, color-charged galleries with awe and excitement—almost a religious fervor. The great success of that exhibition—extended twice to run almost a year in all—was unprecedented. For many, it was clearly a sentimental journey; for others, a splendid anatomy of what made Hollywood romantic and glamorous. One visitor exclaimed as she neared the portion of the gallery devoted mainly to Greta Garbo: "I never thought I'd get so close to a star!" For the young, fascinated by actors and directors, taken with films perhaps seen only on television, the exhibit awakened a new sense of the great care and extravagance lavished on the visual object in the most powerful days of The Hollywood Dream Factory. All in all,

the exhibit was an extraordinary phenomenon that created a new awareness of the movies' visual qualities and a keener appreciation of the talents that shaped perhaps the one most glorious, shared experience of the century.

David Weisz, the auctioneer, had paid a little less than two million dollars for sound stage after sound stage, warehouse after warehouse of costumes, props, furniture, and other standing stock at MGM. There were, for example, sheds of Nazi uniforms left over from World War II, enough to outfit a regiment. Before his sales began in mid-May, 1970, Weisz had invested another million dollars in advertising the MGM auction, including ten separate catalogues with gold covers that featured poorly printed but showy photographs of the major items of the sale. By the time Weisz had completed the series of auctions and private sales at the end of the summer, he had made a reported twenty million dollars.

The auction of the stars' wardrobes, the division of the studio's costumes by personality, was held Sunday, May 17, 1970. Three thousand people gathered on Stage 27 to wait for the gavel to rap.

At 10:00 A.M. sharp the sale was underway: Lot W101, Greta Garbo's hat from an unidentified movie, went for $300. The crowd was audibly impressed. Lot W102, Ann Miller's leotard from *Hit the Deck,* 1955, brought $50. Lot W103, Claire Bloom's shawl from *Brothers Grimm,* 1963, also went for $50. The accelerated bidding for the next item seemed to panic many in the audience, although the day before, rumor among the prospective bidders browsing in the racks of costumes had it that "anything" from *The Wizard of Oz,* 1939, was expected to bring big money. Lot W104, Margaret Hamilton's witch's hat from *The Wizard of Oz,* brought $450. Then the first of the uncatalogued surprise items was put on the block: Margaret Hamilton's witch's dress, sold for $350. A growing tension was evident in the bidders' faces. The prices were racing ahead of even the craziest expectations.

Lot W105, Jeanette MacDonald's boots from *San Francisco,* 1936, sold at $200. Then, with Lot W106—a pair of Kim Novak's black lace panties and brassiere from *The Legend of Lylah Clare,* 1968, which fetched $100—the auction was off. The most intensely awaited items, the auctioneer

allowed—the ruby slippers worn by Judy Garland in *The Wizard of Oz,* the trenchcoat worn by Clark Gable, and the lion's suit from *The Wizard of Oz*—would go on the block at 8:00 P.M.

The auction of stars' costumes had reached Lot W580 when it was stopped at eight to auction the ruby slippers. They were brought to the block on a tasseled velvet cushion.

From the audience, a man who identified himself as the mayor of Culver City stood and said that since the sale had been announced, he had been beseeched to keep the shoes in Culver City, as "the one pure symbol of Americana." Although, he went on, only a small amount of cash had been raised by Culver City schoolchildren, they hoped to be able to buy the shoes. If, however, the slippers must be sold to someone else, he requested that one of the pair be left in Culver City. Applause.

Unfortunately, because of the worldwide advertising, the auctioneer explained, nothing could now be done to keep the shoes for the kids. The mayor of Culver City resumed his seat. The bidding opened at one thousand dollars and quickly went up to fifteen thousand dollars, the highest price ever paid anywhere for a costume or part of a costume. The pair of red-sequined slippers was sold to a youngish man in the front row, who later said he was representing a southern California millionaire.

The Gable trenchcoat, the star's Burberry good-luck talisman, the second of the most sought-after lots, was sold for $1,250 to Bob Cahlman, a New Orleans entrepreneur whose collection of theatrical and movie costumes, *Exits and Entrances,* had been touring the United States since 1959. Then the cowardly lion's suit, Bert Lahr's costume in *The Wizard of Oz,* went for $2,400, after which prices dropped and the bidding resumed a somewhat more normal pace. At eleven that evening, the sale was adjourned with Lot W775, an Ingrid Bergman dress from *Gaslight,* 1944, selling for $150.

In contrast with the ten-day MGM sale with its more than 150,000 costumes and its tens of thousands of pieces of furniture and props, the sale at Versailles had included only 17,182 items, but the auctions ran from ten in the morning until eight at night for a whole year. The MGM sale, by extraordinary coincidence, contained some pieces of furniture from the Versailles sale. Surprisingly, the personal possessions of Marie Antoinette at the time of her execution—a small green morocco case complete with scissors, corkscrew, tweezers, and a comb—fetched only 5 francs 75 centimes, or a little over a dollar in the currency of the time. The second lot, three small portraits in the

shape of a pocket mirror, fetched 4 francs 40. On Stage 27, Adrian's costumes, covered with gold lace, for the 1936 movie *Marie Antoinette* starring Norma Shearer, brought more than a thousand times as much. *Ars gratia artis.*

Thus went the MGM sale, the dispersal of one of the most staggering proliferations of artifacts in the western world, the products of an amazing array of talent that had for a brief historical moment gathered in Hollywood. The costumes—the most fragile of the items disposed of in the MGM sales, and earlier in similar sales at Twentieth Century–Fox—virtually disappeared, acquired mainly by fans who were willing to pay high prices for souvenirs of their favorite stars, but who, for the most part, could not properly conserve them.

Because there were no major film museums, many of the historically most important costumes were lost to private collections, where it was unlikely that temperature and humidity controls, much less curatorial attention, would be afforded the delicate and often irreplaceable fabrics. Much of Hollywood's most tangible presence had been started on the road to ruin.

Just as Versailles had subsequently been reconstructed, perhaps the Metropolitan Museum's exhibition, which included priceless items from the still-extant Paramount wardrobe and many items from the MGM sale now in private hands, pointed to a similar reconstitution: a studio of the imagination, a museum containing some portion of The Hollywood Dream Factory, a constellation of the artifacts of the stars.

I I

In its great and best days, the movie business was not like any other business. "As long as what we spent showed, we could spend anything," said Walter Plunkett, the designer whose career spans four decades and whose designs include the early Astaire and Rogers musicals, *Gone with the Wind,* and *Singin' in the Rain,* 1952.

"We never had to worry about budgets. I guess I did when I was the wardrobe manager at RKO but not after that. As long as Louis B. Mayer was willing to take a big loss on a movie a year to maintain a reputation for quality, we were living in a different world."

When David O. Selznick left MGM to become an independent producer, forming the company that ultimately made *Gone with the Wind,* he wrote to his treasurer in one of his famous memos, "There are only two kinds of merchandise that can be made profitably in this business—either the very cheap pictures or the expensive pictures." Along the same lines, Irving Thalberg, MGM's "boy genius," observed that you could get away with anything in a movie, particularly sex, if you made it historical—and expensive. Indeed, at the larger studios during Hollywood's golden age, costume designers had no fixed line in the production budget. They knew they were designing for

The Golden Bed, 1925. Photo: MoMA.

Cecil B. De Mille heavily publicized the wardrobe of his stars, even Lillian Rich's toilette for The Golden Bed, *1925, emphasizing how much he spent to please his audience.*

a $500,000 or a $1,000,000 or a $2,000,000 movie, and they worked accordingly.

Remarkably, the producers, not the directors, most often determined the look of the movies. Costumes were frequently underway before a director and stars had been assigned to a production. To a greater or lesser extent, art directors might coordinate the disparate elements of the costume designer, set designer, set decorator, and cameramen, but it was a matter of luck and professionalism if those elements jelled.

Because actors in the earliest days of the film were asked to supply their own wardrobes, some stars continued to use their own designers—as Mae Murray did with Adrian, to von Stroheim's consternation, in *The Merry Widow* in 1925 —or reserved the right to okay projected designs. Seldom did designers assume the role that Cecil Beaton did with *My Fair Lady* in 1964 and battle with hairdressers over coiffures which were amending his conception. Quite often, the actor went his own way, ignoring the designer's ideas, as Estelle Parsons did with Theodora von Runkle's thirties costumes in *Bonnie and Clyde,* 1967—putting together her own pastiche of periods. At the same time, few directors have felt the need to become directly involved in the costuming of their pictures. In general, those who did had a remarkable sense of style, and their films were intensely evocative of the decades in which they worked. Those are, of course, D. W. Griffith, Cecil B. De Mille, Erich von Stroheim, Josef von Sternberg, and Vincente Minnelli. Significantly, of these, both von Stroheim and Minnelli had worked as designers before they became directors. The number of producers who placed costume design high among their production values is equally small and duplicates to a certain extent the list of directors: Griffith, De Mille, Irving Thalberg, David O. Selznick, and Arthur Freed, who was responsible for development of the style of the MGM musical.

The producer was of chief importance in the matter of costume design because, more often than not, he approved the sketches for execution. A close collaboration of director and designer, as was the case with Peter Bogdanovich and Polly Platt on *Paper Moon,* 1973, is almost without exception a fairly recent occurrence.

Also, the costume designers played a surprisingly anonymous role in the production scheme. Some, such as Adrian, might cultivate the friendship of the stars they dressed and thus hit the fan magazines, but most worked with little or no recognition within the studios. "I never got a call from the front office," said Edith Head, who has worked as a designer for fifty years and won eight Oscars and thirty-three Oscar nominations. "We did what we were hired to do. We were professionals and, if we did what we were supposed to do, why should anyone say anything?"

"It was a job," said hairdresser extraordinaire Sidney Guillaroff, echoing other Hollywood craftsmen. Guillaroff, with perhaps the longest list of screen credits, went on to say that the only movie he worked on that he thought was memorable was *Marie Antoinette.* "I saved the stills of those wigs. They were the only stills I saved."

Nonetheless, Hollywood crafts were inextricably tied to the history of the movies because they were coeval with the first generation of producers.

Curiously, a majority of those early moviemakers had started out in the fashion business, manufacturing gloves, clothing, furs, and jewelry. They understood the public's taste for vicarious luxury and they inevitably imported many of their former associates from the garment trade into moviemaking. Louis B. Mayer was a shoemaker. Samuel Goldwyn a glovemaker. Adolph Zukor was a furrier. Later, Zukor insisted on fur trimming for the costumes in his pictures: "It was good for the business." *What* business was not clear. Goldwyn even got Chanel to design for the movies—along with Patou, Lucien Lelong, Alix—now Madame Grès, Maggy Rouf, and Schiaparelli, all for *Artists and Models Abroad,* 1938.

As long as movies had been made in New York, until the late twenties, department stores and Broadway costumes had supplied the wardrobe. Costume pictures, at least in the beginning, had been filmed directly from stage productions—the costumes were those used on the stage. For other movies, as has been noted, both actors and extras were expected to supply their own wardrobes. That often still remains true in films with a contemporary setting. Joan Crawford provided her own wardrobe for *Humoresque* and, because of one suit she wore designed by Adrian, he received the screen credit for the costumes, although Sheila O'Brien had designed the majority of the clothes.

Few costume designers for the movies were involved in the making of the costumes in the way that a Seventh Avenue designer or Paris couturier is. "Travis Banton was one of the few designers who had any idea about what a finished costume would look like," said Edith Head about her boss and mentor at Paramount in the twenties and thirties.

They had well-staffed workrooms, actually small factories, that executed their drawings. In those workrooms, the garments in progress moved in an assembly line from

Marie Antoinette, 1938. Photo: MoMA.

Adrian designed four thousand costumes for Marie Antoinette, *1938, each a summary of 18th century style, with authentic bits of lace, embroidery, and buttons to heighten the "reality." Each of Sydney Guillaroff's wigs for this film weighed twenty pounds and more. They were masterpieces of engineering as much as of coiffure. For Norma Shearer as the French queen the wig was frosted with actual diamonds.*

table to table—from cutting stages to finishing. The finished garment was fitted, altered, and then photographed on the actor to be certain of its appearance before the camera. (Edith Head said that the elimination of these costume shots from the studio routine for cost reasons ended any possible quality control.) In addition to the basic complement of cutters, fitters, and tailors, the major studios also had staff beaders, furriers, milliners, armorers, and jewelers. That pattern, established in the late teens, persisted until the fifties. Now, the remaining Hollywood studios add wardrobe staff as needed, and depend in the main on Western Costume Company, Hollywood's largest manufacturer and renter of costumes, to execute the designs of their freelance designers.

The studio workrooms were copied directly from those supplying the Broadway stage, most notably by D. W. Griffith and Cecil B. De Mille, both of whom had theater experience and tried to emulate theatrical professionalism in their productions. Interestingly enough, although both avidly researched their movies, neither seemed to care much for accuracy.

The increased importance that Griffith and De Mille gave to set decoration and costume design, however, came less as a result of the shift of movie production to the West Coast, where greater freedom in exterior shots was possible, than as a consequence of the switch from brief two-reelers to feature-length films. The breakthrough film was D. W. Griffith's biblical feature, *Judith of Bethulia,* shot in 1913, but not released until a year later, when Griffith—thwarted in his ambition to enlarge the scope and length of the films—had moved to another studio.

The costumes for *Judith of Bethulia* were little more than glorified sheets and bathrobes, but, like Griffith's set—a walled city thrown up in the San Fernando Valley—they were made specially for the movie—a first. The costumes and sets, Griffith's ingenious use of rapid cutting, the montage, were clearly breaks with the straight-on, plodding film-record of the stage play that had been the practice until then.

D. W. Griffith was passionately involved in the evocative power of visual detail, and his studied use of closeup brought in its train a whole series of changes in film makeup and costume. However inaccurate, Griffith's use of costume and décor was profoundly evocative and his movie

Marie Antoinette, 1938. Photos: MoMA.

The ball at Versailles was one of the most expensive single movie sequences ever mounted. The making of the costumes, each one a tribute to the skills of MGM's wardrobe department, was only one element in an enormous assembly line of operations that brought the final images to the screen. A small army worked off-camera to place the wigs, distribute the props, adjust the make up, and move the carefully done-up extras onto the set. Note, at the center of the set in the diagram, the figures of the extras in the still below.

Intolerance, 1916, with thousands of "historically" garbed extras, remains the most important and influential American film in the history of movie costume.

That feeling for atmosphere was evident also in the early Italian epics. Those overblown importations, including *Quo Vadis?,* 1912, *The Last Days of Pompeii,* 1912, *Cabiria,* 1913, *Anthony and Cleopatra,* 1914, *Julius Caesar,* 1914, *Salammbo,* 1914, and *Spartacus,* 1914—voluptuous and foolish—set a style all their own that formed a conspicuous counterpoint to the carefully rendered *mise-en-scène* of Griffith. Their exuberant sexuality and naive nationalism set them off as foreign, but theirs was an exoticism that Hollywood would emulate again and again, often remaking the stories with the same titles as the Italian prototypes.

By the end of World War I, Hollywood crafts had assumed a structure that would endure for almost thirty years. At no time had even the Paris couture employed as many seamstresses or boasted workmen with such skill with beading, lace, and furs. In spite of that small fashion industry within the movie industry, Hollywood had very little direct contact with the fashion worlds of Paris and New York. Hollywood made new fashions. Hollywood design, elaborate and exaggerated, was relatively self-contained in its effect. Even with a designer such as Adrian, one of the few Hollywood designers to gain a reputation outside the industry, it would be difficult to make much of Hollywood's fashion impact. Padded shoulders were not invented in Culver City.

On the other hand, the stars themselves were drawn to Paris—at least before World War II. Mary Pickford might wear rags on-screen, but off-screen she wore Lanvin. Gloria Swanson's transformation from a Mack Sennett bathing beauty was charted more by the opulence of her French wardrobe than by the transformation of her acting style. Paris represented *real* sophistication to Hollywood. What the stars confirmed in their conspicuous consumption was a realization that what Hollywood was projecting to the world was not the timeliness or the acuteness that makes high fashion, but a much larger and more powerful illusion: romance and glamour of an extreme and other-worldly sort. Hollywood clothes were not really meant to be worn. Often dresses were so tight, so carefully molded, that they could be worn only when standing up. The chief value of the Hollywood costume, then, was pictorial: it was made to be photographed.

One of the most intriguing aspects of the Hollywood costume was the actors' experience of them—not only the colors that were not seen in black-and-white movies (when Erté, the French designer and illustrator, was designing costumes for Goldwyn at MGM in the twenties, he suggested that it would be more efficient and effective to design and execute costumes only in black-and-white; his suggestion was logical, he was told, but it wouldn't work because the actors would get bored) but the careful construction and the detail that often eluded even the camera. Underneath many of Garbo's historical costumes, designed by Adrian, are petticoats of the finest linen edged with exquisite

When Knighthood Was in Flower, 1922. Marion Davies, center. Photo: MoMA.

Joseph Urban designed the sets and the costumes for Marion Davies, using lighting to create an effect much like painting. He was one of the first designers hired to mount productions that framed the star.

lace. (Strangely enough, Thalberg told his scriptwriters he wanted to know "what kind of underclothes" their characters wore.) Those undergarments were, in a sense, a secret shared by the designer, the seamstress, the dresser, and the star. But who can judge their contribution to Garbo's performance? Beneath the heavy fur-cuffed sleeves of Camille's opera coat, its cloth shot with gold, are undersleeves impossible to see unless the mink trim is carefully pulled back—a detail never revealed to the camera. That is the hidden dialogue that speaks its glamour and romance to the audience, that buoys up the public's waves of tears and laughter at the height of the Hollywood movie.

Whatever the secret of the glamour and romance, it retains its old magic. The morning after the gala opening of the costume show at the Metropolitan, Greta Garbo arrived before the museum's regular hours and wandered through the galleries—reaching out to touch her costumes as if they were long-lost friends.

DMcC

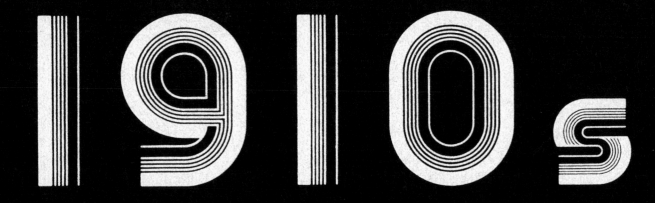

1910s

The Vamp and The Broken Blossom

...starring

theda bara

The soul of heavy-lidded evil, with enormous dark eyes, thick of waist and short of leg, Theda Bara was The Vamp, the countervailing force in an era of the movies that was more nineteenth- than twentieth-century in its choice of heroines. She started out as a stage actress and ended up—her career was extremely short—as one of the most luridly contrived of the Hollywood fantasies. She was the pearl of the Orient, born in Egypt, the daughter of a sheik and a princess, nursed on serpents' milk, married mystically to the Sphinx, the cause of desert wars; a servant of the flesh of unending appetite, a creature of pleasure monstrous in her fickleness. Her acting was a sort of extended hypnotism, her characterizations more a matter of costume changes. Bejeweled and bedizened, Theda Bara's forte was ruining men, running through them as other women run through hats and gloves. Fox built up such an elaborate off-screen campaign that it spilled over into her movies from A Fool There Was, 1916, on. Whenever she arrived on a movie set, she was preceded by a majordomo who stopped every ten paces, banged the floor with a long, knobbed staff, and called out in muezzin-like tones, ''Make way for Baa-raa!'' Supposedly, she ate only lettuce and raw meat. That improbable siren had started out life as the shy daughter of a Cincinnati tailor, her real name Theodosia Goodman. Supposedly, her screen name was an anagram for Death and Arab, but more than likely it was the contraction of Theda for Theodosia, and Bara from her mother's maiden name Baranger. Her success was due not so much to her affinities with Cleopatra—whom she played with some extraordinary ocular gymnastics—as to the fact that her eyes did not burn out on the early celluloid as easily as those of her paler rivals.

Preceding page: *Cleopatra,* 1917. Theda Bara. Photo: MoMA.

Salome, 1918. Theda Bara. Photo: MoMA.

Theda Bara made the first film version of Salome, *1918, in which the Dance of the Seven Veils became a visual metaphor for the movies' psychology of the feminine, or costume-as-character.*

In the spring of 1909, at the age of sixteen, Gladys Smith turned up for a screen test at the Biograph Studio at 11 East 14th Street in New York City, a former brownstone between Fifth Avenue and University Place, off Union Square, and possibly the oldest studio in the United States. She was wearing her navy blue serge Easter suit, a blue-and-white-striped shirtwaist, a Tuscan straw boater with a dark-blue bow, silk stockings, and her first pair of high heels. (''The hat cost three fifty and the suit fifteen dollars,'' she said.) The director of the screen test, in fact Biograph's only director, was David Wark Griffith, then thirty-three. The script for the test was Robert Browning's exaltation of Victorian optimism, ''Pippa Passes.'' The makeup, Gladys Smith remembered, was more suitable for Pancho Villa than for Pippa; her costume was from the wardrobe department—''a tiny cellar alcove set aside for the Biograph costume rack,'' no more than a communal clothes-rack.

That day, Gladys Smith made five dollars for the test; by accident met her first husband, Owen Moore; and began with Griffith to invent the idea of Hollywood; her first role was as a ten-year-old in *Her First Biscuits,* 1909.

None of the studio's meager wardrobe, however, fitted her—the clothes were too big. Griffith sent his wife, Linda Arvidson, off to Best's with $20 from the cash box to buy an outfit for the actress. Linda Arvidson later wrote that she had picked out a smart pale blue linen frock, blue silk stockings to match, and nifty patent leather pumps. "What a dainty little miss she looked, her fluffy curls a-bobbing, when she donned the new pretties." Linda Arvidson had spent only $10.50 of the $20, Gladys Smith recalled, her instinct for money already firmly in place. She was making $25 a week.

"I noticed rather early that Mr. Griffith seemed to favor me in the roles of Mexican and Indian women," Gladys Smith wrote about her early days at Biograph. "Perhaps it was because I was then the only leading girl . . . with eyes that photographed dark, though mine are hazel. Whatever the reason, I portrayed them all: Indian maidens and squaws, and Mexican señoras and señoritas. I learned to apply thick applications of red clay mixed with water to my arms and legs with a sponge; often at five thirty in the cold morning I would don a black horsehair wig, and a beaded dress weighing many pounds topped by a necklace of alligator teeth."

Shortly, Florence Lawrence, the original Biograph Girl, left the studio and Gladys took her place as the company's leading lady, although her name never appeared in the press or in the advertising. She was simply "The Biograph Girl," as Florence Lawrence had been. Her name became known not because her producer demanded it but because the public demanded it. In 1911, she transferred to Independent Motion Picture Company for $175 a week and star billing—she was known as "Little Mary" in the United States and Dorothy Nicholson in England. Gladys Smith, however, did not like the quality of IMP's photography: "My hair became black on their films and my light coloring became like that of an Indian." And she did not complete her one-year contract.

At the start of 1912, she was back at Biograph at $150 a week and her stage name, Mary Pickford, began to be used on posters and handbills—but not in the films.

"We never changed our costumes in a picture," Mary Pickford said. "Ten years might elapse and the leading man would be wearing the same checked shirt. On the other hand, a slight change of dress from scene to scene—the wearing of a different ribbon, hat, or handbag—would be spotted by the picture patrons."

In 1912, according to Mary Pickford's version of the story, D. W. Griffith took an historic step in the making of movies. Mary Pickford was starring in *Friends* with Lionel Barrymore. "It was

...starring

mary pickford

With brown eyes, a saucily insolent walk, and an infectious spunk that drew audiences to see her before her name appeared on the marquee, Mary Pickford has a remarkable and enduring after-image—on the same order as Charlie Chaplin's. That is, perhaps, because she played the same sort of David v. Goliath roles, often irreverently self-reliant. A brilliant business success, an unrelenting perfectionist, Mary Pickford took a hand in every aspect of the film in which she appeared, often spending hours on one costume fitting or one publicity still. Until almost the end of her screen career she demanded Charles Rosher as her cameraman. Her financial rewards were staggering even when compared with the superstars and sports figures of the seventies. In 1912 Adolph Zukor paid Mary Pickford $500 a week—he doubled that in February, 1914; again doubled it in November, 1914; then doubled it yet again to $4,000 a week in March, 1915. By mid-1916, Zukor was paying Pickford $10,000 a week. A year later, at First National, she was making $350,000 a picture. Starting out with Griffith when she was a teenager, she had played grown women. Her first wait came in 1915 in Rags, and she was still playing kids in Annie Rooney, 1925, when she was thirty-two. This choice of roles was not her own. A World War I poll indicated that her fans wanted her to play only Cinderella and other fairytale roles. So, as she romped about in curls and beautifully made "poor" dresses on-screen, she lived the life of royalty off-screen. When she did retire, she produced and even marketed the beauty cream she said she had invented. Her curls, she said, she had always washed and set herself, using a vegetable rinse to keep them blond.

Rebecca of Sunnybrook Farm, 1917. Mary Pickford. Photo: MoMA

Rebecca of Sunnybrook Farm, *1917, came relatively late in Mary Pickford's movie career, but it represented the style for the mischievous little girls that she was to play in her most popular movies—usually dressed in carefully made rags and often topped with an improbable hat.*

Photo: James Abbe

late in the afternoon when Griffith shouted to Billy Bitzer, the cameraman: 'Come on, Billy, let's have some fun! Move the camera up and get closer to Mary.' Now that was a startling departure from the then-accepted routine of photography. Obediently Billy moved the camera—an unwieldy contraption which weighed about one hundred pounds and in which Billy sometimes kept his lunch. Meanwhile, I broke another precedent and put on a second makeup—one a day so far had sufficed for everybody in the business. Billy took the shot, which was a semicloseup, cutting me at the waist.

"I was so excited I couldn't wait to see the results. Our projection room was on the second floor, where it had previously served as the master bedroom of the old Fourteenth Street mansion. It was the new image of my face that I was waiting to see. What a frightening experience when my grotesquely magnified face finally flashed on the screen! The shock of it was like a physical blow. But I was critical enough to notice the makeup."

In that instant, Mary Pickford began to modify her look, to bring it more in line with her naturalistic style of acting. "I think there's too much eyebrow pencil and shadowing around the eyes," she told Griffith. Almost perceptibly, her image came into focus in the next few films until she had captured that particular charm that became identified with her as "America's Sweetheart," the pivotal figure of an entire industry.

Mary Pickford's sensibility was immutably Victorian, as was Griffith's. Her autobiography, *Sunshine and Shadow,* one of the most convincing of all the confessions made by the stars, reads like the memoirs of The Little Match Girl, full of poverty and pathos. At five or six, she took a fading rose from the florist and ate it: "It had tasted very bitter at first, but I thought that if I were to eat it, the beauty and color and the perfume would somehow get inside me."

Even her curls were a souvenir of her sad and impoverished past: "In the parlor, on an easel was a monstrous sketch of my father [who had died when she was four]. Over the top of the picture Mother had lovingly draped a yellow silk scarf with yellow floss tassels. One afternoon, having nothing better to do, I moistened my fingers with my tongue, stood on my tiptoes, and very meticulously rolled the tassels between my forefinger and thumb— the brilliant idea being to make them look like golden ringlets. Much to my disappointment the result of my afternoon's labor was a scraggly assortment of dirty little wads. That tampering with the yellow floss tassels of Mother's silk scarf may have been the inspiration for what later became the Pickford curls."

Her scenario, with its not too carefully hidden wish that she take her father's place, was shortly granted. Soon, she was the family breadwinner and the wreath of curls a trademark she was never able to forfeit. She continued to shape the curls, she said, up until the last of her screen career, with her own fingers.

Surprisingly, "Little Mary," the image of film memory, did not take shape until 1916. That year she acted in a film, *The Foundling,* in which she had one scene that was a flashback to the heroine's childhood. Her childhood friend from the theater, Lillian Gish, whom she had introduced to Griffith in 1912, told her she should play "the adorable little girl" throughout a movie. In *The Poor Little Rich Girl,* 1917, she played Gwendolyn, a ten-year-old girl who was neglected by her rich parents. The public responded as enthusiastically as if she had just been discovered. As a result, she became younger, her curls longer, and her dresses the more absurd in their childishness.

"I had found my place," she said. "I became the little girl I had never been." With her strapped-in breasts, smudged smile, and tattered clothes, she had become the symbol of American purity— touched by mischief perhaps, but good.

The emergence of Little Mary's evil counterpart in the early days of the film is equally fantastic, a calculated compensation for innocence. Theda Bara did not arrive in Hollywood until 1915, a minor stage actress whose exotic name and bloodthirsty past had been created by a press agent. She was a middle-class Jewish girl from Cincinnati. Ironically, although lycanthropy had been practiced in *Mitteleuropa* by men, in Hollywood it was women who became the personifications of evil, and the fancifully bloodthirsty label for these creatures came from a poem by Rudyard Kipling, "The Vampire," that had been dramatized for Broadway earlier in the decade.

Those kohl-eyed creatures were in the train of nineteenth-century painted women such as Baudelaire's whores and Delacroix's harem women—sensual, voluptuous, and predatory. Their nature was most often an embroidery on the character of Salome, who turned up again in the theater, music, and the visual arts—a representation in reverse of the Pygmalion/Perseus myth that so engaged the Victorians, Galatea/Andromeda unmaking her maker/savior. And there was, of course, the horrific decapitation, the implied emasculation, as the resolution of the amorous battle.

Hollywood was fascinated by the worldly woman, and in the triangle of Salome, Herod, and John the Baptist, there was the archetypal pattern of much that was to follow. Salome and versions of Salome turn up again and again in the movies.

Cabiria, 1913. Photo: MoMA.

The early Italian epics introduced a heavy-lidded sexuality that caught on quickly in American films —Cabiria, 1913, coming a year before Theda Bara and her kohl-eyed vamps.

Cabiria, 1913. Photo: MoMA.

The richly worked surfaces of Cabiria looked back to art nouveau and forward to art deco, but the costumes were straight out of 19th century academic painting.

Sometimes the appetite for European sophistication reflected Hollywood at its most ambitious and most gullible. In mid-1912, Adolph Zukor bought for fifty thousand dollars a French four-reel version of *Queen Elizabeth*, 1912, starring Sarah Bernhardt, which had brought lines to the box office. Bernhardt had insisted on playing the role exactly as she had played it on the stage. (Her first film had been a two-reel version of her performance in *Camille,* also released in 1912.) There was little action and, because the actors were filmed full-length, there was little chance of catching any facial expressions. In the four reels of *Queen Elizabeth,* there were only twelve separate shots, the staging was

nonexistent, and at the end, the actors took a bow on the screen, to the delighted applause of American audiences. Zukor was impressed by the success of the longer European films—American films were still only two reels—and the size of the box-office receipts. He began to promote other stars of the stage and opera in his films.

The expansion of the movies' scope was further enhanced by the efforts of D. W. Griffith, whose sentimentality was linked with a shrewd eye for detail and a keen sense of exploiting the technical side of moviemaking. However mawkish his sense of drama, however exaggerated his sexual and psychological involvement with young girls and their aura of innocence, he was able to evoke with realistic settings and costumes a world unimaginable in the stage-like treatments of his peers.

Bernhardt was considered the greatest of the nineteenth-century Camilles, a part she played on the stage well into the twentieth and for the movies in 1912. Her robe de chambre for the famous death scene was by Paul Poiret.

Thais, 1917. Mary Garden. Photo: MoMA.

Mary Garden's outrageously expensive costumes for the silent movie version of the opera Thais, *1917, were among the first incursions of high fashion into the movies, providing the look of luxury Samuel Goldwyn sought. Garden was one of the last of the old-style opera stars—a scandal in* Thais *on the stage, a box office draw in the movies. Playing a worldly woman, she suggested more a Parisian demimondaine than a classical courtesan.*

...starring

irene castle

Broad-shouldered, with large, strong hands, and hair lopped off at the base of her head, Irene Castle was one of the performers the movies nabbed from the stage. The wife and dancing partner of Vernon Castle, she had helped to introduce the ballroom-dancing craze to America— and ultimately to the world. Onstage or on the dance floor, her uncorseted, willowy body, her bobbed hair, and her newly shortened hemline were the cause of many of the fashion changes that came late in the 1910s and early in the 1920s. Her look, however, was determined only in part by her theatrical life. She was also a remarkable individualist, a horsewoman, and an animal-lover, who usually included a monkey among her pets. Her collaborator in designing her costumes was Lady Duff-Cooper, the couturière known as Lucille, an Englishwoman and sister of Elinor Glyn, who was one of the most expensive and influential couturières of the early century. Lucille's most famous costume was for Watch Your Step, *one of the few dresses ever requested by the Metropolitan Museum for its collection, later copied for Ginger Rogers for* The Story of Vernon and Irene Castle, *1939: "It was the first dress with a 'torn' hemline. It was made of blue-gray chiffon that looked like smoke and was twelve yards around the bottom. The bodice was silver with long, full chiffon sleeves, banded with gray fox at the wrist. The cloak was made of a blue-gray and silver brocade (using the wrong side), very full-skirted, with a tight bodice that laced down the left side with chartreuse and emerald-green streamers. The huge skirt of that handsomely brocaded cloak was garlanded in light gray fox, which had been tinted slightly mauve."*

Patria, 1917. Irene Castle. Photo: Museum of the City of New York.

For her hats in Patria, *1917, Irene Castle did her own versions of historical American martial headgear—a stylish salute to the war effort.*

Pl. 3 [opposite]
Irene Castle stage costume designed by Lady Duff-Gordon; copied by Walter Plunkett for Ginger Rogers in *The Story of Vernon and Irene Castle,* 1939.

The costume is described in the biography of Irene Castle on this page.

Photo: Museum of the City of New York.

Judith of Bethulia, 1913. Henry B. Walthall, Blanche Sweet. Photo: MoMA.

In Judith of Bethulia, *1913, his protean costume epic in four reels, D. W. Griffith foreshadowed the preoccupations of the American costume movie— sex, materialism, and history in uneasy proportions.*

Intolerance, 1916. Seena Owen, Walter Paget. Photo: MoMA.

D. W. Griffith invented the false eyelash for Seena Owen in Intolerance, *1916—a strip of gauze with hair glued to it that was then attached to the actress's eyes with spirit gum.*

...starring
lillian
gish

Her mouth a thin line, her eyes ever grave, ever large, Lillian Gish was the prototype of D. W. Griffith's Victorian heroines. Unlike Mary Pickford, she never overcame her troubles on the screen. She struggled and she was broken. About her, Allene Talmey, one of the wisest and wittiest writers about Hollywood, said, "her face required only a breeze to whip it into change whereas others of her craft dealt exclusively with typhoons." Lillian Gish, for all of her pathos, was a supreme master of her craft with a staggering knowledge of all aspects of moviemaking. She brought Henry Sartov to the Griffith studio to photograph her in Broken Blossoms. *His contribution was the soft-focus photography, unique for 1918, that spills luminously over the film, giving it its special atmosphere. It was the effect of filming Lillian Gish through gauze that gave her London waif a dreamy and memorable eroticism. Her small body, fragile features, and intimate scale of acting gave her a presence before the camera that was unlike that of any other actress. Her training under Griffith, a collaboration really, made her unusually canny. At MGM, she had a famous feud with Erté over the costumes for* La Bohème. *He wanted authenticity in the garments of the Latin Quarter students: tattered and heavy garments to suggest the cold of their garrets. Lillian Gish said that silk would do much more to indicate the poverty because it would create an "atmosphere." Erté won out, but Gish did her own costumes. At MGM, in the late twenties, she was finally supplanted by Greta Garbo, who represented a new* spirituelle *type, a more worldly broken blossom. So, in her thirties, trailing clouds of lily-of-the-valley perfume, Lillian Gish retired to the stage and a career that has lasted until the present.*

The origins of that esthetic in Griffith are both obvious and complex. On the one hand, he had inherited from his Confederate colonel father a version of the South that combined the feudalism of Sir Walter Scott, a novelistic sense of gallantry and bravery, and an idea of roles that made him unable to accept women except as angels and madonnas. This nostalgia was in large measure compensated for by the visual awareness that the illustrations in Victorian novels had activated in his imagination: the plenitude of details possible in a steel engraving as opposed to the flattening reality of the photograph. He absorbed the pedophilic manias of those illustrators with the same fervor as their realism. Mary Pickford, Lillian Gish, and Mae Marsh were childhood heroines. He easily recognized the versatility of Dickens's method for sustaining a narrative and he also recognized, as did Dickens, the value of pathos.

About his stars, Griffith told *Photoplay* in 1923, "When I consider a young woman as a stellar possibility, I always ask myself: Does she come near suggesting the idealized heroine of life? . . . The girl, to have the real germ of stardom, must suggest—at least in a sketchy way—the vaguely conscious ideals of every woman. Again, she must suggest—and this is equally important—the attributes most women desire."

Somewhat after the fact, Griffith was formulating the powerful psychology that imbued his movies, a major strain in the evolution of the feminine in the film in general. "To me, the ideal type for feminine stardom has nothing of the flesh, nothing of the note of sensuousness. My pictures reveal the type I mean. Commentators have called it the spirituelle type. But there is method in my madness. . . . The voluptuous type, blossoming into the fullblown one, cannot endure. The years show their stamp too clearly. The other type . . . ah, that is different."

"Blossoming," with its sexual associations, had suggested one of Griffith's most poignant movies. In *Limehouse Stories,* a volume of short stories about the Chinese slum section of London, Griffith found a short story in which the dreams of innocence and evil of the first Hollywood decade coalesced. In *Broken Blossoms,* 1919, taken from these stories, Griffith expressed intimately and unforgettably a theme that he approached again and again, often on a grander scale: Lillian Gish is mistreated by a drunken father. Even when he beats her, she props her tiny mouth into a smile with her fingers. The scenes of her terror are almost unbearable in their intensity, almost a willful assault by the director on her somewhat vacant, woebegone presence. Finally, she is rescued by a kindly Chinese who dresses her in oriental style and places her in his bed, an adored object. What follows is one of the most erotic passages in American films—her still face transformed and

Broken Blossoms, 1918. Richard Barthelmess, Lillian Gish.
Photo: MoMA.

D. W. Griffith's costumes for Lillian Gish in Broken Blossoms, 1918, *were part of his conception of realism, dusted over with fantasy and a sexually charged Victorianism derived largely from the pictorialism of the novels of Charles Dickens and their illustrations.*

Don't Change Your Husband, 1918. Gloria Swanson, Elliott Dexter.

De Mille dressed his stars expensively, often shading over questions of morality with money. Gloria Swanson seldom played the other woman, but rather the long-suffering wife, and here, dressed to the teeth, she sets out to win back her husband.

The Woman God Forgot, 1917. Geraldine Farrar, center.
Photo: MoMA.

Geraldine Farrar, borrowed by De Mille from the Metropolitan Opera, stalks the halls of her father, Montezuma, in a Mayan costume, the feverish product of well-advertised "historical research."

lighted by an emerging sexual languor; her pathetic face framed by two poufs of curls, the wistful eyes, and the trembling mouth. In *Broken Blossoms,* more than in *Birth of a Nation,* 1915, and *Intolerance,* 1916, Griffith had suggested the stirring of an impulse that was to create the glamour and romance of Hollywood.

1920s

The Flapper and the Waif

mae murray

Her lips the color of red taffeta, her hair a blond fluff, her blue eyes stunned wide, Mae Murray was The Flapper, the image of an era that danced its way into the movies. She started out dancing in one of the Manhattan nightclubs that sprang up as competition for the Broadway club that featured Vernon and Irene Castle. (Rudolph Valentino was one of the escort-dancers there.) Then Irving Berlin grabbed her as a stand-in for his musical Watch Your Step, starring Irene Castle. From there it was only a time-step into the Ziegfeld Follies, corsage boxes filled with white orchids and white butterflies, and ruby-paved compacts—with Hollywood only a leap away. Mae kept on dancing for the cameras—in a Paris bistro; dressed as a peacock; wearing horns, a two-piece gold-spangled outfit, and a red wig for a dancing bullfight. But she was most herself as the Queen of Jazzmania, a film about a mythical kingdom devoted to music, dancing, and gaiety, in which she reviewed the Jazzmanian troops to ragtime. Mae Murray was a star unlike any other star, "The Gardenia of the Screen," so self-absorbed and remote that she seemed to move and breathe only when she was in front of a camera. Each day, drenched in gardenia perfume, her lips painted in a bee-sting, she arrived at MGM in her Rolls-Royce town car with its cream-colored body and black leather convertible top, with two footmen in cream and black uniforms that matched the car. The lap robe for that car—there were others—was of sable; the interior of the tonneau, a soft yellow, was fitted with solid gold and cloisonné. Drenched in gardenia perfume, she came to the studio completely made up, her diamonds flashing wildly in the California sun. It was the twenties, and America was dance-crazy. And Mae Murray lived to dance. During the making of The Merry Widow, 1925, she fought with von Stroheim about how the Great Waltz was to be filmed. She won, and the scene was one of the most extraordinary of any movie. Mae and John Gilbert danced breathlessly through a crowd of a thousand extras as if there were no one. They came closer to the camera and Gilbert bent her back. They dipped, swayed, moved in time with the waltz, his eyes never leaving hers. The film ran on Broadway alone for sixteen months, breaking records everywhere it played. Then, Mae Murray married Prince Mdivani. When he forced her to leave the screen, the Jazz Age seemed to leave with her.

World War I provided Hollywood with the image it had previously lacked. Since 1916, Hollywood had been dominating the world market for movies and the wildly successful propaganda film effort and bond drives of the war years gave the band of outsiders in southern California the prestige they had been seeking. The movie professionals, those who had grown up in the young industry, cashed in on their success and consolidated their experience. Representative of that consolidation was the formation of United Artists by the actors Douglas Fairbanks and Mary Pickford, the actor-director Charlie Chaplin, the director D. W. Griffith, and the producer B. P. Schulberg. Among them, to a large extent, they embodied the major achievements of moviemaking, and between them, they created an image of Hollywood that would influence the decades that followed.

The Merry Widow, 1925.

Queen of Sheba, 1921. Photo: MoMA.

There was often little distinction between the historical costume and the showgirl's costume, as in this fowl-feathered creature's get-up from Queen of Sheba, *1921.*

Tess of the Storm Country, 1922. Mary Pickford. Photo: MoMA.

Mary Pickford might appear on screen in tatters, but she never neglected to insure the extreme care with which her costumes and make-up were put together, and she always supervised the cameraman to be certain that he used the most flattering filters. Stills, such as this one from Tess of the Storm Country, *might take as long to set up and shoot as a sequence from the movie itself.*

Pl. 4
Lillian Gish costume for *Way Down East*, 1920, purchased from Henri Bendel.

"Anna is from the country," Lillian Gish told D. W. Griffith about her controversial role as an unwed mother in Way Down East, *1920, "but I don't want her to be quaint or funny. I just want her clothes not to be noticed." Gish wanted the clothes to be "timeless," and for the ball given by Anna's rich cousins she chose an evening dress cut on classic Greek lines, instead of something more fashionable.*

Migration by the film industry from the East to the environs of Los Angeles had begun in 1910. Movie producers were known as "manufacturers," and they were a major element in the Los Angeles boom, although the three thousand miles between them and their eastern backers and creditors may have seemed more compelling a reason for the move than sun and orange groves. Los Angeles was the only major urban center in the world to be created in this century. The studios, however, were the effect rather than a cause of that transformation. Their evolution was determined not only from within but, surprisingly enough, to a considerable extent from without by a man who, unlike most of the moviemakers, was a Westerner and had begun dabbling in films out of love.

In 1917 William Randolph Hearst, the millionaire publisher, met Marion Davies. A year later he had decided she was going to be a movie star. For her, he hired the first production designer, who acted as art director and set and costume designer, functions for the first time geared to the star rather than the production, functions that previously had been performed hit-or-miss by other members of the production team. His earliest choice for this job was Joseph Urban, one of the major designers for the New York stage. Urban designed for the Metropolitan Opera and the *Ziegfeld Follies*—where, incidentally, Hearst had first spotted his future mistress from his favorite seat in the front row.

Hearst and Urban had a great deal in common. Both were eclectic in their tastes, both extravagant, and both charmed by the eroticism of women presented in splendid costumes and settings. Urban's genteel use of nudity and his pilferage of every period for gentlemanly prurience were much to Hearst's liking. The designer represented the same sort of manic appetite that had put together San Simeon, Hearst's pleasure dome, which—with Hollywood—was to become a symbol of California imagination and of American lifestyle. Moreover, Urban's sets and lighting, his sexually charged romanticism, were very much in vogue; his color sense on the stage—his strange blue—echoed most particularly the paintings and illustrations of Maxfield Parrish.

In Urban's work were to be found many of the tendencies that persistently wove in and out of the Hollywood image. Central to that influence was his detached view of the female body. He viewed woman as ornamental. He saw the actor as a part, a highlight of the setting. Thus, movies were the ideal vehicle for expressing Urban's idea of the visual experience—the suggestive parade of women in intricately constructed costumes moving down vast staircases and across endless planes, caressed by furs, revealed and hidden by lace and net, highlighted by sequins and jewels.

All of these effects were greatly heightened by the techniques of the film, but more important, the effects were liberated by the film's extreme emphasis on light and movement. While most cinematic history came to be written in terms of the narrative, there was an alternate esthetic history, always inherent in the medium, that began to develop definite patterns during this period. If Urban is thought of in connection with his patron, W. R. Hearst, then the larger implications of his influence can be understood. Hearst was driven by a certain far-reaching fantasy of history that drove him to compress and expand whole architectural eras in San Simeon. That, the major expression of his imagination, plunged him into the past. For him, the trappings of history were a fantastic distraction, and he used Urban to surround Marion Davies with them. He spent unprecedented sums on packaging and publicizing her. For *When Knighthood Was in Flower,* 1922, he spent $1.5 million to deck Marion Davies in ermine as Mary Tudor. The next year, he had Urban do over the Cosmopolitan Theatre for the premiere of *Little Old New York.* The star, Marion Davies, said she didn't watch the movie. She couldn't take her eyes off the $60,000 chandelier Urban had installed.

Enchantment, 1921. Photo: MoMA.

Joseph Urban, far left, watches a costume parade for Enchantment, *1921, starring Marion Davies, wearing the stylized crown. With his dwarves, fat man, and tall man, Urban's visual conception shared much with Howard Pyle and Maxfield Parrish, the popular illustrators of the day, also taken with fake medievalism.*

Long before the pauvre or street look, Mary Pickford had shown a keen eye for what the poor wore, not just rags-and-tatters but the jauntiness of the tam-o'-shanter, the ill-fitting jacket, and the worn but clean dress—an orchestration of the comic strip character Annie Rooney and her own characteristic sauciness.

When Knighthood Was in Flower, 1922. Marion Davies.
Photo: MoMA.

Marion Davies's movie costumes were a major pre-occupation with W. R. Hearst, who also gave some of the century's most splendid masquerades at San Simeon. Hearst liked to imagine Davies playing the famous women of history, particularly courtesans, always expensively dressed—as here in gold-embroidered velvet and ermine.

Urban was, to a large extent, the measure of twenties Hollywood taste. The interiors of stars' homes that he decorated had great effect, and his stagy pseudo-Mediterranean look gave the film world a sort of cultural identity, or at least the passing cultural cohesiveness that it had lacked in the previous decade of shacks and bungalows.

Hearst understood the uses of influence. While he was helping to reshape the California landscape and the look of the movies, he also set about explaining Hollywood to the rest of the nation and employed his newspapers to put his stamp on the industry itself, notably through his columnist Louella Parsons.

Because of his prominence as a publisher, Hearst could also draw celebrities to the West Coast to visit the studios and introduce them to the producers. That publicizing function often included drawing rather unexpected people into the making of movies. One of those was Erté, the French illustrator and designer of Russian extraction, who was already working for Hearst doing the covers of *Harper's Bazaar.*

Erté was, in a sense, Hollywood's introduction to a larger and more sophisticated world of fashion and decoration. Hollywood stars might select their personal wardrobe in Paris, but Erté was the first French designer to work in Hollywood. A seminal figure, Erté embodied the transition from the stylized line of art nouveau to art deco, a period he was later considered by many to epitomize. While his feeling for detail and his use of black-and-white had much in common with Aubrey Beardsley, his supposed model, Erté claimed to have been more affected in his technique by Persian miniatures and other oriental art forms. Those, of course, were sources for the fashions of Paul Poiret, the epochal French designer for whom Erté had worked, both designing and illustrating, in the previous decade. Actually, few of Erté's extravagant designs were executed. His presence and his reputation, his designs for the New York and Paris stage, had more lasting impact.

During the six months he was at MGM, Erté designed some remarkable costumes for Aileen Pringle in *The Mystic* and *Dance Madness,* 1924, and the costumes for Carmel Myers for the sequence of *Ben Hur,* 1926, filmed after the company had returned from Rome. In addition, he created costumes for the stars of various movies, including Marion Davies, Norma Shearer, Eleanor Boardman, Claire Windsor, Mae Murray, Mae Busch, Pauline Stark, Paulette Duval, Blanche Sweet, and Alice Terry.

Particularly important were his unexecuted designs for *Paris,* a 1925 movie planned with some sequences in color, including a nightclub and an ultramodern house: "My nightclub was triangular,

Sally, Irene and Mary, 1925. Photo: MoMA.

Erté had already used showgirls as part of the décor in his designs for the stage, so that idea was inevitable for his movie designs. Here Sally O'Neill is an elaborate finial on a spinning stage set.

Three Weeks, 1924. Conrad Nagel, Aileen Pringle.

Elinor Glyn, the British novelist who invented "It," although not a designer, had a great effect on the look of the movies. Here, in the screen version of her novel Three Weeks, *she saw to it that Aileen Pringle was dressed for the part with a tightly-coiled coiffure, à la Glyn, and surrounded by the necessary props for love-making, particularly a tiger-skin rug.*

Pl. 6
Mary Pickford costume for *Tess of the Storm Country*, 1922, designer unknown.

Mary Pickford's dress for Tess of the Storm Country, *1922, was of simple indigo and white cotton, but the patches were sewn with the greatest care, sometimes with embroidery stitches.*

Pl. 7
Mary Pickford costume for *My Best Girl*, 1927, designer unknown.

The twenties saw the emergence of the working girl and her basic black dress—a fashion idea seized upon by Mary Pickford for her role in My Best Girl, *1927, and by Chanel, who was fascinated by the wardrobe of the grisette.*

The Mystic, 1925. Photo: MoMA.

While his costumes were often too extreme to be witty, his visual allusions too perverse to be accepted, Erté transmitted a disturbing sexuality in his extravagant reworkings of the female body.

[left]
The Mystic, 1925. Aileen Pringle. Photo: MoMA.

Erté favored strange juxtapositions of fabrics and textures, often using oversize embroidery to create a graphic effect. While his stylized designs were not completely successful, or even popular, at the time, his ideas strongly influenced Hollywood costume design.

The Mystic, 1925. Aileen Pringle. Photo: MoMA.

Erté was accustomed to designing costumes for the stage, most notably the Folies Bergère, and he injected a bizarre theatricalism into his designs for the movies—often treating the actress as an ornament or decorative object rather than as a character.

Dance Madness, 1924. Claire Windsor. Photo: MoMA.

Erté relished visual puns—appliquéed eyes over the breasts and so on—but his favorite jokes were simpler, often served up with a Beardsleyan command of black-and-white, bawdy in their effrontery.

Pls. 8, 9 [*overleaf*]
Mary Pickford costume for *Dorothy Vernon of Haddon Hall*,
1924, designed by Mitchell Leisen. With detail.

*Mitchell Leisen, later a director, had worked as a
designer for De Mille, learning the need for the
appearance of authentic detail and expensive fabrics in historical movies. Dorothy Vernon of Haddon Hall, 1924, was one of Mary Pickford's few
costume pictures—not successful enough to overtake her Waif roles but memorable for its atmosphere.*

Publicity shot for *Ben Hur*, 1926. Erté, Carmel Myers. Photo: Collection of Carmel Myers. Photo: James Abbe.

Erté worked on only the American segment of Ben Hur, *but his touches were to appear again and again in the epic movies that followed at MGM. Carmel Myers collaborated with him on creating elaborate jewelry for his costumes, including multiple finger rings.*

Elinor Glyn, second from left, on the set of *His Hour* with John Gilbert, right.

Elinor Glyn, the presiding genius of twenties Hollywood glamour and romance, wrote and directed movies and told the stars how to talk, dress, and act on and off camera. Her ideas about costuming and behavior came straight out of the most florid late-Victorian and Edwardian novel-making—of which she was one of the most amply rewarded practitioners.

and decorated entirely in red and gold. . . . Technicolor was then in its infancy, and all the color sequences I had seen left me dissatisfied. There always seemed to be a profusion of violet and clashing colors, each overpowering the other. So I got in touch with the directors of Technicolor and explained to them the effects I wished to create. I wanted to use only a few colors at a time, to provide a feeling of harmony and *ambience.* . . . After the nightclub, I designed an extravagant interior which was to be the home of the film's hero. The drawing-room was black-and-white with one wall covered by an ermine curtain; in front of this wall stood a divan, also covered with ermine, on which were heaped cushions covered in black and white fox fur. I have always loved furs as furnishings and I still do. The drawing-room opened on to a dining-room but was separated from it by a wrought-iron grille. The dining-room was done in gold mosaic, with wrought-iron furniture. The seats were covered in panther skin. The table consisted of a fish tank covered with a slab of glass. The hall was star shaped, its walls, floor and ceiling were of black and white marble."

The year was 1925, and Erté later regretted that he had not been in Paris that year during the exhibition of decorative arts that gave art deco its name. Inadvertently, during his six months in Hollywood, he had helped to create Hollywood Modern, the style that would last until the late forties.

Much of the Victorianism of the previous decade persisted, however, in the portrayal of women. Mary Pickford continued to play girl-children almost until the advent of the talkies. Lillian Gish in *Way Down East,* 1920, and, with her sister Dorothy, in *Orphans of the Storm,* 1922, moved on with her role as a battered blossom, a characterization she expanded very slightly in *Romola,* 1924, and *The Scarlet Letter,* 1926. Those hardy waifs were as much a staple of the films of the twenties as they were of those of the teens.

Orphans of the Storm, 1922. Lillian Gish, Joseph Schildkraut. Photo: MoMA.

Griffith's historical movies seldom strayed into prettiness, but for Orphans of the Storm, *1922, he had costumes designed for the stars by Herman Tappé, selecting the costumes for the extras himself. "Tappé's designs were too much in the fashion of the time," said Lillian Gish.*

...starring

clara bow

With her bobbed hair, pouted lips, and saucer eyes, Clara Bow was the "It" girl, as contrived by Elinor Glyn, the British novelist in her sixties who was Hollywood's sexual mentor in the 1920s. "It," Glyn said, was a "strange magnetism which attracts both sexes. . . . There must be a physical attraction but beauty is unnecessary." Clara Bow had neither class nor beauty, but she had an interesting jiggle and she looked terrific in her step-ins. Clara Bow, Anita Loos said, "succeeded in being at one and the same time innocuous and flashy." In It, 1927, the film Elinor Glyn had devised to make her a star, Clara Bow played a lingerie salesgirl. Instead of playing the grand lady, more often than not she was a manicurist, usherette, waitress, cigarette girl, taxi dancer, or swimming instructor. Her jobs allowed her to meet men easily and to set up the exaggerated flirting for which she became famous. Her good-natured vulgarity had little to do with the usual brand of Hollywood glamour, but her antics and her gum-chewing, wisecracking familiarity gave her a rapport with her fans that few of her more worldly peers could match. She was a home-grown antidote to the exotic man-killers that overran movies before World War II. In her private life the red hair, matching limousine, and specially dyed dogs were the snappy contrast to the Continental pretensions of Mae Murray and Pola Negri. However, much like The Pinup of the forties, her type could not survive changing taste. Her sexual independence and slap-happy insolence were possible only in the social mobility of the twenties. Already emerging in the movies at the end of the decade was the hauntingly tragic heroine, epitomized by Greta Garbo, whose world-weary style passed for a sort of honor. Clara Bow was as much a caricature as the John Held flappers and Lorelei Lee.

The change in films was the appearance of a new and emancipated woman who was seen as realistic and independent, or more often as a sort of debased adventuress. On the lighter side, she was Lorelei Lee in *Gentlemen Prefer Blondes,* 1928. Romantically, she was the fictional persona of Elinor Glyn, who found love in *Three Weeks,* 1924. She was out for a good time, as Clara Bow was in most any of her movies. She knew how to dance, as Joan Crawford did in *Our Dancing Daughters,* 1928. She might lead men to destruction as Pola Negri did, or she might destroy herself as Greta Garbo did in *Flesh and the Devil,* 1927. But no matter, she was inevitably well-dressed.

Largely responsible for that ubiquitous character was Elinor Glyn, whose Edwardian novel, *Three Weeks,* had introduced all the heady accouterments of refined lovemaking, including devouring roses, lolling on leopard skins, and gazing soulfully. Before the emancipated heroines of D. H. Lawrence, the heroine of *Three Weeks* went to find out about life and love on her own—in highly orchidaceous prose. The British novelist and director was a sort of one-woman finishing school for Hollywood stars. Her flair for fashion was shared by her sister, Lady Duff-Cooper, who—as Lucille—had dressed Irene Castle for the stage and screen.

Elinor Glyn was successful because she told women not only what to wear, but what to think and do as well. When she articulated her concept of "It"—not sex, really, but a sort of presence—she was explaining the not-too-fine school of erotics that had been flirting with the sexually explicit since the first days of the film. Elinor Glyn was not a designer, but she had a tremendous impact on how the films looked, and in a sense she developed the more sophisticated concept of the woman's picture, with its reliance on the wardrobe to help tell the heroine's story.

Pl. 10
Lillian Gish costume for *Romola,* 1924, designer unknown.

Romola, 1924, starring Lillian Gish, was one of the first Hollywood movies to be made in Europe with actual locales in Florence and costumes patterned after Italian Renaissance paintings.

...starring
gloria swanson

Diminutive, mischievous but elegant, Gloria Swanson combined the savvy of The Flapper and the resilience of The Waif. From Mack Sennett to von Stroheim, she remains her own woman: the sort of good-humored fatalist that De Mille uncovered in her, not the other woman but the wife who is clever enough to steal her husband back. De Mille, perhaps only indirectly, showed her the authority that dressing up could bring her. She dressed and lived to the teeth, but finally it was her ability to get the right look in her eyes that made her success. About her, Elinor Glyn, the writer and director and arbiter of Hollywood appearances, said, "She has perhaps the loveliest eyes I have ever seen. They are strange eyes, not altogether occidental, which gives them their charm—blue eyes, a little up at the corners and the lashes half an inch long. This is the bond between us, perhaps; we both have up-at-the-corner Slavonic eyes." A major ingredient of Swanson's fame, however, was not her looks or her acting but how much money she spent. There were her enormous expenditures on clothes, her $100,000 New York penthouse, the twenty-five-acre estate on the Hudson, the perfumed elevator to her apartment, the gilded rather than silvered mirror that slid aside to reveal a movie screen. She didn't take it all seriously. "The public didn't want the truth and I shouldn't have bothered giving it to them," she said. When a fan expressed pleasure at finally meeting her in person, she said, "Yeah, and I bet you didn't expect such a runt." When she acquired the third of her five husbands—Henri, Marquis de la Falaise de Coudraye—she wired Paramount: "AM ARRIVING WITH THE MARQUIS TOMORROW STOP PLEASE ARRANGE OVATION."

Photo: James Abbe

Pl. 11
Costumes from the Paramount wardrobe (*far left and far right*) late twenties, designer unknown. Costume for Aileen Pringle, MGM wardrobe (*center*) late twenties, designed by Adrian.

Movies in the twenties often flirted openly with the pornographic, teasing the audience's voyeurism with glimpses of breasts and thighs. The boudoir scene was obligatory, as was revealing lingerie— a specialty of the Hollywood designer.

The star who seemed to most embody this sensationalism and glamour was Gloria Swanson, who made herself over from a Mack Sennett slapstick comedian to portray the new woman. She learned to act, but she also learned to wear clothes. She spent tens of thousands of dollars on her wardrobe—more on perfume in a year than the average workingman was earning. With her sleeked-down hair and luminous eyes, she was *the* young American. With her furs and jewels, her titled husband, she was the match of any member of royalty. From *Male and Female*, 1919, on, Gloria Swanson changed men almost as often as she changed dresses.

Typical of her wardrobe adventures was *Beyond the Rocks*, 1922—screenplay by Elinor Glyn—which linked her with Rudolph Valentino, the only force in films strong enough to deflect the independent woman. The plot is simple and well-dressed: a poor English girl—aristocratic, of course—marries an ailing elderly millionaire and then falls in love on her honeymoon with a darling young nobleman. Swanson and Valentino went into their clinches not just in modern dress, but in a series of costumed flashbacks as well.

PI. 12 [*opposite*]
Rudolph Valentino costume for *Blood and Sand*, 1922, designer unknown.

Rudolph Valentino was the only male star whose costumes were an integral part of his image. His glamour was Mediterranean and, in Blood and Sand, 1922, specifically Latin, a masculine counterpart of the Vamps and Sirens.

ZaZa, 1923. Photo: MoMA.

The Paramount wardrobe mistress picks up Gloria Swanson's showgirl headdress for ZaZa, 1923, with its 35-foot train, from the costumer.

ZaZa, 1923. Gloria Swanson, left. Photo: MoMA.

Gloria Swanson, a fantasy of roses, takes her place backstage in ZaZa, 1923, one of the movies for which Norman Norell designed costumes, strongly influenced by Aubrey Beardsley.

Madame Sans Gêne, 1925. Gloria Swanson. Photo: MoMA.

Just as Garbo's and Dietrich's movies were to epitomize the style of the thirties, Gloria Swanson's films represented the style of the twenties, with a wide range of costume pictures. Among the most notable was Madame Sans Gêne, 1925, *a period fashion show.*

Collection of Edith Head.

Travis Banton's trademarks were the shimmering surface, the softly feminine silhouette—both calculated for the movie camera and lighting—and the extravagant touch, a theatrical sense of fashion derived from French stage traditions.

Swanson's Flapper—a tag that came from the floppy galoshes many young things affected as part of their gear—takes on darker allure as the decade ends. In 1927, in *The Love of Sunya,* her costume changes are for flashforwards, since the heroine is able to use a crystal ball to make her amatory choices: love, not ambition or money. In 1928 she played *Sadie Thompson,* putting her fancy wardrobe aside. In 1928 also, under Erich von Stroheim's direction, she began—but did not finish—one of the most perversely erotic films ever made, *Queen Kelly.* In a reversal of the Cinderella story, Swanson played a convent girl who attracts the attention of a prince when she loses her bloomers. He kidnaps her and, back at the palace, she is beaten hideously by his mad mother. In the last reels, she is Queen Kelly, the owner of a string of South African whorehouses—oozed into a black sheath, dusted with orchids, and topped with pearls, her hard mouth pursed above a high neck.

Queen Kelly, 1928. Gloria Swanson. Photo: MoMA.

Cinderella lost her slipper and won a prince, but in von Stroheim's perverse retelling of the fairytale, Patricia Kelly, played by Gloria Swanson, loses her bloomers to win the prince, and ends up as the madam of a string of South African whorehouses —the magic of clothes.

Travis Banton, in a publicity shot taken in the mid-twenties, looks over the costumes of two Paramount bit players. Both costumes reflect the themes and treatment that are so prevalent in his costumes for Marlene Dietrich and Mae West in the thirties.

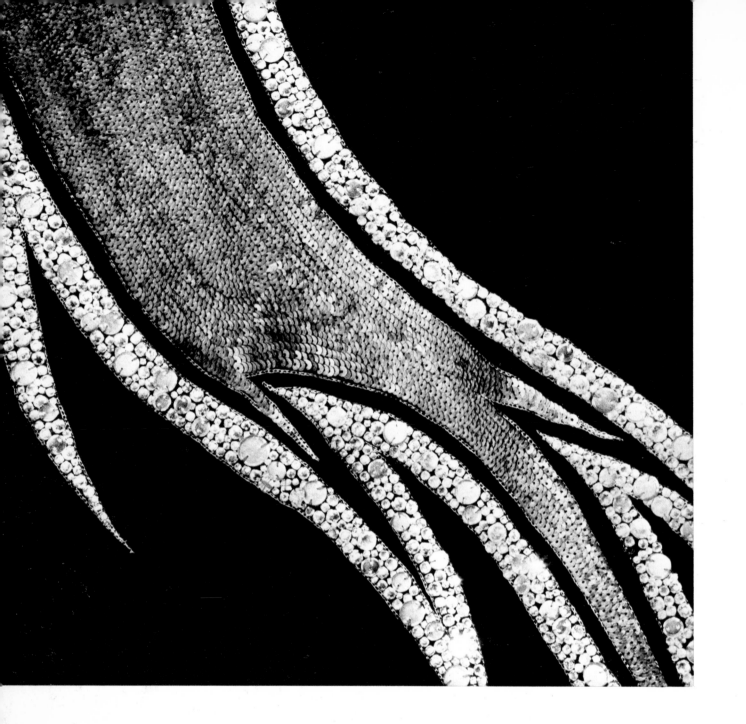

The counterpoint of the increasingly degraded flapper was Rudolph Valentino, whose dark and ambiguous sexuality galvanized the ardor of many a flapper. Valentino is important to any discussion of the Hollywood costume because of his remarkable second wife, Natacha Rambova, the stepdaughter of cosmetics manufacturer Richard Hudnut, and their introduction to Hollywood of Adrian, the most influential of the Hollywood designers.

Natacha Rambova had begun her career as a dancer and had been introduced to Hollywood by her friend, the actress Alla Nazimova, for whom she designed the sets and costumes for *Camille,* 1920, a production heavily influenced by the art nouveau and *Jugendstil* movements. A darkly beautiful woman, Rambova was introduced to Valentino during the filming of the modern version of the Dumas play.

Pls. 13, 14
Kay Johnson, costume for *Madame Satan,* 1930, designed by Adrian. With detail.

The introduction of technically better film stock in the twenties gave a new importance to the detail and finishing of costumes, as evidenced in this extraordinary embroidery of beads and sequins for the masquerade sequence in De Mille's Madame Satan, *1930, an improbable modern love story set on a dirigible. This item epitomizes the extravagance of costume design for the silent movies that gave way to relative austerity as more expensive sound productions came in.*

Aubrey Beardsley's influence on her work was even more pronounced in her settings and costumes for Nazimova's version of Oscar Wilde's *Salome,* 1923. Her highly stylized designs troubled the audience, and the film failed.

After her marriage to Valentino, Rambova elected to assume full control of her husband's career. She plunged into elaborate plans for a film of *Monsieur Beaucaire,* 1924, for which she had sixty costumes made from her designs while they honeymooned in Europe. (Poiret was executing her trousseau, also from her designs.) She was to be art director for the movie, and she added a scenic artist and two assistants; a costume director and four wardrobe assistants; an art selector, interior decorator, and assistant; an expert draper; and a supervisor of makeup. Her grandiose thinking scared management. Rambova anticipated the costs and staff of *Marie Antoinette* by a decade. Reviewers observed that that was the most visually impressive costume movie yet made, but the studio heads were concerned that the "effeminacy" of Valentino's showy role, and the highly mannered look of the movie, would spoil his image.

[*left*]
Salome, 1923. Alla Nazimova, right.

Nazimova allowed designer Natacha Rambova great freedom to experiment. Her costumes captured the 1890s decadence of Oscar Wilde's Salome, 1923, more than they suggested its Biblical antecedent, which was successful artistically but failed at the box office.

[*opposite*]

Rudolph Valentino's costumes for Monsieur Beaucaire, *1924, were designed by his wife, Natacha Rambova, and manufactured in France during their honeymoon. They were brilliant but foppish evocations of pre-revolutionary France.*

Blood and Sand, 1922.

The Sheik *and* Blood and Sand *gave Rudolph Valentino his image as a torrid lover, and in both movies the costumes set him apart from ordinary men—either flowing robes or tightly-fitted bull-fighting gear. Valentino understood not only the impact of what he was wearing, but how to carry the absurdities of his costumes with a flourish.*

Valentino referred to Rambova as "The Boss," and it was her interference with his career that provided a wedge for Paramount to divide the team. She had projected three movies under her visual direction and continued to recruit supporting talent for Valentino. Her most important discovery for the movies was a young New York designer, Adolph Adrian Greenburg, a graduate of the Parsons School of Design, who had done some stage costumes for Irving Berlin's *Music Box Revue,* 1923, a couple of editions of the *Greenwich Village Follies,* and George White's *Scandals.* He had also won a contest to design a drag costume for The Creole Fashion Plate, a female impersonator. Greenburg was to become known later as Adrian.

Before long, Rambova and Valentino were separated—both maritally and professionally. Plans for *The Hooded Falcon,* with a screenplay by Natacha Rambova and costumes by Adrian, were scrapped. Adrian went on to design the costumes for *Cobra,* 1924, starring Rudolph Valentino, but without Rambova.

Photo: James Abbe

Natacha Rambova designed her own trousseau for her wedding to Valentino in 1925, but she waited until they were on their honeymoon in Paris to have it run up by Paul Poiret, the great French designer. Then she modeled the finished dresses for the reporters who had come along to cover their months in France.

Valentino was one of the most expensively dressed stars of the twenties. For his last movie, produced the year of his death at 31, Valentino returned to his greatest success, *The Sheik,* 1922, making its sequel, *The Son of the Sheik,* 1926. The budget for his personal wardrobe, including jewelry and props, indicates the sort of expenditures concentrated on his person:

Sapphire ring with platinum setting	...$3,000
Antique silver bracelet	150
Wristwatch	150
Jeweled cigarette case	300
Jeweled patent lighter	150
Revolver	55
Antique belt and knife	550
Sword	4,000

Pl. 15
Mae Murray costume for *The Merry Widow,* 1925, designed by Adrian.

Mae Murray, along with other Hollywood personalities, claimed to have discovered Adrian, who did her gowns for The Merry Widow, *1925.*

Silver spurs	50
Turban	25
Two Arabian burnooses	450
Two silk headdresses	70
Two lambswool shirts	100
Two embroidered vests	300
Embroidered outer garment	350
Sash	20
Gold-embroidered coat	500
Two jewel-studded belts	600
Embroidered revolver holster	25
Arabian trousers	175
Breeches with braided frimming	75
Two pairs of imported boots	155
Slippers	30
	$11,260

Such a budget was typical in the clothes-conscious productions Adolph Zukor encouraged his directors to make. Just as Griffith's extraordinary imagination in all areas of moviemaking earlier had provided training for many important careers both on and off camera, the high-budget films Cecil B. De Mille made for Zukor were to be an important training ground for many costume designers —most notably, perhaps, Adrian, who worked for him in the late twenties. De Mille's movies, a mixture of materialism and morality, were crammed with expensive detail, more impressive than accurate. He prided himself on research, but the sets and costumes he ordered were straight out of the theatrical tradition of David Belasco, the impresario for whom his father had worked, who had emphasized "realism" in his stage productions.

De Mille understood that glamour and lavish production could go a long way in telling a story, so he laid great emphasis on his production team and on the efforts of his designers, particularly of sets and special effects.

In *The Golden Bed,* 1925, the rich but socially ostracized woman gives a fancy dress ball. The whole set was constructed and decorated with candy and even the costumes represent kinds of candy or are made of candy. The bandstand was the enormous, heart-shaped, satin-upholstered lid of a bonbon box with huge bonbon-shaped pillows scattered at its base. "The candy ball," De Mille said, "was put in to make an important story point: it was a wife's glittering revenge on the lofty matrons of the town who snubbed her for marrying a candy manufacturer, and it was so costly that it broke her husband and sent him to prison."

For De Mille, luxury has its edge, and it must serve his purpose. De Mille insisted on highly publicized expenditures for his stars. Before beginning shooting, he would carefully review the costumes and accessories for a picture—or so his publicity people said— and deliberately discard anything that was not expensive enough.

...starring

pola negri

Tiny, with a wide forehead and big, roaming eyes, Pola Negri was the twenties successor to The Vamp. Her greatest exoticism was simply that she was foreign. With no trace of humor, she played the same role both on and off the screen, particularly in her carryings-on after Valentino's death. A Polish importation from UFA, the German film company, she started a mock-feud at Paramount with Gloria Swanson, her major competitor. The fake rivalry was inadvertently fulfilled when Swanson decided she preferred working in New York. Pola Negri's chalk-white skin, her raven-black hair, her green-shadowed eyes and pouty red mouth were the products of hours of careful preparation. Howard Greer, the costume designer, said she was willing to hold up shooting if her shoes weren't dyed the proper shade to match her dress—and that in the days of black-and-white. As Greer described their first meeting to discuss costumes for The Spanish Dancer, *" 'Now,' she said in a low voice that shook the nails right out of my shoes, 'now you weel make for me clothes like no one has evair made before? Yes?' This, apparently, was a rhetorical question, for Pola went right on talking. She told me all about herself, how wonderful she was, how important, how glamorous." At the screening of daily takes, Negri was in the habit of crooning to herself, "But I am so boao-ti-fool! No one is more boao-ti-fool." Some of the basis for Negri's glamour is indicated by one reviewer of* Passion, *1920: "She is lovely in many scenes, it is true, but some of her features are not beautiful and she makes no apparent effort to pose becomingly without regard to the meaning of her performance. She is expressive. That is her charm. She makes* Du Barry *real, as fascinating as she has to be, with as much of the appearance of dignity as she must have on occasion, and as contemptible and cowardly as she was. She actually wins sympathy for a woman who cannot at any time be admired. It is an achievement."*

The King of Kings, 1927. Victor Varconi, Jacqueline Logan.
Photo: MoMA.

Adrian's apprenticeship with De Mille played an important role in his development as a designer. He learned to emphasize research, luxury, and sex as the chief ingredients of costume design. For The King of Kings, 1927, Mary Magdalene became a sumptuously dressed courtesan—a whore with a cloth of gold.

He wanted *real* fur, *real* jewels—or at least elaborately made jewels that *looked* real—and *real* splendor. But he was practical enough to use some illusions in the costumes of his extras, as the costumes still hanging on the racks at Paramount amply reflect.

De Mille continued the theatrical tradition that Adolph Zukor had begun (for what became Paramount Pictures) with the import of *Queen Elizabeth* in the previous decade. Zukor saw to it that the costumes created by his designers were publicized as a part of the studio's image. Dress books were issued that contained linen-backed photographs not only of the stars, but also of the designers at work.

Two of the most influential of those designers—hired in 1923 and 1924 respectively—were Howard Greer and Travis Banton, both of whom had worked for Lucille (Lady Duff-Cooper), the famous New York couturière.

Greer, a favorite of Pola Negri and more a couturier than a costume designer, did not stay long at Paramount but soon opened a *maison de couture* on Wilshire Boulevard in the mid-twenties. (Edith Head started out as a sketcher for Greer in 1923.)

"New York and Paris justifiably looked down their august noses at the dresses we designed in Hollywood," Greer said. "Well, maybe they were vulgar, but they did have imagination. If they were gaudy, they merely reflected the absence of subtlety which characterized all early motion pictures.

"Overemphasis, as it applied to acting techniques and story treatments, was essential. If a lady in real life wore a train one yard long, her prototype in film wore one three yards long. If a duchess at the Court of St. James perched three feathers on her pompadour, the cinematic duchess perched six, just to be on the safe side. The most elegant Chanel of the early twenties was a washout on the screen. When you strip color and sound and the third dimension from a moving object, you have to make up for the loss with dramatic black-and-white contrasts and enriched surfaces."

When Greer was asked to design the costumes for one of Pola Negri's earliest American roles, as the wife of a Long Island commuter bank clerk who is called upon to give a dinner party for her husband's boss in her modest cottage, "The bank clerk's little helpmeet greeted her guests in a shimmering silver sheath, solidly embroidered in rhinestones and pearls. She wore twenty ropes of pearls and carried a fan of aigrettes."

About the Paramount films of the twenties and thirties, for many of which she designed costumes, Edith Head said, "There was perhaps a more personal, more subjective touch encouraged at the studio in those days. Other studios might make the big film, but at

...starring
louise brooks

Her hair in cleanly cut bangs, her dark eyes sharp and intense, Louise Brooks caught a sort of real chic that was almost totally lacking in the Hollywood of the twenties. Her look, her apparent ease, suddenly caught on again with the young European film-makers a good generation after she had been forgotten by American movie fans. As a salute to her, Jean-Luc Godard gave Anna Karina her Dutchboy haircut in Vivre Sa Vie (Her Life to Live). Echoing Brooks's appearance in her German films, Liza Minnelli was made up like her in Cabaret, 1972. Her importance, however, is not simply her image but the role she played in the evolution of that destructive feminine sexuality that had fascinated Hollywood from the beginning: the Salome theme. Her contribution is closely related to the whole matrix of movie psychology, an ambiguous girl-woman who disarms and destroys men with her sexual charms. Her means were exceptional only because of their vitality. For the most part, her Hollywood movies were in the collegiate-flapper genre where her sophisticated se-ductiveness was most evidently out of place. Reversing the usual pattern, the extraordinary German director, G. W. Pabst, wanted to bring her to Germany to star in his filming of Wedekind's powerful play Pandora's Box, also adapted by Alban Berg as an opera, Lulu. Paramount re-fused to lend her and Brooks quit to play the role, thereby destroying her Hollywood career. In the meantime, thinking Brooks was not free, Pabst had auditioned the then-minor actress Marlene Dietrich. Louise Brooks, however, made the film Pandora's Box, 1929, in Germany and created the films' most brilliant portrait of the diabolical woman, a nymphomaniac who destroys every man who chances into her fatal sphere. Her performance was perhaps the most erotic ever given in the movies, totally against the grain of the archly sophisti-cated and the falsely exotic.

Paramount there was more evidence of the individuals who worked to make the films. Even De Mille's epics had that touch.''

The major factor in the look of Paramount's films was Hans Dreier, the studio's art director, who had come to America in the early twenties from UFA, the German film company. Long before Woodrow Wilson's sanctions against trade with postwar Germany had been lifted, Zukor had secretly formed distribution and production deals with the German company. Eventually, he was able to lure away many of the studio's technicians and use some of the German stars, such as Pola Negri and Emil Jannings. That link led most conspicuously to the joint production of *The Blue Angel,* 1930, with an American director, Josef von Sternberg, and a German star, Emil Jannings—and introducing Marlene Dietrich.

Dreier brought with him the expressionist preoccupations of the German movies and a highly skilled use of lighting to create atmosphere and suggest mood. He had designed Dimitri Buchowetski's film *Danton,* from the episodically constructed play about the French Revolution, using lighting to suggest the panoramic sweep of the drama. Dreier had a feeling for the satirically telling detail that found its expression notably in the films he designed for Ernst Lubitsch, who later worked for Paramount.

Through Dreier's influence, less emphasis was placed on the physical production and greater attention was paid to the dramatic possibilities of lighting. That esthetic was epitomized by von Sternberg's films, and it formed the contrast between the films of Paramount and those of the other studios.

Valentino's death in 1926 marked the end of the first phase of Hollywood's development—mass hysteria, showy grief, and suicides attending his funeral. But the high phase—and for many, the classical phase—of moviemaking had already begun in 1924 with the formation of Metro-Goldwyn-Mayer. The merger represented the linking of the production and management know-how of Louis B. Mayer and his production chiefs, Harry Rapf and Irving Thalberg (already the *Wunderkind* of wonderland), with the Loew's theater chain, an important guarantee of booking. Also included in the deal was Cosmopolitan Productions, William Randolph Hearst's independent company for movies starring Marion Davies.

The Merry Widow, 1925, one of MGM's earliest and largest-grossing movies, was in many ways a dress rehearsal for the sort of movie that represented the studio's ascendancy until the late 1940s. The producer was Irving Thalberg, whose careful attention to detail, emphasis on professionalism on all levels, and involvement with ''authentic'' atmosphere were to stamp MGM movies with a characteristic finish and splendor. His talents, in a sense, went very much against the grain of the usual Hollywood production types

Von Stroheim dropped an American Follies troupe into The Merry Widow, *1925, with a knowing cynicism, encouraging costume designer Kathleen Kay to play off their innocent depravity in a welter of sight gags. Cutting in is John Gilbert.*

Pl. 16
Mae Murray costume for *The Merry Widow,* 1925, designed by Adrian.

Mae Murray often consciously used dancing and dance costumes as metaphors for sexuality—movement disguising her limited range of acting. Her movies are full of staircases, crazy headdresses, and glittery costumes, props she carried over from the Ziegfeld Follies.

because he was willing to trust, up to a point, the carefully selected people who worked for him.

The first phase of moviemaking had hinged on the switch from the highly entertaining, if often vulgar, two-reel quickies to the filmed stage play—a switch that had been calculated to appeal to a more affluent audience. Thalberg continued in that vein, often shopping on Broadway for stars and vehicles. But he set out to give Hollywood its own authority. By 1934, MGM was employing four thousand people for the actual making of movies. Thalberg also turned to the classics for stories, because he understood they had a basically wider and more developed popular appeal than the theater. Finally, he was firmly convinced of the importance of the visual component of films, and he was willing to spend huge amounts of money on settings and costumes.

The Merry Widow proved to be a provocative, even explosive, experiment with Thalberg's ideas. For the director, Thalberg chose Erich von Stroheim, with whom he had already had enormous difficulties over the making of *Greed,* 1923, when they had been working for the Goldwyn Company. *The Merry Widow*—a vast, sprawling movie, brilliantly made and unrelentingly cynical—ran more than nine hours in its finished cut and is regarded by many as

the most fully realized movie, in visual terms, ever made. As a result of that financially disastrous production, Thalberg became intensely concerned about keeping the costs of production in line. According to legend, von Stroheim described one of the characters in *The Merry Widow* as "having a foot fetish." "Yes," Thalberg was supposed to have said, "and you have a footage fetish."

Von Stroheim, an actor from a poor Viennese family, had been an extra in *Birth of a Nation,* and acted in *Intolerance* and *Hearts of the World,* all while working as production assistant for D. W. Griffith. Much of his absorption with atmosphere and detail came from his work with Griffith. In fact, he carried Griffith's method a step further and used costume as a major tool in his exposition of character. Also, he evolved a highly symbolic and fictional version of Europe, usually Middle Europe, as a metaphor for human vanity and sexuality.

Von Stroheim in *The Merry Widow* develops in great detail his own version of The Flapper, with a few nasty jabs at the career of his star, Mae Murray, whose casting von Stroheim had strongly opposed. In the opening sequence, Mae Murray/Sally O'Hara arrives in Monteblanco, the name von Stroheim gave his operetta kingdom, with the company of the Manhattan Follies. "Flo Epstein, Mgr" read the trunks—an allusion to Murray's start in the *Ziegfeld Follies.*

Von Stroheim and Murray quickly clashed. She wanted John Gilbert as a co-star. The director loathed the star system; he would pit Mae Murray's pale, pretty face against one of his favorite grotesques. She wanted the Great Waltz to be the centerpiece of the movie, the one concession she wrenched from von Stroheim. He wanted with a vengeance to avoid the musical aspects of the story. Murray got Gilbert but, in a surprising vote of confidence, the studio ruled in favor of von Stroheim's conception. They even permitted the chamberpots in the royal bedroom and the queen's false teeth in a drinking glass on the night table that Murray had complained about.

The mist-covered mountains of Monteblanco were filmed in the Sierras by cameraman William Daniels, later famous for his camera work with Greta Garbo. The sets and art direction were by von Stroheim, Captain Richard Day, and Cedric Gibbons, the chief art director of MGM and a major force in the quality of films through the thirties.

Adrian designed the gowns for Mae Murray, who did not bother to consult the director about how the character should be dressed. (Mae Murray later claimed to have discovered Adrian.) Because von Stroheim had photographed her so flatteringly—often using as many as six layers of gauze for her closeups—Mae Murray had

Pl. 17
Mae Murray costume for *The Merry Widow,* 1925, designed by Adrian.

Von Stroheim wanted The Merry Widow, *1925, to have a realistic flavor and he fulminated against what he thought was Mae Murray's phony glamour.*

been fairly cooperative until the obligatory Great Waltz sequence at Maxim's. Von Stroheim wanted to blend the dance with the action. She wanted a full musical-comedy production number. About her tight black dress, feathered headdress, and diamond necklace— more suitable for a *Follies* finale—the director kept his silence. He finally agreed to shoot the scene as she wanted, but in one long shot without stopping the cameras, a grueling demand on the dancers.

After shooting the sequence again and again, von Stroheim shouted to Murray, "If this stinks, it won't be my fault. You had the whole floor to yourself." Then, he walked off the set. Mae Murray came unglued. "You dirty Hun," she screamed as she flew at him. As a result, von Stroheim was fired and then rehired. "MAE–VON SIGN PEACE" read the newspaper headlines.

From the first sequence, when Sally O'Hara adjusted her torn stocking, to the last sequence, with its opulent mating dance, the tone of the film is voyeuristic. When the three main characters first saw Sally on the stage, the camera also took a look through the trio's opera glasses. One looked at her face, one at her crotch, and the third at her feet. The first tender love scene—with two blindfolded androgynous musicians playing in the background— was juxtaposed with a wild party given by the lecherous Prince Mirko. According to Hollywood legend, that scene was filmed on a closed set as a sadistic orgy, with the guests cruelly fondling a woman who had been tied to a chair. Under duress, Sally married the foot fetishist, who died on their wedding night in a paroxysm of delight over her feet. Thus the merry widow was launched, suddenly rich because of her husband's timely death.

The fantasy of The Flapper reached its end in *Queen Kelly,* the uncompleted Gloria Swanson movie that von Stroheim began in 1928. In that movie, The Waif was transformed into a madam, from the corrupted into the corruptor. That perverse version of the feminine was to emerge in the next decade as one of the most potent images of woman that the movies had yet produced.

1930s

The Fatal Woman and The Hoofer

...starring
marlene dietrich

With her cool expression, her languorous voice, and her devastating walk, Marlene Dietrich was *The Fatal Woman*, maddening in her sameness and self-absorption. Whatever her beauty, it is always played off against props: the painterly makeup, the preposterous false eyelashes, the gorilla suit, the travesty white tuxedo, the impossible theatrical drag. Perhaps her allure is not so much due to her glamour but rather is due to her being trapped within it, vulnerable to the getup she has been forced to wear, the role she has been conscripted to play. Her collaboration with von Sternberg is significant because of the qualities that became isolated in her image, the versions of the entertainer, the good-time girl she was to play over and over again. Her slacks, polo coats, and mannish hats, her cooking, and her grandchildren are all ploys with which Dietrich sought to counter her on-screen type. Nevertheless, she seemed frozen into her mold —timeless as Garbo but more a victim of the silliness of the contrived movies in which she appeared. Dietrich was a careful student of lighting and photography, and she demanded complete control of the circumstances in which she appeared, starting from the movies after von Sternberg to her rare appearances on television. For her debut in Las Vegas in 1954, she concocted with Jean Louis a flesh-colored net sheath iced over with beads and garnished with white fox. Later, she was asked to lend it to a benefit fashion show in Los Angeles. "Surprisingly, she agreed," said Louis. "But she reserved the right to select the starlet who would wear it. The girl she picked was gorgeous, tall with enormous breasts. The night of the show, out she came on the runway, her breasts flattened by the beadwork. Marlene had neglected to supply her with the rubber bodysuit we had also dreamed up for the dress."

"Gimme a visky with chincher ale on the side—and don't be stingy, baby." Thirty-four minutes into *Anna Christie,* 1930, Greta Garbo spoke her first line on the screen. After months of careful preparation, Irving Thalberg had decided that Garbo was ready to talk. About her image, Garbo said, "Screen vamps make me laugh tremendously. The fact I am considered one makes me laugh even more."

Garbo's new career in the talkies was in many ways a continuation of her previous one in the silents. She went on playing the fallen woman, the extraordinarily beautiful creature vulnerable to men, who is willing to give her life for love. To a large extent, her power was in the emptiness of her expression, that so much could be projected by the audience into the evocative blankness of her face. For the famous ending of *Queen Christina,* when she stood in the prow of the ship that carried her into exile, the director Rouben Mamoulian had told her to think of nothing. The resulting image was haunting, one of the most transcendently beautiful images in any movie.

The enigmatic and expressive power of Garbo's face was inevitably a subject for MGM's publicity department. Howard Strickling, the head of the studio's publicity, had Garbo's face pasted on a photograph of the Sphinx at Giza, as Paramount was later to impose Dietrich's on the "Mona Lisa." (Earlier, in Germany, UFA had superimposed Dietrich's face on a reproduction of Gainsborough's "Blue Boy.") The comparison with the Sphinx was an attempt to define exactly what Garbo's cinematic presence did convey. That image was largely a result of the collaboration of the studio and, most notably, William Daniels, the cameraman who worked with Garbo from the beginning of her Hollywood career in 1925.

"My first memory of her is very clear," Daniels said. "I made a few simple closeups of her. She couldn't speak a word of English and she was terrifically shy. She didn't enjoy it any better than I did. We lit very much to find their best features and accent those features very strongly. Especially eyes. And Garbo had magnificent eyes. She looked much better photographed from the left and I always insisted that directors took note of that. It wasn't a real problem, though, as it was with many stars; you could use both sides if you had to."

Garbo had vanilla-wafer-colored hair and deep-set blue eyes with large irises, set off by lashes so long that they caused other actresses to begin wearing false ones. For her personal makeup she used little more than powder and, at times, an ice cube "to wake her face up." For the screen, she used a version of stage makeup, almost like ballet makeup, to set off her eyes. First, with the eye closed, the eyeball was outlined and then the initial line blurred, softened, and blended. Then a definite black line was drawn under the eyelashes on the bottom lid. At the corner of each eye, a bracket was drawn, pointing outward. Those brackets served to enlarge her eyes and gave them their characteristic shape.

"I didn't create a 'Garbo face,' " Daniels said. "I just did portraits of her I would have done for any star. My lighting of her was determined by the requirements of a scene. I didn't, as some say I did, keep one side of the face lighted and the other dark. But I did always try to make the camera peer into the eyes, to see what was there. With Garbo's naturally long eyelashes, and in certain moods, I could throw the light down from quite high, and show the shadows of the eyelashes coming down on the cheeks: it became a sort of trademark for her."

Daniels worked with other major stars at MGM as well, but the filming of Garbo was his most memorable creation. Out of consideration for Garbo's shyness, Daniels began to put up black flats to keep out onlookers when a shot was being done with her.

Pl. 18
Greta Garbo costume from unidentified film, designed by Adrian.

Lingerie was among the most glamorous of the sub-genres of Hollywood costume—an essential part of the movies' prurience. This negligee of taupe silk marquisette, very much like the one Greta Garbo wore in her famous love scene with John Barrymore in Grand Hotel, *1932, is a masterpiece of finishing and detail, fragile, but painstakingly made.*

greta garbo

The essence of the glamorous and romantic, the presiding presence of Hollywood's golden years, Greta Garbo was a radically new sort of actress for the movies, a screen rather than a stage actress with a great inner style that manifested itself in every gesture. Her movies are full of wonderful moments, memorable because they reveal the character of the woman she is playing more surely than any twist of the plot. Shortly after her arrival in America from Sweden, Garbo wrote to a friend rather gloomily, ''They don't have a type like me out here, so if I can't learn to act they'll soon tire of me, I expect.'' Unlike Dietrich's Hollywood transformation, Garbo's metamorphosis was not mainly cosmetic—although the MGM doctors did keep her on a strict diet for her first few pictures. She came just when the panchromatic movie film that made it possible to render her hair in light tones had been perfected and she was fortunate to have a first-rate cameraman, William Daniels, assigned to her almost immediately. (Daniels shot nineteen of her twenty-four films.) In addition, she had directors who were sensitive to her technique, moving in to allow her face to register in closeups its amazing range of emotions. She didn't need to alter her face to express her change of emotion, Clarence Brown said: ''The change in her eyes did it all.'' Garbo was decidedly workmanlike in her sense of herself as an actress. She said she didn't care about her image off-camera, but one of her colleagues from that period said she went out of her way to be conspicuous. Garbo was alert to the technical side of moviemaking, and she would constantly check camera angles and the position of the lights. She was particularly concerned that her feet might show in any of the scenes. Beneath her elaborate gowns for the costume pictures, or even when she was dressed for a contemporary role, she always wore comfortable house-slippers.

With the talkies came a new friendship and collaboration for Garbo in Salka Viertel, the writer and former actress, who was the wife of Austrian writer-director Berthold Viertel. Salka Viertel encouraged Garbo to take on more ambitious parts, to break away from the frivolous mold in which she had been cast. Because of her immersion in the same Middle European *milieu* as the producers, Salka Viertel, interestingly, proposed merely a more intellectual version of the *femme fatale* that Garbo had played over and over. One of Salka Viertel's first suggestions for a new role was Queen Christina of Sweden: ''The preposterous child of the heroic Gustav Adolph, she was eccentric, brilliant; her masculine education and complicated sexuality made her an almost contemporary character. Also, her escapism, her longing for a world outside puritanical Protestant Sweden, to which she was chained by her crown, fascinated me.''

In 1932, Garbo's contract with MGM was up and a new one was negotiated on the basis of her playing the role of the Swedish queen. Thalberg had often said he did not like historical dramas but

PI. 19
Greta Garbo costume for *Queen Christina*, 1933, designed by Adrian.

Military uniforms provided Adrian with many of his ideas, but nowhere was the martial influence more evident than in his costumes for Queen Christina, *1933, particularly in this gold-braided gown.*

preferred movies about "relationships between people." *Queen Christina*, he told Salka Viertel in their first script conference, "had to be daring and 'human,' not a pageant, the characters unusual. However, it should be possible for the audiences to identify with them."

Then he asked Salka Viertel if she had seen *Mädchen in Uniform*, a German film that was centered on a lesbian relationship. "Does not Christina's affection for her lady-in-waiting indicate something like that?"

"He wanted me to keep it in mind," said Salka Viertel, "and perhaps, if handled with taste, it would give us very interesting scenes."

Nonetheless, that aspect of Queen Christina's personality was expressed not so much by the screenplay as by Adrian's costumes for Garbo. With remarkable simplicity, he dressed her as a man,

...starring

joan crawford

With one of the longest careers of the movies, Joan Crawford has changed her looks to suit each of the epochs she has passed through, working consciously to make her face more and more distinctively photogenic. The pretty starlet of the twenties enlarged her eyes, thickened her eyebrows, emphasized her large mouth instead of playing it down, and emerged with a highly individual style. Crawford started as The Flapper, moved through a series of stylish successes in the thirties, then made a third career playing mature— but often not glamorous—women in the forties. As Mae West and Marlene Dietrich reflected the sensibility of Travis Banton at Paramount, Joan Crawford was the reflection of Adrian's taste, even providing the inspiration for his famous padded shoulders. About Adrian, Crawford said, "He had an unerring sense of what was useful for a dramatic scene or what would distract from a dramatic scene. Most important, he knew all of us, and how we would play a scene—before we knew ourselves." Crawford was five feet four and a half inches tall "with size twelve hips and forty-inch shoulders." The Adrian square shoulders were a natural extension of her silhouette. She wore his look off-screen to great advantage and adapted his ideas to her personal wardrobe: "Adrian always played down the designs for the big scene," Crawford said. "For the lighter scene he'd create a 'big' dress. His theory, of course, was that an absolutely stunning outfit would distract the viewer from the highly emotional thing that was going on. There should be just the actress, her face registering her emotions, the body moving to express her reactions—the dress is only the background. But in the next scene, where she goes to the races and cheers for her horse, the costume would be just absolutely smashing."

Pl. 20
Joan Crawford costume for *The Bride Wore Red*, 1937, designed by Adrian.

Of Adrian's designs, none is more a tour-de-force than his red bugle-bead evening gown for Joan Crawford in The Bride Wore Red, *1937 (a black-and-white movie), with the color of the beading subtly shaded across the gown to enhance the contours of the star's body.*

using a stiff, starched white collar to frame her face. Even when dressed as a woman, the upper half of Garbo's costumes retained their mannish simplicity. With *Queen Christina*, Adrian hit his stride as the most influential of the Hollywood designers. His method had remained very much the same since his early work for Rudolph Valentino. Adrian recognized the screen impact of the carefully delineated military torso, with its echoes and variations in other masculine attire, and he appropriated it as his look. His signature, the padded shoulders, evolved from this triangular look. (In 1932, fitting Joan Crawford for her costumes for *Letty Lynton*, he had decided to make her broad shoulders an asset. "My God, you're a Johnny Weissmuller," he said, and then proceeded to exaggerate her shoulders.)

Thus, the torso and head became the focus of Adrian's designs, and the skirts were used to provide a shape to fill out the overall effect. His use of fabric was prodigal—relying heavily on silks, velvets, and expensive furs—and he was not much concerned about how much of his work was seen by the audience. For example, one embroidered panel in Queen Christina's coronation gown cost eighteen hundred dollars.

Adrian also emphasized Garbo's face and eyes with a series of startling hats: the much-copied cloche for *A Woman of Affairs*, 1929, the pillbox for *As You Desire Me*, 1932, the turban for *The Painted Veil*, 1934, the skullcap for *Mata Hari*, 1931. "Garbo isn't very fond of the fashionable hat of the moment," Adrian

Pl. 21
Greta Garbo costume for *Anna Karenina*, 1935, designed by Adrian.

There were few changes of pace in Adrian's designs. An exception was Anna Karenina, 1935, with its subdued but complex wardrobe, including this delicate afternoon dress in pale blue-green damask and silk marquisette, trimmed with gray-green silk taffeta.

Pl. 22
Greta Garbo costume for *Anna Karenina*, 1935, designed by Adrian.

Adrian often worked on a monumental scale, dressing the MGM stars in costumes that were almost overpowering in their mass. This is particularly true of the historical costumes he designed for Garbo.

Pl. 23 [below]
Mary Pickford costume for *Secrets*, 1933, designer unknown.

Mary Pickford made a valiant and often underrated try at surviving into the sound era, but her audiences were not charmed by her as a grown-up. Secrets, 1933, an essay in nostalgia, was her last picture—awash in petticoats.

[*left*]
Romeo and Juliet, 1936. Norma Shearer. Photo: MoMA.

A major test of Adrian's position at MGM was the production of Romeo and Juliet, *1936, for which Oliver Messel, the British designer, was hired to do both the sets and costumes. Adrian protested and he eventually designed some of the costumes, notably those for Norma Shearer.*

Pl. 24 [*opposite*]
Jeanette MacDonald costume for *Firefly,* 1937, designed by Adrian.

Adrian's strident designs were matched by the powerful and distinctive personalities of Garbo, Shearer, and Crawford. This evening dress from Firefly, *1937, more conventional and less assertive, was perhaps his response to Jeanette MacDonald.*

said. "Nor is she fond of the fashionable hairdress. As she does not wear her hair in a way that suits the current hats and is very fond of personal-looking ones, they are apt to appear rather unusual to eyes accustomed to the prevailing mode. The combination of individualistic hat and hair arrangement often gives Garbo a rather extraordinary style effect."

Adrian maintained his sway at MGM because of his carefully maintained friendships with the stars. His workrooms were in Wardrobe, the large stucco-covered barn on the back lot. Near the entrance were the workers, mainly Spanish-speaking. Labor was cheap in the thirties—there were no unions—and the studio was able to hire tailors and fitters for from $15.85 to $21 a week. In long rows against the wall stood the dressmaker's dummies, tagged with famous names, that were used in making the costumes.

Mata Hari, 1931. Greta Garbo.

Pl. 25
Greta Garbo costume for *Mata Hari,* 1931, designed by Adrian.

Adrian's costumes for Garbo in Mata Hari, 1931, are among his most exotic; an evocation, perhaps, of the orientalism of Paul Poiret, who dressed the World War I spy, and Adrian's own sense of Garbo mystery.

Adrian had a feeling for off-beat visual undercurrents, sometimes making prints with unexpected details, or allusions to unexpected costume sources that were disturbing and attention-getting. In Camille, 1936, for example, the reference is more Russian than French—more a ponderous Russian copy of mid-nineteenth-century French style than the style itself.

Adrian's studio was an enormous room with long shuttered windows edged in ruffled net. There he turned out fifty or so sketches a day, shaking out his brushes on the beige carpet. At one end was a spotlighted platform where costumes being fitted could be tried out under the same lights with which they would be filmed. Adrian also kept in the living room of his house a dummy with a costume from his latest picture.

Camille, 1936, was Adrian's most important picture with Garbo and, indeed, perhaps the single most impressive picture (certainly Garbo's most successful) made at MGM—one of the last

Pl. 27

The studios often made duplicates and triplicates of even the most expensive costumes in a major movie such as Camille. Some might be used for publicity shots, but at least one was held in reserve in case a scene might have to be re-shot or some damage might occur to the original. Even so, equal care was lavished on each of the versions, including the use of expensive fur.

Pl. 28
Greta Garbo costume for *Camille*, 1936, designed by Adrian.

No expense was spared for the costumes made during Hollywood's golden years, although the actual luxury of the fabrics and furs was often lost on the screen. An excellent example is this cream silk and gold lamé evening coat, embroidered in gilt and edged in mink, that was worn in only one sequence of Camille, 1936, a black-and-white movie.

Camille, 1936. Jessie Ralph, Greta Garbo. Photo: MoMA.

Adrian's treatment of the world of the demimon-
daine in Camille, *1936, is markedly restrained. His*
sense of period is less that of the nineteenth-
century drawings of rapacious women by Con-
stantin Guys than that of the respectably kept
woman of the nineteen-thirties.

produced under the aegis of Irving Thalberg. The movie was budgeted at one and a half million dollars.

"We have a problem," Thalberg told his staff. "The audience must forget with the first five minutes that this is a costume picture. It must be contemporary in its feelings, but one thing militates against that effect: the point that a girl's past can ruin her marriage. That problem doesn't exist any more. Whores can make good wives; that has been proven."

"Doing the costumes for *Camille,*" Adrian later said, "was an exercise in charm." That charm could be expressed in everything from forty-yard crinolines to snoods, fringed parasols, bustles, and pyramided skirts.

Camille, 1936. Greta Garbo, Robert Taylor.

Garbo's flat chest and broad shoulders were considered defects until Adrian displayed them to great advantage in his costumes for Camille, 1936. Somehow, the baring of Garbo's shoulders made her all the more vulnerable.

Adrian retained his sway at MGM by carefully ingratiating himself into the trust of the stars whom he dressed. As a result, he was one of Garbo's few confidants—understanding, and perhaps exploiting, her peculiar exhibitionism.

Thalberg's death in 1936 marked the end of the creative period in MGM's history, a period that had lasted a little over ten years. Two of Thalberg's major projects were still outstanding and their fate, without his careful sponsorship, was significant for the course of movie history, not just at MGM but in general.

Salka Viertel had first suggested that Garbo play Maria Walewska, Napoleon's Polish mistress, and Thalberg had reluctantly concurred, with an eye to the European market that was the major support of movies starring the actress. He budgeted *Conquest,* 1937, at $2 million, an almost unheard-of amount for an historical picture. He

cast Charles Boyer as Napoleon opposite Garbo and put the film into production. The results were ruinous: Garbo was "elegantly anemic"; Adrian's empire gown made the worst of her flat chest and caved-in shoulders; after two years of arguments about the screen treatment, the censors insisted that history be rewritten to prove Maria Walewska suffered retribution for her illegitimate child by Napoleon; and the production ran $800,000 over budget. What had been clearly needed was Thalberg's careful use of cutting and reshooting in the films he had supervised to inject some excitement into the footage. (Because of him, directors referred to MGM as the "Valley of the Retake.") Even more important, his presence was lacking in the total look of the picture.

Pl. 29
Greta Garbo costume for *Camille*, 1936, designed by Adrian.

Adrian's designs for Garbo are full of surprises that were often hidden from the camera—luxuries meant to please her alone that he worked into the details and the undergarments. An example of such secret opulence is this embroidery placed far up under an enormous mink cuff.

Pl. 30
Greta Garbo costume for *Camille*, 1936, designed by Adrian.

Seeming contradictions intrigued Adrian—the small head and the big silhouette or, as in this walking costume from Camille, *1936, the huge shape with the delicately worked embroidery. His method was derived, in part, from a keen sense of the values of both the long shot and the close-up.*

...starring
norma
shearer

Hardly beautiful by classical standards, not even glamorously exotic, Norma Shearer with her crisp, well-groomed elegance was a slickly presented product of the star system. Her limitations were extreme but she worked successfully to turn each of her faults to her advantage. Short, with slightly bowed legs, but with a remarkable camera presence that allowed her to steal scenes, Shearer was not the type to play sophisticated-woman roles, but she made herself over and became a hit at the box office. Adrian designed a special silhouette for her that gave her a higher waistline and lower hemline, concealing her legs and disguising her ample hips. She struggled with her brassy voice until she had achieved a measure of smoothness. She learned to practice a high degree of objectivity in selecting her publicity stills, ruthlessly discarding the ones that emphasized her imperfect nose and squarish jaw. Her accomplice in this unceasing process was her husband, Irving Thalberg, whose position as top producer at MGM greatly facilitated her career. In addition, she was expert at getting the advice and help of the studio craftsmen, particularly Adrian and Sidney Guillaroff, a fellow Canadian whom she had hired away from his highly successful hairdressing salon in New York. Of all the Hollywood stars of the period, she was most dependent on the visual power of costume to help convince the audience of her veracity in a role. Much care and many dollars were lavished on enhancing her appearance. Interestingly enough, two of her most important roles—The Barretts of Wimpole Street, 1934, and Marie Antoinette, 1938—had been envisioned by W. R. Hearst for Marion Davies, who was also always expensively packaged. Shearer's casting in those parts caused Hearst's split with MGM. Made after her husband's death but still reflecting his production values, Marie Antoinette was, with Intolerance, 1916, the most elaborate of the costume movies.

Pl. 31
Greta Garbo costume for *Conquest*, 1937, designed by Adrian.

The silhouette of a historical period was often not suited to the star. This was particularly evident in the Empire gowns that Adrian designed for Garbo in Conquest, *1937. They made too much of her tall leanness.*

Thalberg's skill was also notably missing in *Marie Antoinette,* a vehicle for Norma Shearer, Thalberg's wife, that had been in the works for almost five years. William Randolph Hearst had pulled out of MGM in 1934 because he had wanted *The Barretts of Wimpole Street,* 1934, also starring Norma Shearer, and *Marie Antoinette* for Marion Davies. A vast amount of money had been spent on the film before any of it had gotten into the can—a man had been scouring France for expensive furniture and antiques for over two years. Adrian had made thirty-four costume changes for Norma Shearer alone. And she had eighteen wigs, the most elaborate of which weighed twenty-five pounds. For each costume, there were hats, gloves, jewelry, and fans. Shopping in France, Adrian had gathered up gold lace, Lyons velvet, antique gilt braid and buttons, antique embroidery, fans, and snuff and patch boxes that had been used for carrying beauty marks. Perhaps the one unifying element in the opulent film was Cedric Gibbons's art direction—Versailles out of Beardsley. The effect was dazzling—and boring.

PI. 32
Supporting actress costume for *Marie Antoinette,* 1938, designed by Adrian.

Marie Antoinette, 1938, was, in a sense, a result of the proliferating studio system, an elaborate model of what the self-enclosed world of the movie factory could produce. It was nevertheless a box-office failure and, with Gone with the Wind, *1939, marked the end of the full-blown costume movie.*

PI. 33
Norma Shearer costume for *Marie Antoinette,* 1938, designed by Adrian.

A movie of unrestrained lavishness, such as Marie Antoinette, *1938, was made by Louis B. Mayer about once a year to maintain the studio's prestige, even knowing that it would probably not make back its production cost. The use of real diamonds in Norma Shearer's elaborate wigs was just one of the many profligate touches.*

Adrian's position changed radically. Inevitably, budget cutbacks at the beginning of the war included his extravagances, and his last costumes for MGM were more austerely executed, including those for *The Women,* 1939, *Idiot's Delight,* 1939, and *The Philadelphia Story,* 1940. (During the thirties, his publicity releases often mentioned that he made more than the President of the United States.) His costumes for *The Wizard of Oz,* 1939, were his first color work, and it was the new preeminence of Technicolor, with the demand for flashy show-biz costumes, that forced him out in 1941.

Garbo was a timeless mystery, a myth against which other myths could be measured. Dietrich was more specifically the creation of one man, a creature who embodied the esthetics and values of moviemaking in the thirties. She, even more than Garbo, summed up the sort of fatalistic Germanic heroine who was a projection of the "siren-fear" of the men who formulated the movies. Both she and Garbo were eclipsed by World War II, probably not so much because they seemed foreign or exotic, but because they gave off an aura of coldness that finally had a negative connotation for American movie audiences.

No two stars in the history of the film, however, so splendidly embodied such extreme sexual obsessions. If Garbo was the myth of the woman, Dietrich was the idea. Once, trying to protest the parallels drawn between her and Garbo, Dietrich said, "She must think I'm trying to imitate her. But there is nobody like Garbo. I am new to the screen, but I think she is the greatest star in the world." When she heard the praise, Garbo asked innocently, "And who is Marlene Dietrich?"

When he was casting *The Blue Angel* in Germany, Josef von Sternberg asked Marlene Dietrich to come for a screen test—which he never used. He was convinced of her potential. He exulted in his vision of her, putting her up on a stage, one leg on a chair, to show off her allure. He wanted to convey his experience of her by means of the camera. Back in Hollywood he transformed her— put her on a diet, changed the shape of her eyebrows and the color of her hair. Marlene Dietrich willingly submitted to the regimen.

"Unfortunately, I didn't have sufficient time to make tests of Marlene Dietrich," said Lee Garmes, the cameraman who worked with her on her American films for Josef von Sternberg. "I had seen *The Blue Angel,* and, based on that, I lit her with a sidelight, a half-tone, so that one half of her face was bright and the other half was in shadow. I looked at the first day's work and I thought, 'My God, I can't do this, it's exactly what Bill Daniels is doing with Garbo.' [Here, Garmes contradicts Daniels's version of how he lighted Garbo.] We couldn't, of course, have two Garbos! So, without

Pl. 34
Gladys George costume for *Marie Antoinette,* 1938, designed by Adrian.

Years in preparation, Marie Antoinette, 1938, was the most elaborate of the thirties costume movies, with each costume covered with beautifully and carefully worked detail.

ruth chatterton

The first major star of the woman's picture, a Broadway leading lady before talkies made her a star, Ruth Chatterton was one of the few movie actresses to bring to Hollywood her own style and an acutely developed fashion sense. Although she was one of the oldest actresses in films at the beginning of the thirties, Chatterton was able to play romantic parts convincingly in some of the most truly fashionable contemporary costumes ever seen on the screen. Her trademark was her "class," and one imagined her richly cultivated voice enveloped by a cloud of expensive perfume. Off-camera, in spite of her movie hauteur, she snapped spearmint gum with disconcerting informality. Her favorite Hollywood designer was Travis Banton, who did some of his most extravagant creations for her. But when Paramount began to spend huge sums to promote Dietrich, Chatterton perceived a threat to her position as queen of the lot, so she switched to Warner Brothers, where her tearjerking roles foreshadowed the similar pictures that Bette Davis and Joan Crawford would be making there later. Irritated by Warner's low budget for costumes, Chatterton usually supplied her own clothes, not so much because she fancied the snob appeal of New York and Paris designers, but because she depended on being seen in the most flattering way. Significantly, she was considered the one actress in Hollywood who knew how to move in her clothes. Her success was relatively short-lived, but her manner and her exacting demands on the wardrobe and makeup departments were much copied. Even with the huge sums spent on costumes, no other Hollywood star of the period was as close to being a woman of fashion. And that was largely because she disdained the low level of most Hollywood design and went on dressing with the same edge she had in Manhattan.

saying anything to Jo, I changed to the north-light effect. He had no suggestions for changes, he went right ahead and let me do what I wanted. The Dietrich face was my creation."

Dietrich's working relationship with von Sternberg was an elusive one. His direction was more often than not a command, telling her to count silently to time a move or exit. About their collaboration, Dietrich said, "He taught me that the image of a screen character is built not alone from her acting and appearance but out of everything that is cumulatively visible in a film. He taught me about camera angle, lighting, costumes, makeup, timing, matching scenes, cutting and editing . . . the most creative experience I ever had."

Von Sternberg seemed intoxicated with Dietrich's appearance, maddened by her clothes, crazy with her disguises. In his movies with her, he seems constantly to be heaping on costumes, compounding masks, to strip them off again—savoring the surfaces and textures. In *Blonde Venus,* 1932, Dietrich appeared dressed as a gorilla and removed the head; then she put on a frizzy white Afro to sing "Hot Voodoo" to an astonished Cary Grant. Later, she appeared in a white top hat and tails. That elaboration of pretenses increased with each movie—and became more frenzied. Playing Catherine the Great in *The Scarlet Empress,* 1934, she arrived in Russia— a grotesque movieland Russia—an innocent young girl. And although the corruption proliferated around her, finally with her participation, her face retained the same wide-eyed naïveté. In *The Shanghai Express,* 1932, everything is given over to pattern and light and shadow. Her wardrobe seemed endless and ever-changing, a transmutation of the setting.

The most passionate of those chiaroscuros is *The Devil Is a Woman,* 1935, the last of Dietrich's movies with von Sternberg and the one that they both regarded as their best together. "I was at my most beautiful in that picture," said Dietrich.

The costume designer for the film was Travis Banton, the designer for all of Dietrich's films while she was at Paramount. Unlike Adrian, Banton was not so much involved in the silhouette, the

Pl. 35
Ruth Chatterton costume for *Sarah and Son*, 1930, designed by Travis Banton.

Ruth Chatterton, imported from Broadway by Paramount in the early days of sound, was one of the few movie stars to have a fashion sense of her own —a quality to which Banton readily responded. Curiously, Chatterton made no effort to conceal her age or dress younger, and her glamour was worldly and wise.

The Devil Is a Woman, 1935. Marlene Dietrich. Photos: MoMA.

Travis Banton's collaboration with von Sternberg on The Devil Is a Woman, *1935, produced his most outrageous and expressive designs, intricately constructed costumes that seemed more to disguise than to reveal.*

shape of his costumes, as in the creation of a complexity of surface details that, taken singly, tend to contradict one another. In his evocation of "Shanghai Lily" in *Shanghai Express*—"It took more than one man to change my name to Shanghai Lily"—Banton orchestrated a theme from the glint of jet beads, the dull surface of black silk crêpe, and the murky sheen of *coq* feathers.

In *The Devil Is a Woman,* Banton went even further in elaborating his sense of Dietrich's glamour. At Sternberg's urging, Banton employed whole ranges of textures and surfaces from spangles to carnations. He amassed details—stockings with elaborate clocking, and so on. He echoed detail with detail, the lace of a mantilla caught in the lace of a parasol that was amplified by the lace

[above]

Shanghai Express, 1932. Anna May Wong, Marlene Dietrich.
Photo: MoMA.

One of the most memorable movie costumes, Travis Banton's gown for Marlene Dietrich in Shanghai Express, 1932, *summed up the power of the* femme fatale. *Significantly, this power is suggested by layers of feathers and beads spilled over black crêpe—the face hidden behind a veil and the hands encased in gloves.*

Blonde Venus, 1932. Cary Grant, Marlene Dietrich. Photo: MoMA.

Pl. 36
Marlene Dietrich costume for *Blonde Venus*, 1932, designed by Travis Banton.

Travis Banton's gowns for Marlene Dietrich were often deliberately anachronistic, both to offset the improbable plots, as in Blonde Venus, 1932, and to make Dietrich more timeless and mysterious. Interestingly enough, these designs often covered Dietrich so thoroughly that the kick of her leg was a surprise and a shock.

127

Pls. 37, 38
Marlene Dietrich costume for *Angel,* 1937, designed by
Travis Banton. With detail.

*Travis Banton brought his fondness for beading
from couture, where it was one of the marks of
luxury in custom clothes. However, as in this evening gown with matching scarf made for Marlene
Dietrich in Angel, 1937, he seldom used beading
simply as decoration, but made of it the fabric of
his design.*

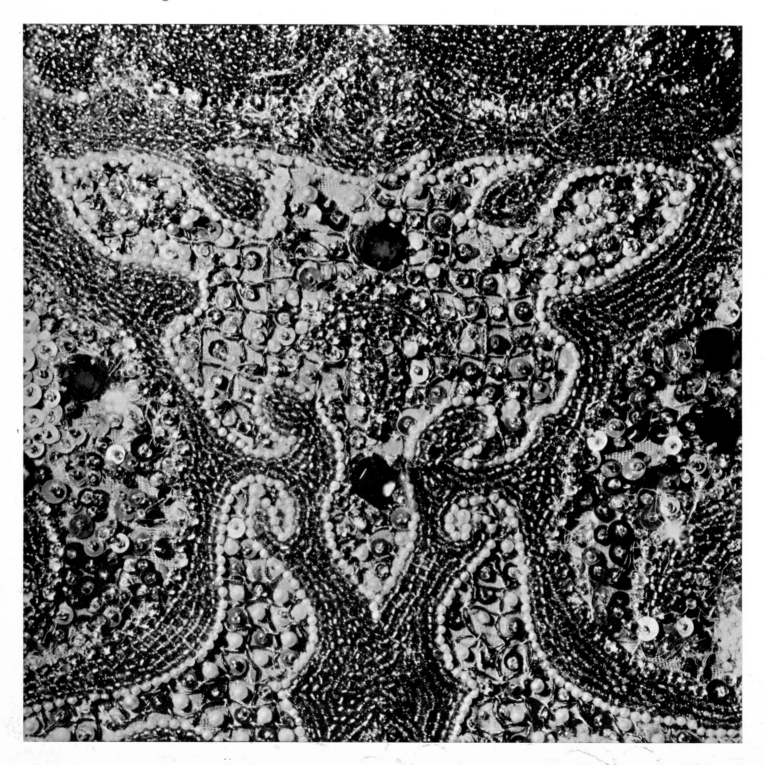

So Red the Rose, 1935. Margaret Sullavan.

Travis Banton did few actual period costumes—his talent was for a refined version of couture. An exception was So Red the Rose, *the 1935 Margaret Sullavan movie, for which he designed delicately sweeping gowns, strikingly unlike similar projects that Adrian and Walter Plunkett were working on at the same time.*

131

The Garden of Allah, 1936. Marlene Dietrich.

The thirties were not only the high point for costume pictures but they also produced a look that was indisputably Hollywood's—an image perhaps epitomized by this famous publicity shot of Marlene Dietrich in The Garden of Allah. *The costume credit for the film was given to Ernest Dryden, but it was more than likely Travis Banton, working under a pseudonym because of his contract at Paramount, who designed the memorable gown for Dietrich.*

Pl. 39
Marlene Dietrich costume for publicity stills, designed by Ernest Dryden, copied by Bill Blass.

Not all of the money spent by the studios on costumes was used for the films themselves. Publicity shots were often treated just as extravagantly, and an expensive outfit was sometimes run up for one day's worth of photographs—as was this Marlene Dietrich peignoir edged in red fox.

Pl. 40
Mae West costume for *Belle of the Nineties,* 1934, designed by Travis Banton.

Mae West picked up most of her tricks of appearance in vaudeville, where she had to make her presence felt to the last row.

Pl. 41 [*opposite*]
Mae West costume for *I'm No Angel,* 1933, designed by Travis Banton.

Mae West was a consummate illusionist. Really quite small, West made herself tall with her long skirts, created an enormous bosom with careful corseting, and managed to be the center of attention with her huge hats. What was merely showy on the burlesque stage, Travis Banton transformed into real glamour, adding further to the illusion with satins and beads and cascades of plumage.

through which the camera saw the scene. Also, there were embroideries on embroideries, sparkles on sparkles, ruffles beneath ruffles.

The Devil Is a Woman is so extreme in its effects, most notably the costumes, that it is comic—how intentionally comic can only be guessed. Dietrich's costumes are a link with another Paramount star who openly and devastatingly parodied the siren and her prerogatives. That star is, of course, Mae West, whose calling card in *Belle of the Nineties,* 1934 (she's selling the Brooklyn Bridge), reads "Peaches O'Day / R.S.V.P."

The trademarks of the stars of the thirties—their distinctive make-up, costumes, and hairdos—were often so overstated that they were an easy mark for parody or even ridicule. In the Baby Burlesks, Shirley Temple took off on Marlene Dietrich, and also on Mae West, picking up on the essentials of Banton's formula of sparkle, feathers, and beads.

Mae West turned glamour to a different effect from that of Garbo and Dietrich. Her image was firmly lodged in the 1890s, as was her shape, with its pulled-in waist and pushed-up bosom. Her films seemed to be excuses for her to parade around in beads and feathers, rolling her eyes, provocatively shifting her hips, and delivering one-liners. A great part of her effect was a curiously mechanical walk, a result partly of her stiff underpinnings and partly of her philosophy of the strut.

The designer Schiaparelli was asked to do some costumes for Mae West, and the star's mannequin was sent to Paris. The

...starring
mae west

With her mechanical walk, her pouter-pigeon bosom, and her gay-nineties pompadour, Mae West was the summary of American sexual preoccupations that haunted the movies. Her image is constant, but it is a ploy that allows her to get across her wipeout one-liners. The big hats, long dresses, and heavy jewelry are not as arbitrary choices as they may seem. The look is derived from her early days in vaudeville, not long after the turn of the century. On the vaudeville stage she learned the rhetoric of glitter. One of her favorite memories is her purchase of a white rabbit hat, muff, and capelet from her first earnings. Her expenditures on costumes were always a major part of her act—eyecatchers that were sexy and not so much expensive as redolent of money. Mae West worked carefully to control every aspect of her show herself, writing her own scripts and choosing costumes that would draw the audience's attention to her. That formula she carried over to the movies, where sparkling white dresses and big hats gave her even more prominence. Because of this, she is generally thought of as a big woman. In truth, she is diminutive. Corsets pushed her hips and breasts into their abundant appearance, and the long skirts and trains, and high heels, made her look much taller than she was. How well these tricks worked was evident in Myra Breckinridge, 1969, made when she was seventy-eight. Even in Technicolor, at her age, pitted against luscious Raquel Welch she holds her own as standout by virtue of her use of white and feathers and furs. "The difference between me and other actresses," she said, "is that I dress for the men in the audience. I'm not afraid to give them what they want."

She Done Him Wrong, 1933. Cary Grant, Mae West.

Mae West's Gay Nineties look had been set long before she came to Hollywood, but Edith Head gave it an extra, glamorous edge, softening West's natural inclination to exaggeration with a glitter of beads and sequins.

Pls. 42, 43 [overleaf]
Mae West costume for *She Done Him Wrong*, 1933, designed by Edith Head.

Edith Head, working as an assistant to Travis Banton at Paramount, did the costumes for Mae West's second movie. The beautiful details and careful execution were clearly the studio's contribution, but the ideas were Mae West's, a formula she had been concocting during her more than thirty years on the stage.

137

Dinner at Eight, 1933, publicity photograph. Photo: MoMA.

Jean Harlow seemed most at ease in versions of the negligée and the peignoir, with the bias-cut emphasizing even further her genial flooziness. Adrian's designs for her lacked much of his usual bite, but they had far greater currency in popular culture than his more mannish designs for Garbo.

...starring
jean harlow

Deliciously coarse, outrageously whorish, Jean Harlow was the comic survivor, the woman who can turn any adversity to her advantage with a wisecrack. Her roles often teetered toward the explicitly lewd. At the end of Dinner at Eight, *1933, Harlow says to Marie Dressler, "Do you know that the guy said machinery is going to take the place of every profession?" "Oh, my dear," Dressler replied, "Oh, my dear, that's something you* need *never worry about." Harlow's publicity image was a straightforward exploitation of her platinum hair— a fad that she began—and her bra-less breasts. Harlow was so fond of her breasts that there are many publicity photographs in which she points to them, touches them, and caresses them. The candor gave her posthumous reputation a more lurid cast than it deserved, and Harlow has been made, quite inaccurately, into a precursor of Marilyn Monroe and her troubled last years. Like Lombard, Harlow was a perfect foil for the bias-cut dress with its clinging outline. On Harlow, who tended to be more generously proportioned, the dresses seemed to be not-too-chastely designed nightgowns. Adrian played up the resemblance to lingerie with the furs and feathers that he massed about her shoulders, letting the dress fall, unimpeded and provocative, over the hips and pelvis. Both Monroe and Harlow projected an image that was not high fashion but had wide fashion influence, a sort of sub rosa erotic uniform that became closely associated with Hollywood glamour, and lingered on in the Frederick's of Hollywood look. Harlow was not fashion, but she was Hollywood.*

avant-garde designer could not believe the shape. "Shocking," she called it, and appropriated the proportions of the dummy for the bottle for a new perfume named Shocking.

Other actresses also played against the glamorous prototypes of Garbo and Dietrich for their comic effect. For some, like Jean Harlow, it was simply a matter of implied contrast between her raucous, wise-cracking persona and the seriousness of the reigning goddesses. For others, like Carole Lombard, it was a matter of conscious imitation, as in her comic parody of Garbo in *The Princess Comes Across*, 1936. And there was the matter of the styles set by Garbo and Dietrich, which dominated the look of actresses in the thirties. Even Shirley Temple had her go at imitating Dietrich in one of the "Baby Burlesks"—*The Incomparable More Legs Sweetrick.*

...starring
carole lombard

Startlingly beautiful, with a zany sense of humor and little regard for Hollywood proprieties, Carole Lombard caught the glitter-and-guts mood of the thirties. Unfortunately, she seldom appeared in the movies in her own person and, even in the screwball comedies for which she was noted, her looks were played off against her brains. Lombard had been scarred badly in an automobile accident and she put a great deal of effort into disguising the scars for the screen. Her visual appeal, particularly in bias-cut gowns, relied heavily on the fact that she did not wear anything under her dresses. In a time when girdles, bras, and slips were standard equipment, Lombard's moving parts, clear for all to see under the skin-tight satin and silk, were a fascinating revelation. Her favorite designer was Travis Banton, although he never dressed her with the sort of elaborate exaggeration with which he costumed Mae West and Marlene Dietrich. That was partly, of course, because her films did not get big budgets, but it was also because Lombard did not need to be gilded to project elegance. Perhaps the most memorable of his gowns for her was the most simple: the white satin dress she wore when tangoing with George Raft on top of a drum in Bolero, 1934. Her looks also enabled her to carry off the sort of satirically designed outrages she wore in Twentieth Century, 1934, and the rich-girl excesses of My Man Godfrey, 1936. Unfortunately, Lombard was often made up in parody of other stars—her makeup was most often copied from Garbo. The most remarkable thing about her extant costumes is the extreme narrowness of her hips. Copying her look for Gable and Lombard, 1976, Edith Head emphasized the lean elegance of her screen appearance for Jill Clayburgh rather than her more casual real-life image. Asked by an interviewer who was the best screen lover, Lombard cracked, "George Raft—but not in the movies."

Twentieth Century, 1934. Carole Lombard, John Barrymore. Photo: MoMA.

Carole Lombard often played types, and none of these characterizations was more pointed than the Broadway actress she played in Twentieth Century, *1934, a parody of Broadway glamour reflected in the exaggerations of the Hollywood costume.*

Pl. 44 [*opposite*]
Jean Harlow personal wardrobe, designer unknown.

Pl. 45
Carole Lombard costume for *No Man of Her Own*, 1932, designed by Travis Banton.

Hollywood costumes were seldom made to be worn in the same sense that stage costumes were constructed for both comfort and endurance. Banton designs for Carole Lombard, notably this white chiffon evening gown with silver-gilt sequins, are so tightly form-fitting at times that they seem to be made only for posing.

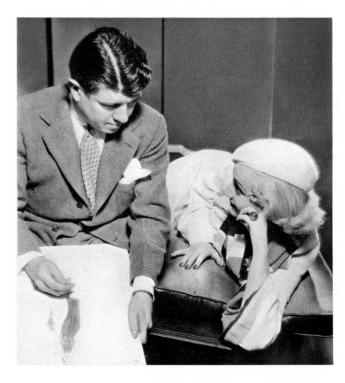

Bolero, 1934. George Raft, Carole Lombard. Photo: MoMA.

Travis Banton's costumes for Carole Lombard, such as those in Bolero, *1934, were seldom flashy, but rather coolly elegant foils for her quirky comedy.*

Carole Lombard free-lanced widely, often making movies off the Paramount lot. Travis Banton remained her favorite designer and she frequently bought his costumes for her personal wardrobe, particularly because his slinky bias-cut gowns suited her no-underwear style.

As pervasive as the image of The Siren is in the films of the thirties, her more positive counterpart, The Hoofer, also plays an important part. That such a halving of the feminine occurred perhaps tells more about the character of the movie industry than about the nature of the American woman. The Siren was a worldly woman of mysterious origins who survived by her wits and often with her body. Her drive was survival and she had no scruples. The Hoofer was more often than not from a small town and her rationale was so simple and bright that no one would question it. Life, for her, was show biz and, if she got the breaks, she could make it to the top. The Hoofer might have been a "dame," but she usually ended up a "lady." The Siren started out a "lady" and ended up a "tramp." So much for the mobility of archetypes!

Glorifying the American Girl, 1929.

Ziegfeld had an important effect on the style of the movies, but he supervised only one, Glorifying the American Girl, *which had a production number that included costumes by John Harkrider. Harkrider's influence can be seen throughout the movie musicals and in the television costumes for Cher.*

Pl. 46 [*right*]
Supporting actress costume for *Whoopee*, 1930, designed by John Harkrider.

Sound brought the musical to Hollywood, and one of the most influential of the early designers for these movies was John Harkrider, who had worked with Ziegfeld and brought the tradition of his Follies *costumes to Hollywood.*

Footlight Parade, 1933.

The costume movie was never purer than in the musicals, where sexuality, abundance, and extravagance were integral parts. The early master of the form was Busby Berkeley, who often functioned as both designer and choreographer.

145

Cleopatra, 1934. Sketch by Travis Banton.

Banton might have been sketching the quintessential De Mille costume but the elements, such as the hip treatment and the suspended halter, are clearly his own.

...starring
claudette colbert

The bangs, the saucer eyes, the rosy cheeks, and the throaty, impertinent laugh made Claudette Colbert one of the movies' most distinctive comedians. Her style was usually played off against a modish suit topped by an improbable hat. Her chic was a necessary component of the roles she played. It gave her a necessary edge in the battle of the sexes—a visual foil in the cinematic comedy of manners. Because of the popularity of her screen roles, Colbert was the first of the Hollywood stars to have a department store dummy patterned after her. It was for Saks Fifth Avenue and was the first of a series of celebrity mannequins, mainly of society women, that were made for the store until the 1970s. At Paramount, except for De Mille's The Sign of the Cross, 1932, and Cleopatra, 1934, Colbert was dressed as a fashionable woman of the times by Travis Banton and Edith Head, then his assistant. Their costumes for her reflected the worldly, often cynical touch that director Ernst Lubitsch had brought to the studio: bright gaiety underlaid with a bittersweet knowledge of the world. Few movie stars influenced moneyed taste, but Colbert was clearly an exception. Off-screen she was one of the few stars to wear clothes by eastern designers and she was careful to include their names, most notably Sophie, in her publicity. No other screen actress, besides Ruth Chatterton, seemed so completely at ease in high fashion. That poise—her presence in clothes whose starkness might have overpowered a less sophisticated actress—made completely believable the society highjinks in The Palm Beach Story, 1942, with its remarkable play on the connotations of dress. Colbert's cheeky chic helped make Preston Sturges's comedy one of the most pleasing comic movies ever made.

Cleopatra, 1934. Claudette Colbert. Photo: MoMA.

Pl. 47
Claudette Colbert costume for *Cleopatra*, 1934, designed by Travis Banton.

Travis Banton's technique was to rely on subconscious responses, the sheen of gold and the molding of fabric, rather than on easy effects like exaggerated silhouettes and gimmicky decoration. This is particularly evident in his seemingly effortless gold lamé gown for Claudette Colbert in Cleopatra, 1934, ravishing in its simplicity but carefully made to work as a sort of second skin.

Gold Diggers of 1933. Ginger Rogers. Photo: MoMA.

There is perhaps no other costume that captures so well the obsessions of the thirties, or the aspirations and type of The Hoofer, as this Ginger Rogers costume from Gold Diggers of 1933.

Flying Down to Rio, 1933. Fred Astaire, Ginger Rogers.

Walter Plunkett's swingy dresses for Ginger Rogers in her early RKO musicals with Fred Astaire created one of the movies' few truly indigenous fashions. They were inspired by the craze for ballroom dancing but were recognizably Hollywood.

PI. 48
Fred Astaire costume for *Top Hat*, 1935, designed by Bernard Newman.

Fred Astaire and his white tie and tails were an elegant exclamation mark in the musicals of the thirties. His wardrobe, with his carefully cut suits and great taste, were a continuation of the cult of the Edwardian dandy, splendid and witty in his garb.

Pl. 49
Fred Astaire's shoes from his personal wardrobe.

Fred Astaire had a carefully cultivated elegance that he brought to Hollywood from the Broadway stage. In both his film and personal wardrobes he emphasized comfort—carefully breaking in jackets and shoes before he wore them. Comfort and fit perhaps explain why each of these famous dancing shoes has a different manufacturer.

The Old Maid, 1939. Bette Davis, Miriam Hopkins. Photo: Academy of Motion Picture Arts and Sciences.

Costumes were frequently the subject of fierce competition among the stars. The rivalry between Bette Davis and Miriam Hopkins was particularly vehement and, although they battled frequently on the set of The Old Maid, *1939, about costumes and hairdos, they were at their best in that movie.*

An important exception to this pattern was Bette Davis, whose major career began with the role of a tramp in *Of Human Bondage,* 1934, and moved toward roles of increasing strength and integrity. Later she would complain about the roles that Warner Brothers could offer her, the low level of production values, and the cut-rate actors who were cast opposite her. But she never complained about the studio designer, Orry-Kelly, whose designs added impressively to her performances. Orry-Kelly was hired by Warner Brothers in 1931 after he had been knocking around Hollywood as an out-of-work actor, painting murals, and even illustrating titles for Fox.

One of the few Hollywood designers at ease with both period and modern costumes, Orry-Kelly produced a series of carefully researched but highly original designs for Bette Davis, including *The Sisters,* 1936, *Jezebel,* 1938, *Dark Victory,* 1939, *Juarez,* 1939, *The Old Maid,* 1939, and *The Private Lives of Elizabeth and Essex,* 1939. About him, his fellow designer Walter Plunkett said, "He was the best of all of us. He did everything well. Designers tend to brag about their innovations. But Orry-Kelly was always way ahead of the game."

Jezebel, 1938. Bette Davis in foreground.

Of his designs for Davis, the costumes for *Jezebel* were the most widely publicized, in particular the notorious "red" ballgown that Jezebel wore to shock her beau and those at a ball. The gown was made up in red, although the film was black-and-white, but it had to be remade because it looked black in the movie. The second try was more successful, and Jezebel turned up in a rust satin that photographed like a terrific red.

Two classic films closed out the decade, recapitulating the major themes that had preoccupied the movie industry from its beginning. Both films were shot in Technicolor. Both reflected the expert competence that had been developed to an extraordinary degree in the MGM studios. Both were hinged on disaster—a foreshadowing, perhaps, of the devastation that lay ahead with World War II. Both were summary statements of Hollywood's ability to project the national fantasy to an unprecedented degree. Both were romances and, to a surprising extent, American fairy tales. They were to become two of the largest-grossing motion pictures of all time. And because they came at the end of the thirties, at a moment in history that marked the disruption of European history and the ascendancy of the United States, they crystallized certain facets of the American psyche, focused by the Depression, that would come to have increasing and haunting relevance.

Jezebel, 1938, was made as Bette Davis's answer to Gone with the Wind. Jezebel's shocking red dress for the cotillion became, with Scarlett's costumes, among the most remembered of movie costumes.

Pl. 50
Bette Davis costume for *The Private Lives of Elizabeth and Essex*, 1939, designed by Orry-Kelly.

Bette Davis often complained of the low production values at Warner Brothers, and her costume films lack the atmosphere of the films from other, slicker studios. Nonetheless, Orry-Kelly's designs, handsomely unpretentious, are among the best.

153

A Midsummer Night's Dream, 1935. Olivia de Havilland, Dick Powell. Photo: MoMA.

A Midsummer Night's Dream, 1935. James Cagney, Anita Louise. Photo: MoMA.

One of the most ambitious of the Hollywood costume movies was A Midsummer Night's Dream, *1935, the Max Reinhardt production in which every element was a part of a visual whole.*

Pl. 51 [*opposite*]
Violet Kemble-Cooper costume for *Romeo and Juliet,* 1936, designed by Oliver Messel.

Oliver Messel's designs for Romeo and Juliet, *1936, brought the most sophisticated British stage design to the movies—a sense of the decorative and the fantastic that was to be very much a part of the taste of the next decade.*

Pls. 52, 53
Supporting actor costume for *The Wizard of Oz*, 1939, designed by Adrian.

Hollywood designers were seldom successful with fantasy costumes, but Adrian's designs for The Wizard of Oz, *1939, were a notable exception—bold and imaginative with a stylish edge. These felt costumes for the Munchkins are among the most innovative of his studio years, both in cut and color.*

Pl. 54 [*opposite*]
Vivien Leigh costume for *Gone with the Wind*, 1939, designed by Walter Plunkett.

Gone with the Wind, 1939. Clark Gable, Vivien Leigh. Photo: MoMA.

In his costumes for Gone with the Wind, *Walter Plunkett was able to suggest effectively the burgeoning materialism of the post–Civil War period, largely through the use of details such as the openwork sleeves of Scarlett's afternoon dress.*

The Wizard of Oz, 1939, was the first of a string of MGM musicals produced by Arthur Freed that spun the studio off in a new direction. Judy Garland as Dorothy, her breasts bound and her hair in pigtails, was in the tradition of Mary Pickford: a spunky girl-woman whose innocence got her through. The front office had wanted Shirley Temple for the picture, but Twentieth Century–Fox refused to lend her. The film, with its settings and costumes, was totally a product of studio fantasy, a self-enclosed world whose colors and shapes were those of a dream or fairy tale but whose sources were *Greed, Snow White*, 1937, and Joseph Urban. Like Christian in *Pilgrim's Progress,* Judy Garland's adventures were allegorical: the triumph of the pure in heart over the Depression. And "Over the Rainbow" was a sort of cult anthem.

No less romantic but ostensibly based on history was the second of these Hollywood monuments, *Gone with the Wind*, 1939. In the

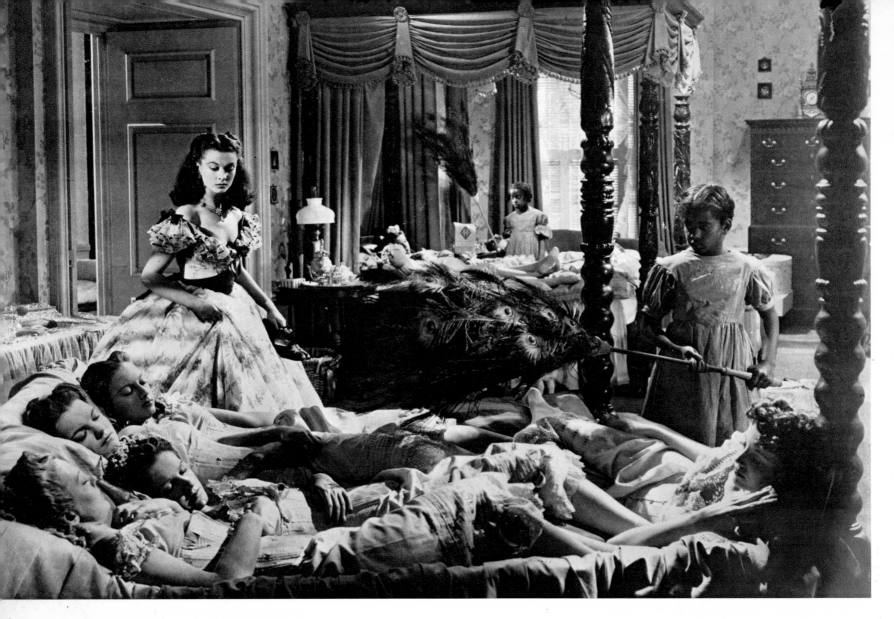

Gone with the Wind, 1939. Vivien Leigh.

Walter Plunkett did extensive research in the South for Gone with the Wind, *1939, but David O. Selznick cared only that his designs fit Margaret Mitchell's descriptions in her novel. Scarlett O'Hara's barbecue dress, one of the most famous movie costumes, unfortunately has not survived.*

late summer of 1936 Thalberg had been approached with a fifty-page synopsis of the novel. "Look," Thalberg said, "I have just made *Mutiny on the Bounty* [1935] and *The Good Earth* [1937]. And now you're asking me to burn Atlanta? No! Absolutely not! No more epics for me now. Just give me a little drawing-room drama. I'm tired. I'm just too tired."

The screen rights were picked up instead by David O. Selznick, whose career in many ways had paralleled Thalberg's and who was closely connected with MGM, even by his marriage to Mayer's daughter Irene. Subsequently, MGM put up $1,250,000 of the $4,250,000 that the film finally cost. Many of Selznick's professional

Pls. 55, 56, 57 [*opposite and overleaf*]
Vivien Leigh costumes for *Gone with the Wind,* 1939, designed by Walter Plunkett.

Walter Plunkett was one of the handful of Hollywood designers interested in the use of historical fabrics and ancient forms of dressmaking and ornamentation. This interest is notable in his ivory silk satin wedding dress for Scarlett O'Hara, twined with matching leaves and cream lace. Most of the costumes shown in this book were designed for black-and-white movies.   Gone with the Wind, 1939, however, was one of the first extensive uses of Technicolor, and Walter Plunkett's designs were carefully thought out to punctuate the picture postcard colorings. He scored his costumes to suggest historical period and the internal development of a character, but he was also attentive to the note a shape or color might sound when it made its appearance in the movie.

Gone with the Wind, 1939. Vivien Leigh, Clark Gable.

Pl. 58
Cammie King costume for *Gone with the Wind,* 1939, designed by Walter Plunkett.

Plunkett kept his eye on the proportions used by dressmakers in the periods he researched, always being careful to reflect the differences for each age, as in his riding habit for Bonnie Butler, Scarlett's small daughter.

Pl. 59 [*opposite*]
Vivien Leigh costume for *Gone with the Wind,* 1939, designed by Walter Plunkett.

Probably no other costume has symbolized so well the experience of a period as Scarlett O'Hara's dress made from her mother's portières. It became an emblem of survival for the generation that lived through the Great Depression.

attitudes had been formed by his experiences at MGM, but he was to cast the film independently, and the memorable results pointed to the end of the star system.

In spite of the publicity, the aim of the visual side of the movie was not historical accuracy but how to make use of the Technicolor process to create the most stunning effect possible. However, Selznick's involvement in the production and the changes in staff (both George Cukor, the director, and Lee Garmes, the cameraman, were fired) caused the movie to split in half. Garmes said Selznick wanted picture postcard colors. Selznick was concerned that the first half of the movie seemed too soft and pastoral.

Working on the costumes was Walter Plunkett, who had been responsible for outfitting some of the best costume pictures from *Little Women,* 1933, on. He did a remarkable job of permitting the costumes to tell the story from the lighthearted ante-bellum days through the war and into Reconstruction. Selznick revealed in his unceasing memos his concern that the sets looked as if they had just been put up, that the rooms didn't look as if they had been lived in. Plunkett ''aged'' the dress Scarlett made from her mother's portières by adding the fading that sunlight would have made on the green velvet.

''Selznick wasn't interested in accuracy,'' Plunkett said. ''I did research in the South because I thought it was necessary.

PI. 60
Vivien Leigh costume for *Gone with the Wind,* 1939, designed by Walter Plunkett.

Few American movies used costumes so effectively to chronicle the fortunes of characters as Gone with the Wind, *1939, with Scarlett's passage from innocence to disillusionment charted in her gowns —from her widow's weeds to the famous claret velvet ballgown that sums her affluence as Mrs. Rhett Butler.*

Little Women, 1933. Katharine Hepburn.

Because of the modest circumstances of the family in Little Women, *1933, Walter Plunkett set himself the unusual task of designing clothes that they might have made for themselves, copying the patterns in Godey's Lady's Book.*

...starring

katharine hepburn

With her high cheekbones, quavering voice, trembling mouth, and teary eyes, Katharine Hepburn has been one of the most parodied of the Hollywood actresses. When she was called to Hollywood to star in A Bill of Divorcement, *1932, her first film, she demanded unsuccessfully that Chanel do her wardrobe. Chanel, of course, was her first musical role some forty years later in* Coco, *with costumes by Cecil Beaton. Hepburn has always made much of exercise and soap-and-water as her chief beauty aids, but for her first movie role her eyelashes were given a permanent to give them some curl. The designer who worked most with her at RKO was Walter Plunkett, who designed the remarkable, silvery fantasy "big" costume she wears in* Christopher Strong, *1933, the only costume Plunkett designed for the picture. Plunkett remembers her with particular fondness among the actresses he worked with; a painting of her in one of his costumes from* The Sea of Grass, *1947, hangs on his living room wall. "She was always interested in the historical side of what we were doing," Plunkett said. "Most of my ideas for* Little Women [1933] *came from Godey's Lady's Book, simple dresses that might have been made at home. Kate asked me to loan her things to read so she could steep herself in the literature of the period. Also, she was one of the few actresses who concerned herself with learning how to move in the clothes of a period—and each period does have its own walk. For* Little Women, *we rigged her up in a hoop she could wear at home to practice in. I remember her calling me up at one point, 'I've done it. I've managed the john without taking off the hoop.'"*

Selznick was much more worried about being true to Margaret Mitchell. If he objected to a design, I'd only have to point out one of her descriptions in the novel and he was satisfied. The movie had nothing to do with history. Look at the opening, with Scarlett twirling a plastic daffodil and wearing what was about to become the forties' hairdo."

Well into the production, Selznick was concerned that not enough was being made of the Technicolor process: "I know from talking to Walter Plunkett that no one feels as badly about the limitations that have been imposed on him as he does. But if. we are going to listen entirely to the Technicolor experts, we might as well do away entirely with the artists that are in our own set and costume departments and let the Technicolor company design the picture for us."

Even the fit of the costumes worried Selznick: "I spoke to Walter Plunkett about Gable's costumes. I think there is no excuse for fitting him so badly, especially around the collar. . . . I think it is very disappointing indeed to the elegant Rhett Butler, wandering around with clothes that look as though he had bought them at Hart, Schaffner and Marx and walked right out of the store with them."

Thus went the ultimate in packaging of Hollywood glamour and romance—a movie that in revival after revival would attract more people than any other film in history. A large part of this success was undoubtedly the veracity of its fable and its heroine—an example for America as it moved out of the Depression.

Just as, a decade before, sound had brought lasting changes to the movie industry, color was about to bring its changes. The classic period of moviemaking was drawing to a close.

1940s

The Pinup and The Girl Next Door

...starring
rita hayworth

The expression in her eyes a little too knowing, her voice a trifle overripe, her creamy skin and auburn hair straight out of Technicolor, Rita Hayworth was The Pinup. In the thirties, the studios had made the stars. In the forties, Rita Hayworth won a popularity contest that had less to do with what she had done on the screen and more to do with the famous photograph of her in a rumpled bed wearing a satin-and-lace nightgown. She was not the first of the starlets, nor the last. She epitomized the studio system of the thirties that picked comers and attempted to groom them for stardom or publicity shots, but Hayworth ultimately succeeded on her own. Those platoons of the bleached and permed went easily from playing The Hoofer to posing as The Pinup. Rita Hayworth did it with a difference. She suggested something more: a weary vulnerability teetering on toughness that captured a lot of the frenetic sexuality of the war years. That knowingness comes out in "Put the Blame on Mame" and the sly gentility of her striptease. About her black satin sheath, Jean Louis said, "That dress seemed marvelous from the first moment I thought of it. I think Rita made it sexy because of the casualness with which she wore it. There was something voluptuous about her ease." After Gilda, the makeup, the hair, the carefully cured voice didn't hold. Maturing but interesting, The Pinup fell into playing The Vamp and The Fatal Woman in Salome, 1953, and Miss Sadie Thompson, 1953.

The beginnings of World War II in Europe considerably shrank Hollywood's market and the studios began to cut back their production budgets accordingly. One of the first major alterations was a reduction in the budget lines for both costumes and set decoration. 1940 was a year of heavy losses and in 1948 the government intervened to prevent block booking of studio films into studio-owned theaters, adding yet another element of economic instability to an already grim outlook. It was inevitable in a period of massive adjustment that the star system should also suffer. Greta Garbo, Norma Shearer, and Joan Crawford left MGM as their contracts ended, and although Garbo and Shearer went into retirement, Crawford established a new and even more successful career at Warner Brothers. Garbo, whose movies had been less and less of a box-office draw, had been making a salary of $250,000 a year and her departure was a great relief to the heavily strapped studio. Thus began a new era of "realistic" movies—no sets and no costumes to speak of—and escapist movies that were carefully calculated by the front office to sell.

Gilda, 1946.

Pl. 61 [*above*]

Pl. 62 [*opposite*]
Hedy Lamarr costume for *Samson and Delilah*, 1949, designed by Edith Head. With detail.

De Mille plucked the feathers for Hedy Lamarr's cape in Samson and Delilah, *1949, from peacocks at his own ranch. Then Edith Head had them glued on individually, letting them cascade down the long cape.*

Samson and Delilah, 1949. Hedy Lamarr.

Cecil B. De Mille's influence extended into the fifties. Samson and Delilah, *1949, was one of the last of his costume epics, with Edith Head's wry hand at work most notably in the costumes for Hedy Lamarr.*

Eighteen Technicolor movies appeared in 1940, and the number grew steadily each year—twenty-five in 1942, and so on. Those movies, more often than not musicals, developed an esthetic of their own that was unlike much of anything that had come before, except perhaps for Walt Disney's films, in which color and design, activated by music, were brought alive. *Fantasia,* 1940, was a watershed in this regard. MGM movies of the forties seemed to be drowned in sound, the dialogue lost in the mood music that poured from the soundtrack.

Except for the musicals, costumes played a very small part in getting the movies' messages across. Perhaps the most romantic and glamorous of the movies of the war years, *That Hamilton Woman,* 1941, was produced by an Englishman but made in Hollywood, and it starred Vivien Leigh and Laurence Olivier in a love story that revived the most glorious days of the British Empire. Even then, Leigh's gowns were knockoffs of the many paintings of Lady Hamilton rather than new creations. The motif of the few

Pl. 64
Supporting actress costume for *Ziegfeld Girl,* 1941, designed by Adrian.

Adrian's designs are associated with the most famous stars at MGM, but his touch is recognizable even in his costumes for the chorus line of Ziegfeld Girl—no pastiche of Follies gimmicks but a sleek, silvery statement of Adrian's own transcendent brand of glamour.

Pl. 63
Hedy Lamarr costume for *Samson and Delilah,* 1949, designed by Edith Head.

The basic idea of the De Mille costume had changed little in four decades—lots of flesh and lots of jewelry. Because of De Mille's strong influence, Edith Head's designs are much like those of Adrian in King of Kings *and Travis Banton in* Sign of the Cross.

major costume pictures that were made was nostalgia, remembrance of safer and saner times. In his decorous costumes for *Pride and Prejudice,* 1940, Adrian, who was shortly to go into the dress business for himself, seemed to have lost his flair.

Also, few roles created for women called for the sort of flamboyant and extravagant costumes that adorned Hollywood

Pl. 65 [*opposite*]
Greer Garson costume for *Pride and Prejudice*, 1940, designed by Adrian.

Adrian was seldom at ease with real period pieces and his costumes for Pride and Prejudice, *1940, one of his last pictures, suffer for being straight forward. Jane Austen did not suggest to him the sexual obsessions of Dumas fils in* Camille, *1936, or Tolstoi in* Anna Karenina, *1935.*

Pride and Prejudice, 1940. Flora Robson, Greer Garson.

Adrian's last designs for the movies were no less remarkable than his first, although by the beginning of the forties the padded shoulders and narrowed hips were a commonplace. His designs for Pride *and* Prejudice, *1940, with Greer Garson, were full of his period clichés—vast skirts, incongruous detail, and lavish use of fabric.*

That Hamilton Woman, 1941. Vivien Leigh.

British producer Alexander Korda made a series of sleekly romantic films in the thirties. World War II forced him to make That Hamilton Woman, *1941, in the United States with a Hollywood crew. The result was one of the most glamorous costume movies ever made, with Vivien Leigh dazzling as Lady Hamilton, one of history's most memorable fashion plates.*

stars in the thirties. Suddenly a new and definitive kind of woman was playing a central role in movies. Of those, the most influential was Bette Davis. She was at pains to make her screen image conform to what real women were wearing, and even in her bitchiest roles, such as *The Letter,* 1940, she did not use her costumes as an ornament or camouflage. Indeed, in *Now Voyager,* 1942, she used the unplucked eyebrows, dumpy figure, and dowdy clothes of her character to dramatize her neurotic withdrawal, taking off her glasses and shedding pounds to show the transformation of the character. And such realism was again her tactic in *A Stolen Life,* 1946, in which she played twins.

The opposite tack was taken by Joan Crawford, who had been appearing in movies since the mid-twenties. With great determination she had remade herself as she saw fit, transforming herself into the image of each period, from Flapper to Siren. In the course of the years, she had altered herself by raising her eyebrows, plucking them to make her eyes bigger and wider, changing the shape of her mouth with makeup, and gradually having bigger and bigger caps on her teeth to give her mouth more prominence. The forties were the high point of her career, since she was by then able to use her expertise with some independence.

The masterpiece of her know-how was *Humoresque,* 1946, in which photographer Ernest Haller lighted her with extraordinary moody care, creating a distillation of forties atmosphere, shadows tumbling across her magnificent face. For this movie, Adrian, now in business for himself, made a series of costumes which complemented the studied simplicity of her makeup—notably, a black beaded gown that relied on her famous shoulders for its shape. Crawford also blurred the line between her personal and her movie wardrobes, using her platform shoes as a trademark of her glamour.

Another star important to the new and decidedly American image of woman was Katharine Hepburn, who also worked with increasing independence. A turning point in her film career was the movie version of *The Philadelphia Story,* the Broadway hit she had helped to finance as a vehicle for herself. For her screen role, Adrian made some of his most striking contemporary costumes. Also great successes were the Pat and Mike comedies, co-starring Spencer Tracy. They did not make any fashions in clothes, but rather suggested a new ease between men and women.

In many ways, the career women in forties movies seemed to grow from the tradition of The Hoofer in thirties musicals. They had some of the same spunk, they came from the same small towns, but they also had more of an idea where they were going. The prototype of that forties woman is *Kitty Foyle,* 1940, as played by Ginger Rogers, who got her start in the movies playing Hoofers.

...starring

bette davis

Her mouth a slash of red, her eyelashes exaggerated for the camera, Bette Davis, with her flapping arms and explosive, spitting delivery, became the widely parodied paradigm of the screen actress—eschewing glamour to play drunks, tramps, and a slew of quintessential bitches. Not beautiful in the conventional mold of the film star, she bypassed the fatalism of Garbo, the constricted worldliness of Dietrich, and the posed theatricalism of Norma Shearer to evince a series of qualities that were indisputably her own: pride, humor, intelligence, defiance, anger, and an indomitable will. Her most romantic period came at the end of the thirties when Warner Brothers produced a series of costume pictures starring her, to compete with those being produced by MGM. Jack Warner's failure to grab Gone with the Wind, *1939, for her was one of the well-known pivot points of her career. But that disappointment was made up for by her superb performances in* Jezebel, *1938, and* The Little Foxes, *1941, playing in the latter a far more subtly conceived southern belle than Scarlett O'Hara. For these parts she was dressed by Orry-Kelly, who depended more on detail than on flash to make his historical points. His psychological understanding of historical period, along with Davis's willingness to change her image entirely for a role, distinguished his beautifully executed ideas. For* The Old Maid, *1939, another of those costume dramas, Bette Davis was given a head of curls. Her co-star, Miriam Hopkins, refused to come on the set until the hairdresser matched Davis's coiffured magnificence for her. The battle ended in a draw when Hopkins got her own curls. Bette Davis's classical period came, however, in the forties, when she began to play independent, contemporary women whose clothes were a far less obtrusive part of the characterization. Even in those pictures, Davis's collaboration with Orry-Kelly was evident, and the elements of reportage and timeliness were an integral part of her look.*

Pl. 66
Katharine Hepburn costume for *Without Love,* 1945, designed by Irene.

Irene brought dressmaking touches to all the costumes she designed—both contemporary and historical. Her designs may not have had much flair, but the stars inevitably felt flattered by her attention and comfortable with her professionalism.

179

Lady in the Dark, 1943. Ginger Rogers.

Lady in the Dark, 1943, was one of the earliest Hollywood experiments with the surreal, a supposedly witty jab at slick fashion magazines and slicker Freudian analysis. Edith Head's dance costume for Ginger Rogers, all sequins and mink, at $35,000 was publicized as the most expensive costume ever made.

Pl. 67
Katharine Hepburn costume for *The Philadelphia Story*, 1940, designed by Adrian.

Katharine Hepburn's independence and non-conformity made her difficult to dress stylishly in contemporary roles. An exception was The Philadelphia Story, 1940, in which Adrian, in spite of his usually exaggerated line and shoulders, provided a simplified, almost classical, look for her.

Her costumes—mainly white collars appended to black suits—were a great hit in the mass fashion market. But another of the career women she played, the fashion editor in *Lady in the Dark,* 1943, wore the most expensive costume ever made for a movie. It was a phantasmagoria of red and gold sequins trimmed in mink that cost $35,000 to make.

The most popular movie phenomenon to emerge from the war years, however, did not begin in Hollywood. The pinup had begun in calendars, on magazine covers, in the illustrations by Varga and Petty for *Esquire,* and in the pickup of studio publicity photographs by *Yank,* the Armed Forces newspaper. In a sense, that proliferation of cheesecake was a sort of talent search of its own, a popularity contest as far-flung as the exploits of GI Joe and Kilroy. The winners in these erotic sweepstakes were not the established stars. Nor was a bathing suit necessary to qualify. Rita Hayworth wore a nightgown.

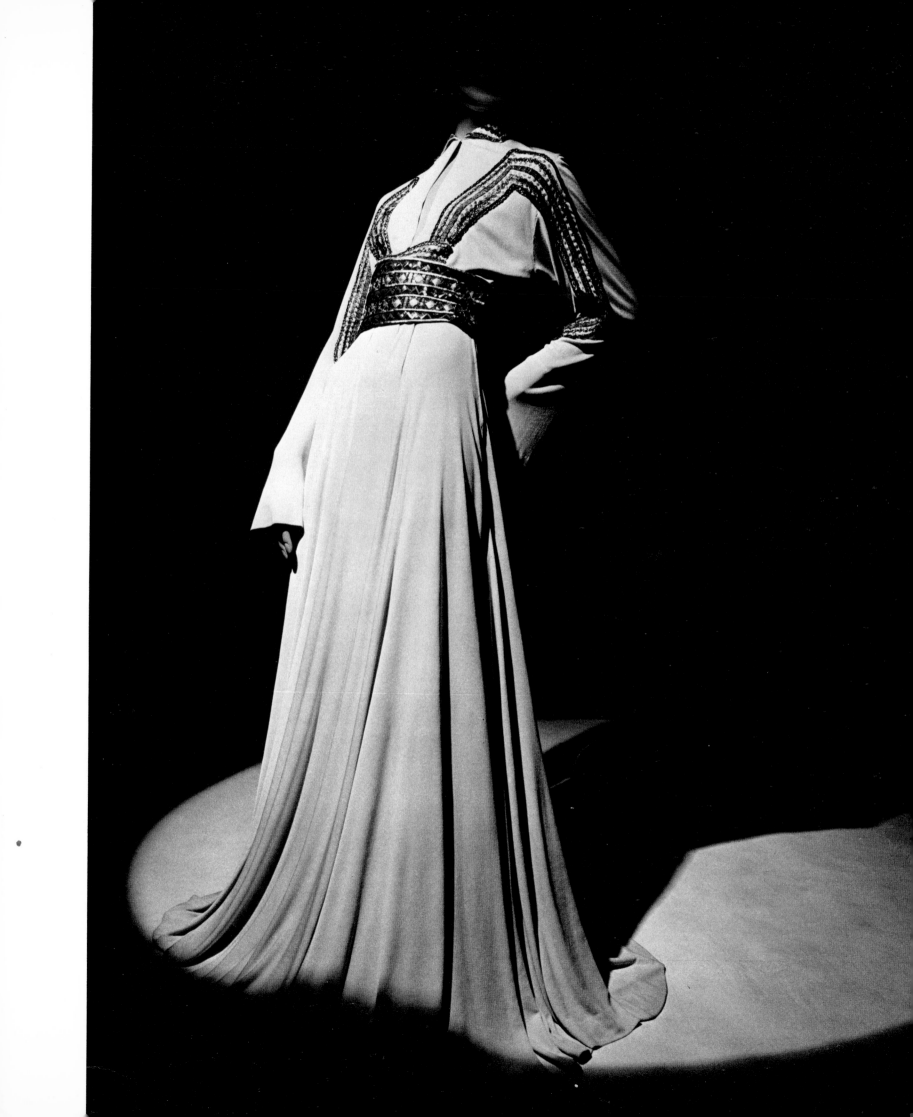

Pl. 68
Esther Williams costume for *Million Dollar Mermaid*, 1952, designed by Helen Rose.

Esther Williams created her own sub-genre of Technicolor musicals, diving in and out of improbable production numbers with a wardrobe of bathing suits designed mainly by Helen Rose. Her wet look was another variation on Hollywood's obsession with lingerie.

Betty Grable emerged one of the two winners in what was probably the most widely reproduced photograph ever taken—wearing a one-piece bathing suit, high heels, hose, an anklet, hair swept up in a mass of curls, peering back provocatively at the camera over her right shoulder, her hands on her hips. The other was Rita Hayworth, snapped by *Life* sitting up in a mussed bed, her hair tousled, wearing a satin and lace negligée. Those were the new superstars, chosen not at the box office but in a lottery so compelling that it didn't matter whether they acted or sang or danced.

...starring
lana
turner

With her platinum hair, her knowing eyes, and her unchanging expression, Lana Turner was the epitome of the forties studio star, her glamour a result of MGM conditioning and publicity buildup. She was so much an invention of the movies that she was more at home among the expensive clothes and furnishings of her cinema life than in her off-screen life, and her seven marriages and personal scandals seemed almost to belong to some lesser fiction. Her walk, her voice, her non-acting were the highpoint of the studio esthetic, the sort of homogenization of productions and actors that marked Hollywood films in their Golden Years. Inevitably, her appearance and her performance are equated, and the stiffness of her maquillage and hairdo are matched by her delivery of lines. This is particularly evident in her dea ex machina *performance in* The Postman Always Rings Twice, *1945, her best movie, in which her mechanical-doll exterior, a startling contrast to her husband's shabby diner, works beautifully for the murderously plotting wife of an older man. "Lana was never suited for the costume pictures she made," said Walter Plunkett, the designer of her costumes for* Green Dolphin Street, *1946, and* Diane, *1956. "She had no feeling for history. She could stand up straight but she couldn't move. The idea that women moved differently in the seventeenth or the nineteenth century was totally alien to her." MGM had seen her from the beginning as a new version of Joan Crawford, but she lacked the flexibility of Crawford in transmuting her image as required. Her slick image was retreaded for* Imitation of Life, *1959, a box-office success;* Portrait in Black, *1960; and* Madame X, *1966. "She's not* Madame X," *said Pauline Kael. "She's Brand X; she's not an actress, she's a commodity." Her career was summed up by Kirk Douglas, playing a film director in* The Bad and the Beautiful, *when he said to Lana Turner, a star he had created, "You acted badly, you moved clumsily, but the point is, however bad you were, every eye in the audience was on you."*

The movies accepted the vote and absorbed it as their own myth. After all, the publicity departments had for years, especially at Christmas and Easter, been grinding out useless "glamour" shots of starlets dressed as Christmas trees and hugging Easter baskets. Here at last were shots that produced measurable results.

There were other comers within that Beauty Boom. Esther Williams became a star because she could swim—and wear a bathing suit. Lana Turner could wear a sweater; Veronica Lake let her long blond hair fall over one eye. In 1943, Howard Hughes produced *The Outlaw*, starring Jane Russell, who sociologists said represented a shift of the visual erogenous zone from the legs to the breasts.

One Touch of Venus, 1948. Ava Gardner. Photo: MoMA.

Ava Gardner played several roles that were related to the myth of Pygmalion and Galatea, one of Hollywood's favorite themes. In One Touch of Venus, *1948, she was a statue that had come to life with an evening gown of white crêpe handpainted to simulate marble.*

Pl. 69
Ava Gardner costume for *One Touch of Venus*, 1948, designed by Orry-Kelly.

Surrealism had a great effect on the movies of the forties, providing a fashionable overlay of myth and psychology. The handpainted marble motif on this gown from One Touch of Venus, *1948, is an example of the genre.*

While those Pinups enjoyed a fairly carefree life in stills, they played roles with somewhat more sinister implications. The Pinup could also be the man-trap. In *Double Indemnity,* 1944, she was out for money—a black widow who wore an anklet, played by Barbara Stanwyck. In *The Postman Always Rings Twice,* 1945, she was Lana Turner, up to no good in all white and bared midriff, topped by a turban. She was Veronica Lake in almost any of her movies.

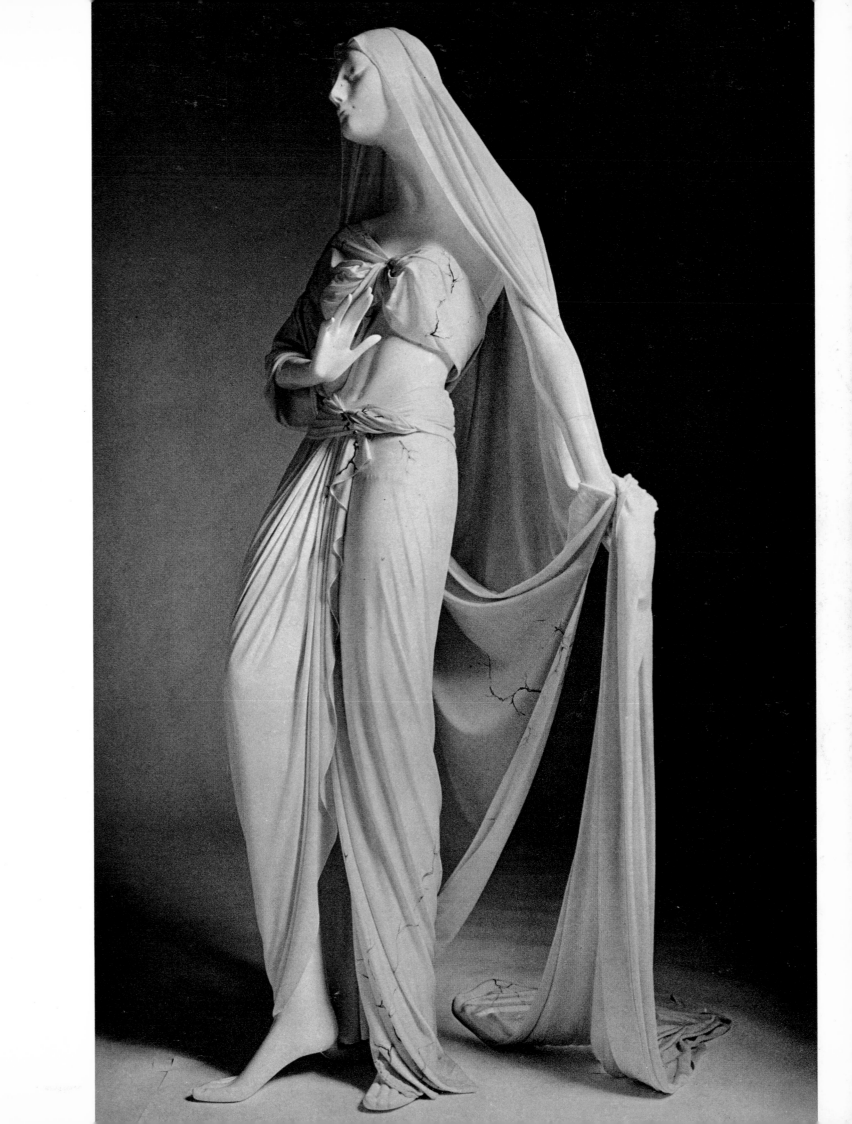

...starring
ava gardner

Sensual, husky-voiced, her eyes betraying the untroubled surface of her image, Ava Gardner somehow eluded the strictures of the studio system and invented her own sort of glamour. Speaking of her performance in The Barefoot Contessa, 1954, *with a script by Joseph Mankiewicz, obviously patterned after her off-screen life, Humphrey Bogart said, "Whatever it is, whether you're born with it or catch it from a public drinking cup, she's got it, and the people with the money in their hands put her there." Seldom was her remarkable beauty actually reflected on the screen, except perhaps in* The Killers, 1946, *one of her earliest movies. Strangely enough, three of her films seemed to echo the myth that grew up around her, catching and distorting her stardom. Each of them —*One Touch of Venus, 1948; *Pandora and the Flying Dutchman,* 1951; *and* The Barefoot Contessa—*contained a statue, the conventional Hollywood expression of the Pygmalion/Galatea theme. The ad copy for* The Barefoot Contessa *ran: "The World's Most Beautiful Animal." Somehow, Gardner's own code seemed to contradict that inflation. She looked no more at home in the Grecian draperies than she did in the period costumes for* The Great Sinner, 1949. *Of all the stars produced by the studio system, Gardner seemed the least reverent, the most sorry about the exploitation. When MGM delivered one of its many bum deals to her, she said, "That's Metro; they louse you up every time." With her ravaged image, her world-weariness, and her disregard for publicity, Ava Gardner represented a decisive break with the old idea of the Hollywood star. She was much like a Hemingway heroine in her easy fatalism—she had been a friend of Papa since the forties and played in several movies made from his stories, most notably* The Killers—*and she was a forerunner of the Beats. For her, disarray became her most sincere form of honesty —a direct attack on the strictures of the studio.*

Pl. 70
Ava Gardner costume for *The Great Sinner*, 1949, designed by Walter Plunkett.

Costume pictures were not considered good risks in the forties, but they were still made to accommodate stories that would not have been accepted in contemporary dress. The Great Sinner, 1949, was beautifully costumed but boring.

Cover Girl, 1944. Rita Hayworth, Gene Kelly.

Movies such as Cover Girl, 1944, *with Rita Hayworth and Gene Kelly, underlined parallels between the movie industry and other glamour-producing media. However, because of long production schedules, movies were seldom timely, particularly in terms of fashion.*

Pl. 71

Lana Turner costume for *Green Dolphin Street*, 1946, designed by Walter Plunkett.

Walter Plunkett's designs for Green Dolphin Street, *1946, were a highly accomplished excursion into a difficult period of mid-nineteenth-century costumes, adding a remarkable insight into the clothes worn in colonial outposts. His use of military braid on Lana Turner's off-white wedding gown is such a detail.*

But the essential bombshell was Rita Hayworth. Because she came somewhat after the most intense period of studio star-development, Rita Hayworth received virtually none of the grooming and polishing that other stars went through at MGM, for example. Her career in the late thirties was a miasma of B movies and a couple of quota-quickies in Canada, films made to compete with American imports. Her appearances with Fred Astaire enhanced her reputation, but they did not give her the backup that a close, long-term involvement with a studio might have provided. Her auburn hair, brown eyes, and creamy skin seemed made by Technicolor but her glamour came from her life off-screen.

Rita Hayworth made only two movies of any great importance. Both conveyed a kind of recklessness and sensuality that seemed to reflect the anxiety and shapelessness of the postwar years. The first was *Gilda,* 1946, a film that made little sense except for Gilda's line "If I were a ranch, they'd call me the Bar Nothing," and an elegant striptease—pulling off her opera-length gloves— as she sang, or rather lip-synched, "Put the Blame on Mame, Boys" in a black satin sheath by Jean Louis. The other was *The Lady from Shanghai,* 1948, in which Orson Welles, soon to be her ex-husband, returned to some of von Sternberg's visual obsessivenesses in a meditation on a treacherous woman. For the movie, he had Hayworth cut and bleach her hair. And, while some of the similar movies of the past had been loving tributes from the director to the star, in that film Welles seemed to assault the whole feminine image in the movies with an ending set in a funhouse with an extraordinary climax of shattered mirrors.

Hayworth's career, perhaps more than any other in this period, is symptomatic of the vacuum that had arisen in the presentation of the stars. Her image, based largely on her popularity as a pinup, was allowed to drift and finally to falter. And yet, in spite of her failure, she remains perhaps the one star to bridge the gap between Jean Harlow and Marilyn Monroe—and that, more because of her personal publicity than because of any solid achievement on the screen.

Betty Grable's career was remarkably similar to Rita Hayworth's. After a number of false starts in the late forties, she became a star at Twentieth Century–Fox largely as a substitute for Alice Faye in the period musicals that were the studio's Technicolor staple. Betty Grable was, strangely, never directly exploited as a Pinup by the studio, but she was cast in a series of showgirl roles that were a foil for the studio's designer Charles LeMaire.

A designer at one time or another for a Hammerstein and Ziegfeld musical, *George White's Scandals,* and Ringling Brothers' Circus, LeMaire made free use of Fox's heavy Technicolor budget. His taste was limited but his imagination was boundless. And he was

Gilda, 1946. Rita Hayworth. Photo: MoMA.

Jean Louis's gowns for Rita Hayworth in Gilda, 1946, were among the first inklings of a new sort of glamour in movies, a glamour more openly sexual than anything that had gone before. "That was only thirty years ago, but when I decided to reproduce the dress, I discovered that the same satin wasn't being made."

Pl. 72 [opposite]
Rita Hayworth costume for *Gilda*, 1946, designed by Jean Louis.

Jean Louis did not attempt anything splashy to embellish Rita Hayworth in Gilda, 1946. Rather, he worked out a sort of coda to her natural beauty, a black satin casing that was understated and unexpected for the moment. Nonetheless, the drama of that sheath and the matching gloves was extreme.

Billy Rose's Diamond Horseshoe, 1945. Betty Grable. Photo: MoMA.

Charles LeMaire's designs for Betty Grable had no relation to history or fashion. They were all variations on the showgirl costume, both because of Grable's legs and the plot of films such as Billy Rose's Diamond Horseshoe, 1945.

most at ease when he had a quiver of showgirls to dress for some fantastic number. When he came to Grable, he seemed to be decorating a cake more often than a woman. Perhaps the most extreme of his confectionary excesses is *The Dolly Sisters,* 1945, in which he had both Betty Grable and her blonde double, June Haver, to dress.

A summary of his style is contained in the Cosmetic Carousel sequence in *The Dolly Sisters,* a twenty-popgun salute to femininity, in which choruses are, among other things, dressed as false eyelashes, lipsticks, and powder puffs.

The Pinup's less explicitly sexual counterpart was The Girl Next Door, usually a throwback to some more stable period before the war. Often, she was the leading character in a fantasy musical of a kind that frequently had retained the show-biz formulas of the thirties. The most brilliant exponent of this sort of role was Judy Garland, who had grown up at MGM playing Andy Hardy's girlfriend and who, with the war years, had begun to take on more mature roles, even to fall in love and marry.

The Dolly Sisters, 1945. Betty Grable, June Haver.

Twentieth Century–Fox's musicals, more hysterical than historical, were mindless and visually stunning. Charles LeMaire's designs for Betty Grable, shown here with her movie-twin June Haver, were baroqued cheesecake, iced with sequins, and quivering with feathers.

That Lady in Ermine, 1948. Betty Grable, Cesar Romero. Photo: MoMA.

Twentieth Century-Fox's "historical movies," mostly musicals, dealt entirely in stereotypes. LeMaire used the nightclub image of the past in That Lady in Ermine, 1948, i.e., if a costume is old, it has a big hoop skirt.

...starring
betty grable

Her legs were among the great symbols of the forties, and with her blandly wholesome good looks and unpretentious manner, Betty Grable was more popular as The Pinup than as The Movie Star. She had made almost thirty films, in fact, before she became a star. And then, largely because of the affection she inspired among the World War II troops, she was one of the exhibitors' Golden Ten for ten years, and the top woman in films for four of those years. Like Lillian Russell, her stardom was not so much because of her glamour as because she so easily suited a popularly held ideal. She was clean and wholesome and not dangerous, as the stars of the thirties had often been. About her, Richard Schickel said, "Her special forte was the backstage musical in which her famous legs were put on display on the most absurd of pretexts. Miss Grable's beauty—if that is the word for it—was of the common sort. Never did she offer much in the way of character or maturity. She was, at best, a sort of great American floozie, and her appeal to lonely GI's was surely that of every hash-house waitress with whom they ever flirted." Because of her box-office appeal, Betty Grable was guaranteed that all her movies would be made in Technicolor, at a time when color film stock was both scarce and expensive. Twentieth Century–Fox's Technicolor musicals, her often-vapid image, and Charles LeMaire's extravagant-cheap costumes for her, sum up a period. LeMaire, who worked briefly for Ziegfeld and George White, carried the tradition of the showgirl costume in the movies to its most obsessive heights, piling feathers on feathers, sparkle on sparkle, and frills on frills. Even in the most extreme of those concoctions, particularly in Billy Rose's Diamond Horseshoe, 1945, Betty Grable is the good-natured victim of LeMaire's most lurid excesses—the soul of good showgirlmanship, the essence of pliability.

Forever Amber, 1947. Linda Darnell. Photo: MoMA.

Producers searched for another Gone with the Wind, *although by the mid-forties costume pictures had fallen into disrepute.* Forever Amber, *1947, a bestseller, seemed a natural. In spite of splashy costumes, a splashier budget, and a stampede of extras, it did not succeed in equaling its predecessor at the box office.*

Ziegfeld Girl, 1941. Judy Garland.

Ziegfeld Girl, *1941, was an unremarkable movie, but Adrian's luminous designs, among his last for the movies, were an indication of the brilliant possibilities of the black-and-white costume movie—another tribute to Florenz Ziegfeld and his vision of the theater.*

The great lie to her public wholesomeness was the pattern of drug use and depression that the studio's demanding regimen had early imposed upon her. If she had any girlhood at all, she had lived it in brief snatches during filming of the movies with small-town settings that had become her specialty. After a period of inactivity, her career was launched for a second time with *Meet Me in St. Louis,* 1944, MGM's biggest grosser after *Gone with the Wind.*

Meet Me in St. Louis, directed by Vincente Minnelli, explored the possibilities of what was subsequently to become known as the MGM musical—the music totally integrated with the script. Adapted from a series of Sally Benson short stories that had been running in *The New Yorker,* the musical is about a series of events in the life of a family at the time of the Columbian Exposition of 1904 in St. Louis. A former set and costume designer, Minnelli mobilized every detail to help tell the story. The look and feeling of the gingerbread architecture is authentic, but it is exaggerated to give the feeling of a lacy valentine, a saccharine surface that is emboldened by surprising uses of color and unexpected pattern and texture, as in the costumes also.

Minnelli made extensive use of the possibilities of Technicolor. His technical advisors told him (it was his first film in Technicolor) that he couldn't expect the colors to come out pure in the final print, but he persevered and finally got the effects he wanted.

Perhaps his greatest innovation was the way he used the set. The camera plunged in and out of windows and in the party sequence moved continuously through the four rooms of the house, instead of treating it as if it were a three-sided stage set. Also, Minnelli insisted that the camera work reflect the rhythm of the musical numbers.

With *The Pirate,* 1947, Minnelli hit the peak of his forties use of Technicolor in a highly self-conscious takeoff on the swashbuckling epic, with rollicking jabs at the operetta and the whole convention of the movie romance. The script was taken from the Alfred Lunt–Lynn Fontanne stage play by S. N. Behrman, and it retained the original's sense of style. "The pirate, played by Gene Kelly," Minnelli said, "was a pastiche of Douglas Fairbanks's gymnastics and John Barrymore's canned ham." Also, Minnelli swiped from paintings everywhere to get the look he wanted—a Vermeer bedroom and an extra after Manet's "Olympia" with her black serving girl.

Meet Me in St. Louis, 1944. Judy Garland.

Irene Sharaff, originally a stage designer, brought a high level of fantasy to her costume designs for the movies. She often used the essence of a period, its popular conception, as her point of departure. For Meet Me in St. Louis, 1944, she seemed to have immersed herself in turn-of-the-century greeting cards—all frills and lace.

Pl. 73 [*overleaf, left*]
Supporting actors costumes for *The Pirate,* 1947, designed by Irene Sharaff.

Pl. 74 [*overleaf, right*]
Judy Garland costume (*front*) for *The Pirate,* 1947, designed by Irene Sharaff; Cyd Charisse costume (*rear*) for *The Kissing Bandit,* 1949, designed by Walter Plunkett.

Efforts to integrate all the visual elements in the color movie were a surprisingly long time in coming. One of the most important of the realized efforts was The Pirate, 1947, a vibrant Caribbean canvas crammed with explosive detail by Irene Sharaff; a style caught also by Walter Plunkett in his costumes for Cyd Charisse in The Kissing Bandit, 1949.

The costumes for The Pirate were vivid parodies of theatrical conventions. They were galvanized by a spectacular use of Technicolor and a sense of place—Martinique—that came more out of painting than postcards. The remarkable craftsmanship in the ensemble costumes was the work of Karinska, the famous ballet costumer, who rendered Tom Keogh's designs under the supervision of Irene Sharaff.

The Little Foxes, 1941. Bette Davis.

Orry-Kelly's designs for The Little Foxes *are among the most brilliant conceived for the movies—glamorous, but tinged with a sense of the price exacted by the past. Bette Davis was at the top of her form as Regina, and her gowns added to the stature of her portrayal, radiating her greed for money.*

Makeup was handled by Dotty Ponedel, who had been assigned to Marlene Dietrich at Paramount. She eliminated the rubber discs Garland had been using to change the shape of her nose and told her she didn't need caps to disguise her irregular teeth. "I raised her eyebrows a bit," said Dotty Ponedel, "and gave her a fuller lower lip. I put on a makeup that was pretty to the eye. I knew it would be pretty to the camera, too. I tweezed out some of the hairline. And that was that."

Not nearly as popular as *Meet Me in St. Louis,* but equally significant for its visual experimentation, was *The Ziegfeld Follies,* 1945, in production for two years, with a cast of most of the MGM stars: Fred Astaire, Lucille Ball, Lucille Bremer, Fanny Brice, Lena Horne, Gene Kelly, Victor Moore, Red Skelton, Esther Williams, and William Powell.

The movie had a revue format and perhaps the most impressive segment was "Limehouse Blues," using the hit song written for the 1919 *Charlot's Revue* and inspired by *Broken Blossoms.*

"We did the dream sequence of the number," Minnelli said, "with chinoiserie costumes designed by Irene Sharaff. The art department,

...starring

judy garland

Even with her blazing voice and startled eyes, Judy Garland was The Girl Next Door. Except for Marilyn Monroe, no other star has seemed to capture the public so emotionally. Because of her roles as Dorothy in The Wizard of Oz, *1939, as Andy Hardy's sweetheart in a succession of MGM musicals, and ultimately in* A Star is Born, *1954, Judy Garland was the heroine of a fairy tale that might easily have been the plot for a Hollywood movie. Her martyrdom at the hands of the glamorizers has been frequently cited. But the terms of her ruin are obsessions shared by many women in this century, particularly with regard to weight loss. One of her most recent biographers, Gerold Frank, uses her medical history as a major source of his exposition of that theme. For Garland, as for the other young actresses being groomed for the MGM stable, changes of weight, irregular periods, and skin problems were of even greater importance than the regularly administered acting and dancing lessons. A large part of Garland's glamour came from her marriage to Vincente Minnelli, who originated her tux-and-tights look for* Summer Stock, *1950. Louis B. Mayer referred to her as "the little hunchback" and her bad posture was a major camouflage problem throughout her career. Her frequent changes in weight made her a particular problem for the wardrobe department, as well as the makeup department. Stale Coca-Cola to shade in her cheeks was used by Dotty Ponedel, who had done Dietrich's makeup at Paramount. The career of perhaps no other star reflected so clearly the discrepancy between appearance and reality in the images imposed by the studios. And perhaps no other star personified so well the aspirations of her fans to transcend the limits of cosmetic possibility.*

in looking over her sketches, noticed the eighteenth-century chinoiserie artifacts which Irene had drawn in the background. She always did this sort of thing with her costume sketches. Her suggestion was so right that it was adopted; thus Irene wound up doing the sets as well."

"I'd worked on several New York shows with Karinska, the great costume designer who'd started out with Krazhelev and the Russian Ballet," Minnelli said. "She had the uncanny talent of transforming the elements of Braque and Picasso sketches into magnificent costumes. It would be no great challenge for her to suggest the many cosmopolitan influences—East Indian, Chinese, and European—of Martinique in the 1830s."

With *The Pirate,* Minnelli had made the sort of integrated film that was the best of the Hollywood musical genre—a whirling, sweeping succession of tightly joined images. And although the picture made it only at big-city box offices, *The Pirate* was to have a major effect on the movies of the next decade.

Ziegfeld Follies, 1946. Fred Astaire, Lucille Bremer. Photo: MoMA.

Costume designers and set designers seldom worked together, although their designs were approved by the studio art director, who supervised all the visual aspects of the movie. An exception was Irene Sharaff, whose costume sketches for the "Limehouse Blues" section of Ziegfeld Follies, 1946, became the sets as well.

Ziegfeld Follies, 1946. Lucille Ball.

The emergence of Technicolor as the major medium for costume movies brought a change of emphasis in everything from the styling of dresses to their color. In one of the sequences from Ziegfeld Follies, 1946, Lucille Ball, all in pink, tamed a line of black-sequined panthers.

Pl. 75
Lucille Ball costume for *DuBarry Was a Lady*, 1943, designed by Irene.

Historical costumes became clearly escapist in the forties. Irene, the sister-in-law of MGM's art director Cedric Gibbons, who took Adrian's place as the studio designer in the early forties, lacked Adrian's flair. Her designs, such as this riding habit for Lucille Ball in Dubarry Was a Lady, 1943, were confection, but expensive confection.

1950s

The Sex Goddess

...starring

marilyn monroe

An improbable mix of woman and child, perhaps the most famous star of the century, certainly the most written and talked about, Marilyn Monroe was *The Sex Goddess*, a role that she created for herself as much as it was created for her. In the tradition of screen blondes, she had the friendly vulgarity of Harlow, the seductive irreverence of Lombard, and the devastating ability of Mae West to parody sex. Watching her act, another movie blonde, Constance Bennett, said, "There's a broad with a future behind her." Whether they were planted by the publicity department or not, her cracks had a way of ingratiating her fluffy zaniness even further into the public imagination—her confession that she wore only Chanel Number 5 to bed, for example. Her undulating walk and breathy voice were deceptively simple stratagems. About Monroe the actress, director Joshua Logan said, "Watch her work in any film. Monroe is pure cinema. She is the most completely realized and authentic film actress since Garbo. How rarely she has to use words. How much she does with her eyes, her hips, her slight, almost accidental gestures." She also had a way of making jokes about herself. The shocker in the famous skirt-blowing scene in The Seven-Year Itch *is not that her panties show but that she is wearing anything underneath at all. Working on the costumes for one of her last films, Jean Louis went to her house to meet her and have a first fitting:* "I waited for an hour and finally she came out of her bedroom, wearing a bathrobe. She threw it open and said, 'I thought you should see what you have to work with.' She had nothing on underneath. I told her there would also be hats. 'I don't like hats,' she said. 'But remember, I have a big head without much in it.'" *About her performance in* Some Like It Hot, *Billy Wilder said,* "She comes on with her two balcons sticking out, and you know she's killing everyone with her looks, but she always seems surprised that her body's kicking up such excitement. Now that's a real comic attitude and that's not something I showed her."

In 1948 came the court decision that ended studio ownership of the theater chains and thus the guarantee of a market for the studio product. In addition, the weekly attendance figures for movies dwindled to less than sixty million, the lowest figure since 1933, when the United States was in the depths of the Depression. It was not simply a matter of needing better films with greater drawing power. Another decisive factor had been added to Hollywood's many problems. The sale of television sets had doubled, tripled, and quadrupled in the last years of the forties. So for the first time in its brief history, Hollywood began to retrench.

As a result, stars and directors began to go out on their own, and they were quickly joined by the writers, craftsmen, and technicians who had supported their efforts in the great days of the studios. Producers looked carefully at every item in the budget and cut back particularly on production costs. On the one hand, there was a greater emphasis on individual expression—the studio image was fading. Because the movie trusts had been broken, movie theater owners could no longer depend on the studio films to draw an audience. Stars had filled the theaters in the thirties. In the forties, until 1948, studio movies filled the theaters. However, the pressure for financial success at the box office became so great that the fees for stars—salaries and percentages—were the main items of studio expenditure. Neorealism, the documentary style introduced by European film-makers after World War II, became dominant, and for the first time productions began to leave the sound stages *en masse.*

Summer Stock, 1950. Judy Garland. Photo: MoMA.

Judy Garland's male drag in Summer Stock, 1950, came to represent the height of fifties chic just as Dietrich's tuxedoes had epitomized glamour in the thirties. Vincente Minnelli had thought up the outfit for an earlier movie but the sequence had been scrapped.

Pl. 76 [opposite]
Lana Turner costume for *The Prodigal,* 1955, designed by Herschell.

The Prodigal, 1955. Lana Turner.

The movie costume epic persisted well into the sixties but the format varied little from the days of the silent movies. The Prodigal, 1955, nonetheless, with Lana Turner as a pagan priestess, was one of the last biggies based, even loosely, on the Bible.

Pl. 77
Elizabeth Taylor costume for *Beau Brummell*, 1954, designed by Elizabeth Haffenden.

One of the first movies made by MGM in England as Hollywood began to commute all over the world was Beau Brummell, *1954. In the tradition of British costume pictures, Elizabeth Taylor was done up like an eighteenth-century painting, glowing and romantic.*

Pl. 78
Ava Gardner, Marge Champion, and supporting actresses costumes for *Show Boat*, 1951, designed by Walter Plunkett.

The costumes for Show Boat, *1951, are remarkably evocative of the period. The nifty bustles and cunning swags are contributions of Walter Plunkett, who caught the dazzle of the minstrel show without being swept away by it.*

Supporting actresses costumes for *Brigadoon*, 1954, designed by Irene Sharaff.

Brigadoon, 1954, one of the last big MGM musicals, depended greatly on atmosphere to suggest the lost Scottish town that draws the two Americans into its midst. The tartans are in autumnal colors, subtly outlined in beads and sequins.

Pl. 80
Lana Turner costume for *The Merry Widow*, 1952, designed by Helen Rose.

The von Stroheim Merry Widow, 1925, had first been given a contemporary setting, but in the escapist fifties Lana Turner was put back into a black corset and the whole belle époque feeling of the original was revived, with Helen Rose producing costumes of such sentimentality that Jeanette Mac-Donald would have felt at ease.

Essentially, the problems of the newly independent film-makers were management problems. If they did not show a profit, they had little chance of getting their next production financed. Because of changing tastes and the new emphasis on tight budget controls, sets and costumes began to be regarded as frills. The watchwords were small costs, and small or no overhead.

At the beginning of this period, at least, MGM continued to spend lavishly on its productions, particularly musicals, but the numbers were cut back. The extraordinary originality of the Freed Unit, set up at MGM to turn out musicals under the supervision of Arthur Freed, was curtailed as the front office began to insist on securing commercially safer properties. Again Hollywood looked to Broadway, and in 1954, with *Brigadoon*, Vincente Minnelli began to work mainly with pretested material. The idea of the studio as a factory with unlimited resources gave way to individual productions with their characters dictated by the exigencies of popular taste.

...starring
audrey hepburn

Piquant, a stylish survival of The Wait, with her querulously vulnerable but memorable voice, Audrey Hepburn was one of the most remarkable of the last major stars generated by Hollywood. She was definitely not a Sex Goddess. Her incandescence seemed a throwback to an earlier, more magically sentimental moment in the movies. She was discovered by the French writer Colette, who immediately saw in Audrey Hepburn her heroine Gigi, a schoolgirl who is being trained to be a belle époque courtesan by her grand horizontal mother and grandmother. Hepburn starred in the Broadway stage adaptation of the Colette story, and went to Hollywood from there. Director Billy Wilder said about her, "After so many drive-in waitresses in movies—it has been a real drought—here is class, somebody who went to school, can spell, and possibly play the piano. The other class girl is Katharine Hepburn. . . . She's a wispy thin little thing, but you're really in the presence of somebody when you see that girl. Not since Garbo has there been anything like it. . . . It's the kind of thing where the director plans sixteen close-ups throughout the picture with that dame—that curious ugly face of that dame." Not since Claudette Colbert had Paramount had a star with such high-fashion impact. Edith Head made great use of that side of her image in Roman Holiday, 1953, *in* Sabrina, 1954, *and, with Givenchy, in* Funny Face, 1957, *playing off with a dryly ironical, brilliantly journalistic flair the* haute couture *of the period against Hepburn's distinctive look. Audrey Hepburn's most elaborate film was yet another Cinderella story,* My Fair Lady, 1964. *Hepburn, skinny and nervy, wore the exaggeratedly Edwardian gowns with aplomb. "Dearest C.B.," she wrote Cecil Beaton after he had photographed her in his designs, "I can remember that I have always wanted so badly to be beautiful. Looking at those photographs last night I saw that, for a short time at least, I am, all because of you, Audrey."*

Pl. 81
Rita Hayworth costume for *Pal Joey,* 1957, designed by Jean Louis.

Rita Hayworth's career was on the skids, but Jean Louis was able to give her some of the old glamour with his costumes for Pal Joey, *1957, a decade after* Gilda.

Not too surprisingly, in a period of extreme transition, Hollywood began to take a self-conscious look at its own history, in terms not just of events and personalities but also of its esthetic and psychological evolution. The films that reflect that preoccupation took a variety of forms, but they served to define and interpret what had gone before, and by the way established some of the terms in which French film criticism, particularly the *Cahiers du Cinéma,* would see the Hollywood movie. Noteworthy among the films that looked self-consciously at the Hollywood myth were *Madame Bovary,* 1949; *Sunset Boulevard* and *All About Eve,* 1950; *The Bad and the Beautiful* and *Singin' in the Rain,* 1952; *The Barefoot Contessa,* 1954; and *The Goddess,* 1957. Just as the costumes for the historical movies produced by Hollywood had been pastiches, the costumes for these movies were often no more than glosses on what had gone before.

The most psychologically perceptive of these films, brilliantly using the esthetic of the costume drama, was *Madame Bovary.* Flawed by a script that makes Flaubert's prosecution for obscenity its narrative frame, the film was Minnelli's anatomy of the Hollywood romance, a serious parody of the grand, romantic period of moviemaking. Unfortunately, the production was thrown off-center by the casting of Jennifer Jones, who gave a neurotic, mannered characterization, and by a musical score by Miklos Rosza that was perhaps more psychologically acute than sentimentally satisfying. The director used all the usual paraphernalia of the romantic movie, including costumes, sets, and props, but he gave them a psychological importance they had seldom had before. In Emma Bovary's girlhood room, the wall is papered with fashion plates and romantic scenes that had shaped her imagination.

That is visual stuff that the movie sets out to demolish—Emma's dreams opposed by the shabby reality of the provincial French town to which her doctor-husband takes her as a young bride. Minnelli used a series of mirrors to chart her disintegration: a simple mirror in her girlhood home, in front of which she primps for her prospective husband; a large gilt rococo mirror at a local nobleman's ball, in which she sees herself surrounded by the gentry; and a cracked mirror in the rundown hotel room where she meets her lover.

In that psychological drama Minnelli detailed the lengths to which Emma Bovary went to obtain the furniture and gowns she felt she must have, secretly mortgaging all her husband's holdings. *Madame Bovary* is a sort of Cinderella story in reverse, a paradigm for the consequences of the dreams and sentimentality engendered by ideas of romance and glamour.

Roman Holiday, 1953. Audrey Hepburn.

Pl. 83 [*opposite*]
Audrey Hepburn costume for *Roman Holiday*, 1953, designed by Edith Head.

Audrey Hepburn represented the return of The Waif, and her movies were often touched with fantasy. In Roman Holiday, 1953, Edith Head was able to create costumes both chic and fabulous for the princess on the loose.

Pl. 82 [*left, bottom*]
Supporting actresses costumes for *Les Girls*, 1957, designed by Orry-Kelly.

A few films in the fifties aspired to the chic of the glossy fashion magazines and the cosmopolitan world they purported to reflect. Among these were Funny Face and Les Girls, both 1957. Les Girls was in color but Orry-Kelly used black-and-white liberally, as in these polka-dot on polka-dot chorus costumes for one of the musical numbers.

Funny Face, 1957. Fred Astaire, Audrey Hepburn.

Funny Face *represented the first real incursion of high fashion into the movies. Hubert de Givenchy, the couturier, designed Audrey Hepburn's wardrobe, notably this wedding gown. Richard Avedon served as technical advisor, supplying the stills for the titles and credits and helping Fred Astaire with his role as a photographer.*

To Catch a Thief, 1955. Grace Kelly, Cary Grant.

For To Catch a Thief, *1955, Alfred Hitchcock told Edith Head to design a fairy tale princess gown for Grace Kelly to wear to the masquerade ball. The sweeping gold dress with its gold birds and the gold wig was one of Head's favorite designs —a startling intrusion of the fantastic into reality.*

The costume designer for the film was Walter Plunkett, who had done the costumes for *Gone with the Wind* and whose work was a chief element in the romantic tradition of the movies. "The costumes were overdone," Plunkett said. "But that was largely because of interference from David O. Selznick, Jennifer Jones's husband. Because they were so grand, they added an element of unintentional satire."

Selznick was particularly concerned about Jennifer Jones's appearance, and he sent the production staff a series of memos. About her heavy eyebrows, he wrote, "Please believe me when I say there's not the slightest thing to worry about in connection with her eyebrows; that they are a part of her unique loveliness; and that it would be sheer folly to tamper with them to the slightest extent. I will appreciate it if you will leave them strictly alone and will assume this to be so unless I hear from you further."

...starring
grace kelly

Aloof, blonde, blessed with an aristocratic reserve that other actresses could merely hope to copy, Grace Kelly was a striking contradiction to the obvious sexuality of most fifties movies. Born in Philadelphia, the niece of playwright George Kelly, Grace Kelly developed a career of remarkable independence, starting out as a model and Broadway actress. Effortlessly, she was the woman of quality that the woman's picture had always attempted to imitate. But her surprising strength came in playing against type, as she did in The Country Girl, 1954. Although she acted in only eleven movies—her movie career began in 1951 and ended in 1956—she had remarkable poise playing opposite Cary Grant in To Catch a Thief, 1955, and in the Katharine Hepburn role in High Society, 1956, the musical remake of The Philadelphia Story. Her screen personality gave a heightened dimension to her marriage to Prince Rainier of Monaco and, although she has not appeared on the screen in twenty years, her popularity has not diminished. She was the ultimate, living realization of the Cinderella fantasy that haunted Hollywood from the beginning. Her Serene Highness, Princess Grace, visited the Hollywood costume exhibition at the Metropolitan Museum with Lillian Gish and Vera Maxwell, the designer. She was surprised, she said, to see her costumes from The Swan, 1956, shown with hats and accessories that had not been worn with them in the picture: "And the dresses were slightly altered. Of course, costumes were often changed to be used on young actresses for screen tests. Eventually they would end up on extras in crowd scenes." Her costumes included in the exhibition were designed by Helen Rose, one of the major designers at MGM, who also did her wedding gown. "The costumes for Green Fire [1954] were designed for the part even before an actress was chosen to play it, whereas for The Swan, Helen Rose did design the clothes especially for me, and in this case, as in other costume pictures, I would myself do research and have a clear idea of the period and what particular lines and colors would be suitable to the character, to the situation, and to me as the actress. I would then discuss the role and the clothes with the designer." Such care has remained evident in Princess Grace's personal wardrobe.

Pl. 84
Grace Kelly costumes for The Swan, 1956, designed by Helen Rose.

The making of The Swan, 1956, a fairytale of sorts, exploited Grace Kelly's marriage to Prince Rainier of Monaco. The tone of the film, largely because of her interest in costuming, was surprisingly true to the Edwardian period.

The Glass Slipper, 1954. Leslie Caron, Estelle Winwood. Photo: MoMA.

Pl. 85
Leslie Caron costume for *The Glass Slipper*, 1954, designed by Helen Rose.

The Glass Slipper, 1954, re-told the Cinderella story with a startling simplicity, perhaps to enhance the fairytale atmosphere of the costumes. Once again Hollywood turned to children's books for its inspiration.

His memo about her makeup in a test for *Madame Bovary* was in a sense a summary of his years of big studio experience: "Too much make-up creates a masklike impression that is most undesirable and destroys all character."

The centerpiece of the movie was one of the most brilliant dance sequences in any movie, particularly for its characterization of Emma Bovary and its dizzying synesthesia. Rosza's waltz had an accelerating, almost sprung rhythm that contributed greatly to Emma Bovary's neurotic image. "As Emma swirled about," Minnelli said, "the baroque mirror and chandeliers swing around with her. The camera movement suggested her dizziness and breathlessness, and explained why the host ordered the breaking of the windows, an action we retained from the book."

Madame Bovary, 1949. Jennifer Jones, Van Heflin.

With the costumes for Madame Bovary, *the epitome of romantic studio movies, Walter Plunkett launched a period of extreme self-consciousness in movie costume design, designing gowns that referred back more to other movies than to history. From the fashion plates on Emma Bovary's wall to the foolish fripperies of her descent, style defines the stifling sentimentality in which she lived.*

Pl. 86
Grace Kelly costume for *The Swan,* 1956, designed by Helen Rose.

Grace Kelly often participated in the costume research for her films, indicating to the designer her preferences for colors and fabrics. Her costumes for The Swan, *1956, designed by Helen Rose, were quietly beautiful re-creations of pre-World War I gowns.*

And later: "I find it not even possessing the same faults and virtues of the old-fashioned thick cake make-up of the MGM so-called glamour stars, circa 1929; but actually . . . such a complete change in Miss Jones' appearance that she looks like a cross between Lynn Bari and Buff Cobb. Apparently whoever made her up was under the impression that Emma Bovary is a Javanese. Jennifer's whole face is brought out to a point by this make-up; the mouth is extremely bad—in shape, in color, and in extent of make-up—to such an extent that the mouth becomes her most predominant feature as in the case of Joan Crawford; the quality of her eyes, her most apparent attribute, is minimized; and all of the character is taken out of her face. I urge that whoever made her up *not* be used, because I cannot tell you how strongly I feel that this make-up is just awful, and precisely what is not indicated, either for Miss Jones or for the role."

Another sort of anatomy of the Hollywood myth was *All About Eve*, 1950, written and directed by Joseph L. Mankiewicz. Although the movie is set in New York and is ostensibly about the Broadway stage, it is also, on a deeper level, a narrative about the passing of the old order, an examination of the dynamic that produces stars. It is written, rather surprisingly, from within Margot Channing's experience as she is pushed aside by a younger actress, Eve Harrington. Patterned loosely on Tallulah Bankhead, Margot Channing, played by Bette Davis, is an old trouper, one of the

For Diane, *1956, Walter Plunkett worked from
Renaissance portraits, adding his own sense of what
life might have been like in the immense cold palaces. His palette was exceptionally muted, tending
to grays and soft oranges. For Lana Turner he made
overskirts and overdresses to be worn in layers.*

breed that was teetering on the edge of extinction in both New York and Hollywood. Bette Davis's wardrobe in the film is full of Bankhead echoes. Her dress for the famous cocktail-party sequence has a neckline much like the gowns Aline Bernstein designed for Bankhead's role in the Broadway production of *An Eagle with Two Heads.* "I steeped myself in Bankhead," Edith Head said.

Literate and sophisticated, the screenplay comes out on the side of the mature actress who is being supplanted by her understudy. Mankiewicz's script suggests a deeper sense of survival than even show biz can comprehend—suggests that Margot will survive as a woman, if not as an actress. The validity of that myth is questionable, but its enduring popularity is some indication of its relevance as a truth about the nature of stardom. In the sixties, the same story returned as the basis of a hit Broadway musical, *Applause,* with another ageing star, Lauren Bacall.

Ironically, the new star introduced by *All About Eve* was not Anne Baxter who played Eve, but Marilyn Monroe, making one of her first film appearances. The costumes in this film are of small consequence—cocktail dresses that are among the many fashion clichés of the fifties. But Bette Davis's well-worn mink coat became a sort of legend itself as the germ for the "What Becomes a Legend Most" fur advertising campaign.

Even more significant for Hollywood's examination of its own myths was *Sunset Boulevard,* 1950, Billy Wilder's homage to the silent movies, with many visual and costume allusions to the movie past. Among the performers were Erich von Stroheim, Buster Keaton, Cecil B. De Mille, Anna Q. Nilsson, and H. B. Warner, with Gloria Swanson as its star. Von Stroheim plays Swanson's ex-husband and director, now relegated to the role of keeper, butler, and chauffeur. During the course of the filming, Wilder told von Stroheim his films had been ten years ahead of their time. "No," von Stroheim said. "Twenty."

The film is bracketed by the world of silent movies in which Norma Desmond/Gloria Swanson had appeared—a metaphor for both the past and the unconscious, a dramatization of the movies' archetypal woman with all her trappings. Trying to seduce the young writer she has brought into her house, she dresses as a Mack Sennett bathing beauty. In fact, the silent footage used when Norma Desmond tries to draw the young writer into her fantasies is from *Queen Kelly,* one of the convent sequences in which Patricia Kelly is shown in her as-yet-unsullied innocence.

Wilder seems to be working out conscious parallels between the two films. The plot in each film hangs on a powerful and mad woman: the Queen Mother and the film star. Each hopes to tie a younger man to her through luxury.

All About Eve, 1950.

[*left*]
Bette Davis. Photo: MoMA.

[*below*]
George Sanders, Anne Baxter, Photo: MoMA.

[*opposite top*]
Bette Davis, Gary Merrill, Anne Baxter, George Sanders.

[*opposite bottom*]
Photo: MoMA.

Edith Head's remarkable reportorial skills as a designer were in evidence in All About Eve, 1950, a comedy of disguises in the grand tradition.

In both films, a grand staircase plays a central dramatic role. In *Queen Kelly,* the drunken prince is carefully carried up the palace stairs as his mother, naked with a white cat in her arms, stands at the head of the stairs. In *Sunset Boulevard,* the young writer arrives as Norma Desmond is preparing for the last rites for her pet chimpanzee.

Wilder makes much of the setting in which the star relives her triumphs—a sort of autoerotic bower banked with photographs of Norma Desmond and many mirrors. At moments, the questions of makeup—as Norma Desmond prepares to visit De Mille at the studio—and her wardrobe, including an intricate wire cigarette holder worn on the forefinger, border on the ludicrous, but those are the sorts of exaggerations out of which von Stroheim had built character in his films. More to the point, using the displacement of age, Wilder seems to be questioning the efficacy of these after-images—von Stroheim's military garb is transformed into a chauffeur's uniform, Gloria Swanson's clothes-madness into madness.

The melodramatic silliness of the movie is transformed because of the details it marshals, details that serve as visual footnotes playing the whole history of the movies back into what is happening. Because the characters are playing against the larger backdrop of their images, they seem to be participating in the visual enactment of their destinies, a sort of cinematic determination, their fate marked by the costumes they have assumed. (Edith Head's costume sketches seem laced with a carefully observed irony.)

This strange resonance is nowhere more evident than in the film's conclusion. Norma Desmond has killed the writer for trying to escape from her world into the arms of a younger woman. Wilder, however, carries the melodrama one step further and reveals the underlying mechanism in his observation about the nature of stardom. When the press and the police arrive, Norma Desmond comes down the staircase thinking she is shooting her next movie. She is dusted over with gold, and she has flecks of gold scattered on the one shoulder that is bared by her sparkling full-length scarf. Below, von Stroheim stands by the newsreel cameras directing her. She is playing Salome and those are the steps of the palace. Outside, a young man floats face down in her swimming pool. Once again, the extraordinary and elusive creature who haunted the screen has struck and felled her prey.

Sunset Boulevard, 1950. Gloria Swanson, William Holden. Photo: MoMA.

Gloria Swanson started out as a Mack Sennett bathing beauty—hence her costume in this scene—and Sunset Boulevard, *1950, was full of reverberations from her career. Edith Head's costumes for Swanson were acerbic, sardonic in their nostalgia, and a summation of the Paramount wardrobe.*

407. Upper Hall. Closeup. Norma dazedly comes forward to railing of staircase.
       NORMA: What is the scene?
              Where am I?

408. Lower Hall. Medium close shot. Max (von Stroheim) and two cameramen.
MAX: This is the staircase of the palace.

409. Same as 407. Norma bewildered, slowly grasps situation.
NORMA: Oh . . . yes . . . yes . . .

410. Same as 408.
MAX: (off) Down below. They're waiting for the princess.

The obverse of *Sunset Boulevard,* at least in its sunny buoyancy, was *Singin' in the Rain,* 1952, directed by Gene Kelly and Stanley Donen, set at the moment when silent films became talkies. The two films share the conviction that movie myths are operative myths—that things happen just the way they do in the movies.

Edith Head's costumes for Gloria Swanson in Sunset Boulevard, 1950, were, in a way, a brilliant take-off on the history of Hollywood costume. The concluding sequence, when Norma Desmond descends her staircase as Salome, has an uncanny sense of the eternal return.

[opposite]

Walter Plunkett had given up designing contemporary costumes early in the thirties at RKO, but in Singin' in the Rain, 1952, the musical about the advent of sound, he reverted to his beginnings as a designer in the silent twenties, spoofing the Old Hollywood glamour with a genial and knowing wit.

The exuberance of Gene Kelly, Donald O'Connor, and Debbie Reynolds is tied as well to the sort of boosterism that began to overtake the movie industry. For all of its wholesome charm, *Singin' in the Rain* is slightly out of focus, a period piece without a period. Perhaps more than any of the other films produced by the Freed Unit, it points toward a new freedom in the musical, for it evolved more from movement than narrative. Unfortunately, it lacks the visual coherence of earlier Freed musicals. But stiffening its casual air is a conviction, almost cynical in its comic effects, that every Hollywood type is a stereotype and thus stuck with behaving true to form.

"Designing for *Singin' in the Rain* was a trip back to those first musicals I made costumes for at RKO," said Walter Plunkett. "I said then that I would never design contemporary clothes again because every producer's wife and every secretary would double-guess you. But when I came back to it even that period had become historical. The second time around I loved it."

The Bad and the Beautiful, 1952. Lana Turner

The Bad and the Beautiful, 1952, directed by Vincente Minnelli; *The Barefoot Contessa,* 1954, written and directed by Joseph Mankiewicz; and *The Goddess,* 1958, directed by John Cromwell (who, twenty-four years earlier, had directed Bette Davis in *Of Human Bondage*)—all move more profoundly into a consideration of Hollywood images, the meanings imposed by makeup and costume.

About *The Bad and the Beautiful,* Minnelli said, "It was a harsh and cynical story, yet strangely romantic. All that one hated and loved about Hollywood was distilled in the screenplay . . . the

Lana Turner was clearly typecast in her role as a movie actress in The Bad and the Beautiful. *Helen Rose played her over-glamorous designs off against the "realistic" style of the movie, giving Turner some of her most memorable costumes.*

ambition, the opportunism, and the power . . . the philosophy of 'get me a talented son-of-a-bitch.' But it also told of triumphs against great odds and the respect people in the industry had for each others' talents.''

In *The Bad and the Beautiful,* Lana Turner is wrecked by the Pygmalion-producer who created her image. Her mistake was in taking the role he created for her personally. Her appearance, makeup, and costumes were a metaphysical statement of the unreality surrounding the star. A nimbus of perfection surrounded her blond beauty, an aura that reflects in the movie the process that had made her a star.

There is a visual tension between her role in the story and her half life in the film as Lana Turner. Minnelli used that tension in a scene that pierced her self-contained presence in the role with a melodramatic sequence in which she lost her nerve when her car goes into a spin on a rain-drenched highway. Turner became hysterical, and perhaps more significantly, her hair flopped down on her forehead and her fur became disarranged. Not so much acting as a rearrangement of surfaces, this scene became the basis for a reconsideration of Lana Turner's talents as an actress.

The Barefoot Contessa, as surprising in its way as *All About Eve,* explored the elusive afterlife as a star of a legendary woman, and the conflict between her outer image and inner life. The role was played by Ava Gardner, herself a visible manifestation of the experience of women in Hollywood. The image was much like her own, including a sort of medley of her roles—with a statue-portrait in Grecian draperies to echo *One Touch of Venus,* 1948. The giveaway clue in that film-à-clef was the bare feet, since Gardner loved to kick off her shoes and dance.

The classic formulation of the psychology of a star, however, was Kim Stanley's performance in *The Goddess,* 1957, a role so subtle and provocative in its revelations that it seemed to many an exposé of the career of Marilyn Monroe. *The Goddess* proposes a rather simplistic equation for the drives of a star. In the case of Kim Stanley's role, the motivation was a reaction against a suffocating fundamentalist religious background—with bleached hair, provocative décolletage, and tight dresses as the means of rebellion. In the cinematic meditation on surfaces, the glamorous gear of stardom becomes equated with the deepest self-betrayal.

Marilyn Monroe's first appearance in a movie was in 1947, at the age of twenty-one, but her real career as a starlet did not begin until 1952, when she appeared briefly in *Clash by Night.* Her last movie, *The Misfits,* 1961, was made only nine years later, and a year after that she was dead. More than any star, her stardom was more in her presence than in her films.

Bus Stop, 1956. Marilyn Monroe. Photo: MoMA.

Marilyn Monroe continued the roles of Betty Grable in Twentieth Century–Fox musicals, carrying her showgirl get-ups into her serious roles as well, such as Bus Stop, *1956. No matter what else, her image was constant.*

Pl. 88
Marilyn Monroe costume for *The Prince and the Showgirl,* 1957, designed by Beatrice Dawson

Marilyn Monroe confessed (for publication) that she was never much at home in clothes. She found her gowns for The Prince and the Showgirl, *1957, particularly uncomfortable because of the under-pinnings. She hated girdles, much less corsets.*

The few movies Monroe did make seem to suggest something larger and fugitive, a quality that somehow eluded the screen. The term *Sex Goddess* seemed to be coined for her, and she seemed to sum up in her person all the film images of women: Waif and Vamp, Flapper and Good Girl, Whore and Saint, Pinup and Hoofer. She was a sort of pan-Venus, all things to all men. In the famous photographic feature for *Life* in 1958, Richard Avedon had her dress in her other incarnations, as Lillian Russell and Clara Bow. None of her films was so revealing of her potential. She had a protean proclivity for becoming a star.

Norman Mailer, in his biographical meditation, *Marilyn,* makes much of Monroe's own fantasies about her origins, the amount of cinema lore with which she was imbued. He is beguiled by corny coincidences: how she told her friends that Clark Gable was her father and then ended up starring with him in *The Misfits.* Whatever the meaning of her troubled dreams, Marilyn Monroe was Hollywood's child, the heir to a dream that lived, and perhaps died, in her.

The Seven Year Itch, 1955. Marilyn Monroe, Tom Ewell.

Pl. 89
Marilyn Monroe costume for *The Seven Year Itch*, 1955, copied by John Kloss.

What other dress is more emblematic of the postwar years than Marilyn Monroe's dress from Seven Year Itch, 1955? Bought off the rack, the halterneck dress of white pleated crêpe was photographed again and again and the publicity still became almost as famous as the shot of the Marines raising the flag on Iwo Jima.

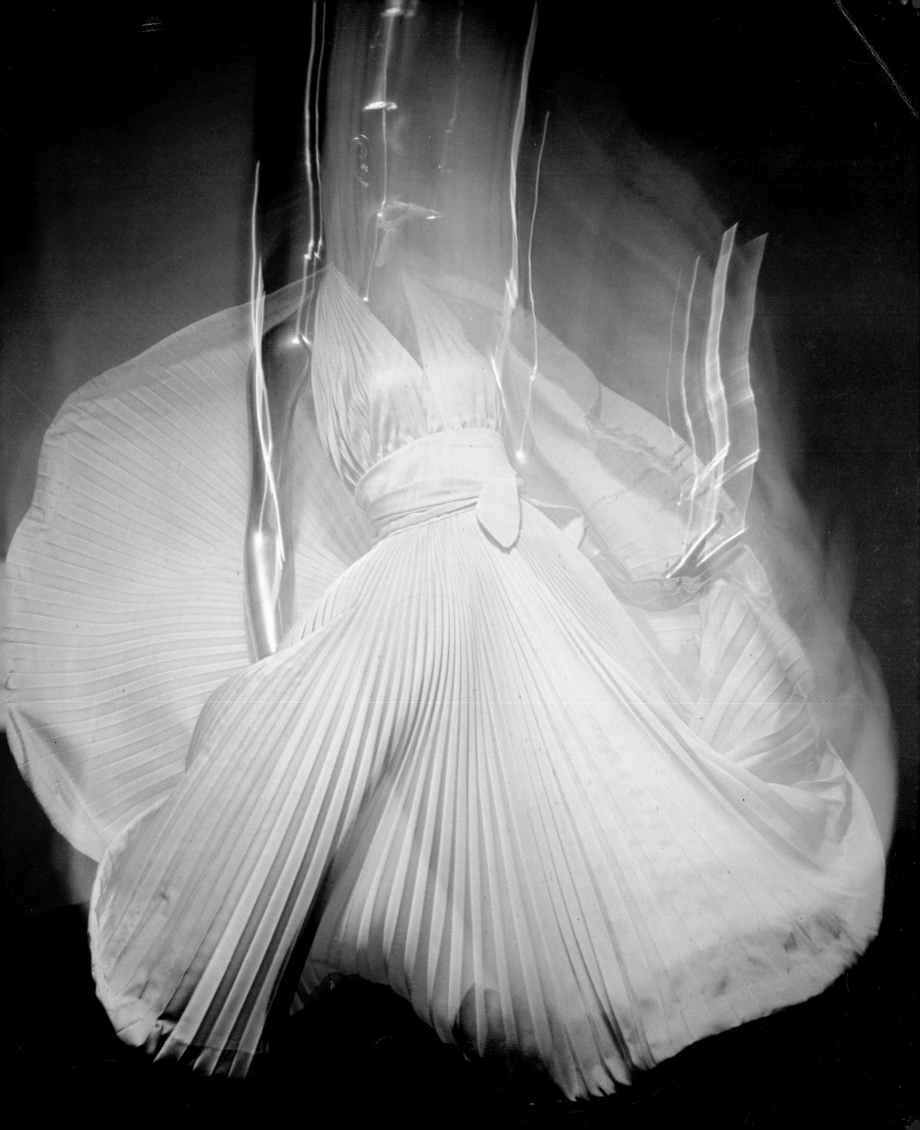

Pl. 90
Marilyn Monroe's Lillian Russell costume for photographic
feature in *Life* magazine by Richard Avedon.

For Life *magazine, Richard Avedon photographed
Marilyn Monroe in a series of incarnations as the
great ladies of stage and screen. Among the most
memorable was her impersonation of Lillian Russell
in a scanty cycling outfit.*

Some Like It Hot, 1959. Tony Curtis, Marilyn Monroe.

Some Like It Hot, *1959, contained Marilyn Monroe's best performance—sexy, wacky, and effervescent—and her best costumes, designed by Orry-Kelly. Picking up on the movie's use of twenties America as a sort of hedonistic utopia, Orry-Kelly relied not so much on history but on a sort of remembered voluptuousness and zany travesty, the sort of blatant sexuality possible only in comedy.*

Mary Pickford regretted that silent pictures had come before sound. The reverse seemed more appropriate to her.

With *An American in Paris,* 1951, the esthetic of the studio movie found its ultimate expression, the team movie reached its apogee. The ingredients are in no way surprising, but what makes the film a masterpiece of its kind is a superb integration of every element of the movie, a unity possible, perhaps, because of the use of Gershwin's *American in Paris* as the motive for both the image and the action. Tags of the music were introduced in the film long before the culminating ballet because it was feared that the public would not have recognized the music.

237

The visual center of the movie is Paris, not just as a geographical entity but as a series of resonances in terms of art, architecture, and music. "I approached the film as a culmination of all the influences I'd been experimenting with during the nineteen-forties," said Vincente Minnelli. "Everything I knew about Paris, or had heard about Paris, would be incorporated whenever possible. I pored over thousands of pictures with set director Preston Ames. Together we created a Paris so authentic that Frenchmen are amazed to discover the picture was filmed in the United States."

The production was so complex that three costume designers were used: Walter Plunkett, Orry-Kelly, and Irene Sharaff. Plunkett did the costumes for the Artists Ball in black-and-white, a mélange of patterns and shapes showered with black-and-white confetti. Sharaff was assigned the ballet. In early production meetings Minnelli had called for "the ultimate in color for this sequence." Not surprisingly for Hollywood, black-and-white was the result.

In *The Magic Factory: How MGM Made* An American in Paris, Vincente Minnelli and Irene Sharaff talked about Leslie Caron's first appearance in the movie, literally her first appearance on the screen.

Vincente Minnelli:

> In staging Leslie's introduction I thought, "Wouldn't it be interesting to do it monochromatically?" Each vignette would be staged in a different type of room. I had decided on doing each room in one color: a Jacobean room in all yellow, a Biedermeier that's all pink and so on. Leslie's costume would be the only color contrast. Since the scene was such that Guetary was trying to explain the girl, and Oscar would take him literally at his word, I felt the scene called for this type of treatment. I had done this kind of thing before, on the stage, treating rooms in one complete color, painting everything the same. It's just a way of doing it. If you're trying to visualize one person from a description given you by another person, you don't see it very well; you see it distorted. "She's very studious." "Oh, she reads a great deal." "Not at all—she's very gay." Staging that kind of scene the way I did suits that situation. The colors were poster colors, absolutely like from a child's paint box. I then asked Irene Sharaff to design the costumes and the other combinations.

Irene Sharaff:

> The costumes were brilliant things, but I must say it was Vincente's brain child. I forgot the sequence except for one bright saffron yellow dress I did for it. This was just a little present that I gave *An American in Paris*. It was done as a gift. I think Vincente and I talked about it as being done in very jewel-like colors, very sharp prismatic colors, so you got it as one sharp prismatic thing against another, compared to the subtleties of the ballet itself.

The ballet is an artist's version of Paris that might have evolved in the imagination of the GI Bill student-hero. It begins with a black-and-white sketch that dissolves into a colored sketch.

Pl. 91
Supporting actress costume for *Lovely to Look At,* 1952, designed by Adrian.

After having retired from films to become a couturier, Adrian designed costumes for one final movie in 1952, Lovely to Look At. But he was called back not so much because of his years at MGM but rather because of his second career as a dress designer, an authentic touch for a movie about fashion.

"Paris appears, but all its color has been drained," Minnelli said. "It's a fickle city that will falsely enchant, then mock you. Suddenly the color is harshly splashed into the image and the spirit of the city is evoked."

The American tries to blend into the setting, but he is ignored in the bustle of the city. Then he finds himself in the flower market at dawn, as if painted by Renoir, and the girl appears. Next he happens on a street that is redolent of Utrillo. His mood changes and the setting becomes the Zoological Gardens, after Rousseau's "Sleeping Gypsy." "The suppressed physical yearnings blot out every other emotion," Minnelli said, "and his mind feverishly indulges in a dream of a great and unreciprocated love. He is drugged with the thought, the dream expands. Paris is again alive, but now it is part of him and he is part of Paris . . . the Paris that loves a lover. The gay crowds in the Place de l'Opéra come to life and he and his love dance with them. They imagine themselves as characters in a Toulouse-Lautrec poster. Their hysteria becomes an orgy of fulfillment when, without warning, the nothingness returns. People disappear and the color drains out of everything. He's left again, as he started, hopeless, alone."

The ballet is over. The hero wakes up. And boy, of course, gets girl. In the brilliantly staged and costumed ballet, the most ambitious of Hollywood's visual aspirations were realized in the construction and outfitting of a moving painting. The Hollywood costume returned to its sources.

A footnote to the history of the Hollywood costume: At about the time of *An American in Paris,* Vincente Minnelli began to give his daughter Liza tiny copies of the costumes from his pictures, five costumes a year by Adrian or Irene Sharaff. Over the years those included, among others, the Furies and can-can costumes from *An American in Paris,* Gertrude Lawrence's presentation gown from *The King and I,* and Cyd Charisse's ballerina costume from *The Band Wagon,* 1953.

Gigi, 1958. Leslie Caron. Photo: MoMA.

Movies about style, the forte of both Luchino Visconti and Ken Russell, began in the fifties with Gigi, 1958, the major popular impetus for the revival of art nouveau in the years that followed. The charm of Gigi was not so much in the Colette stories from which it evolved, or the original score by Lerner and Loewe, but in the settings and costumes by Cecil Beaton, a total immersion in the world of eighteen-nineties Paris.

...starring
leslie caron

The last of the MGM ingenues, with prominent teeth and short haircut, Leslie Caron was discovered by Gene Kelly and became a star with him in An American in Paris, 1951. Her dancing and singing led to other fairytales, most notably Lili, 1953, and The Glass Slipper, 1954, in which the essential Hollywood myth was retold with Technicolor veracity. The roles were slight, but Caron's charm, amplified by the final bursts of studio extravagance in costumes and sets, made her an intriguing exception to the heavy-breasted sensuality of screen stars in the Eisenhower years. For An American in Paris, Caron's costumes by Irene Sharaff, one of the three designers for the film, were the most memorable. Without exception, they were silhouettes taken from ballet, with large skirts and tiny waists. Caron's haircut, ballerina skirts with layers of petticoats, and ballet slippers helped to popularize that style, particularly among teenagers, and she was one of the first Hollywood stars to wear the Left Bank–style black tights. Perhaps not coincidentally, after the very theatrical costumes in An American in Paris, her costumes seemed to come out of the stage tradition—the gamine of Lili, and the birthday-cake style of Helen Rose's costumes in The Glass Slipper. Her chief success was in MGM's film musical Gigi, 1958, a role she had played on the London stage. For that movie Cecil Beaton went to authentic French sources for the art nouveau décor, and his costumes were a brilliant rendering of the Parisian 1890s. Caron had a sensuous and nubile charm that blended well with the florid curves at Maxim's.

An American in Paris, 1951. Gene Kelly, Leslie Caron. Photo: MoMA.

Pl. 92 [overleaf]
Leslie Caron costume for An American in Paris, 1951, designed by Irene Sharaff.

An American in Paris, 1951, provided a brilliant 1950s "highbrow" synthesis by Hollywood of the visual world from fashion to painting, loosely linked by Gershwin's programmatic music. Sharaff's costumes for the ballet sequence were straight from the palettes of Lautrec, Renoir, and Dufy.

1960s

The Twilight of the Goddesses

...starring
elizabeth taylor

Pale-faced, big-eyed, with an extraordinary double set of eyelashes and a surprising voice, extravagantly beautiful Elizabeth Taylor was the last of the studio stars, the highly paid M.C. of The Twilight of the Goddesses. She managed to keep her name in the headlines, her private life a matter of gossip, longer than any other star in the movies. Her front-page notoriety, after all, spanned two decades, and she has been a star for three. And, while many stars have regaled themselves with clothes and cars and jewels, Taylor has achieved a level of conspicuous consumption all her own. At times, she has seemed to court disfavor, but she has somehow turned her faults to her advantage, even playing mocking parodies of herself, as in Secret Ceremony where, dressed by Marc Bohan, she plays an ageing whore. Her particular quality is an astonishing honesty. Asked about her career after A Place in the Sun, she said, "Most of the subsequent films were a morass of mediocrity. Not just the scripts, I was mediocre too." The costumes for A Place in the Sun, by Edith Head, were among the most remarkable created for her—a frothy formulation of the sort of image she had been given at MGM, underlined with a telling sarcasm. After Cleopatra, a disaster film before its time, financially and critically speaking, Taylor began to play roles that referred topically to her much-publicized love affairs and marriages. About her Cleopatra, John Coleman said, in what might be an epitaph for the oldtime star, "Monotony in a split skirt, a pre-Christian Elizabeth Arden with sequined eyelids and occasions constantly too large for her. Plumply pretty, she gives herself womanfully to the world's prime seductress but nary a spark flies." In spite of her press, Elizabeth Taylor has prevailed.

Three times the name was called out. Three times the spotlight scanned the empty stage. A nervous murmur ran through the old Madison Square Garden. Twenty thousand people wondered if the star had shown. Then came the voice of Peter Lawford, "And here is the late Marilyn Monroe."

She stepped forward, her dress seeming to smolder and burn in the spotlights. "Happy Birthday, dear President," she sang in her whispering voice, as the audience went crazy.

Later, in his speech, John Kennedy acknowledged her tribute in a joke that again brought applause: "I can now retire from politics after having 'Happy Birthday' sung to me by Miss Monroe." That evening in mid-May, 1962, was perhaps one of the last extraordinary moments of the myth generated by Hollywood in its fifty years of creating glamour, glitter, and romance.

The producer of the Kennedy birthday party, Jean Dalrymple, had asked Marilyn Monroe to be careful about what she chose to wear. "I told her to wear something modest since it was a formal occasion. Before the gala, I went to her dressing room and there she was in this modest little gown with no bareness at all. It even had a neck and sleeves. And then she went out on the stage and it melted away." The "modest little gown" was a nude marquisette, entirely covered with rhinestone brilliants.

Less than three months later Marilyn Monroe was dead, and the era of the Hollywood star seemed ended.

The experiments with financing and production that began in the fifties, the importation of foreign films, the collapse of the studios as a major creative and economic force, and the development of joint productions between Americans and Europeans were the emerging characteristics of the film industry. A major symptom of the change was the supplanting of studio filming by work done almost entirely on location. Also, the directors and actors in American films were no longer exclusively the products of Hollywood.

Four films were particularly important in making this transition. *Cleopatra,* 1962, effectively ended the costume picture. Filmed in Rome at a cost of $40,000,000, the most expensive movie ever made, *Cleopatra* was used as an object lesson in movie financing, since it caused the Twentieth Century–Fox annual report in 1962 to show a $39,769,094 loss. (By contrast, MGM's investment of $15,000,000 in a remake of *Ben Hur,* 1959, brought worldwide returns of $80,000,000.) The other major shock to the movie economy also came in 1962 with MGM's second version of *Mutiny on the Bounty,* which cost $19,000,000, a budget ten times that of the original 1935 movie.

In 1965, Twentieth Century–Fox produced *The Sound of Music,* starring Julie Andrews, one of the biggest moneymakers in Hollywood history. Unfortunately, the spate of big-budget musicals during this time did not do so well and another Hollywood staple fell into disrepute. An exception was *My Fair Lady,* 1964, with Audrey Hepburn, which cost $14,000,000 and was the most expensive movie ever made in a studio—perhaps the last of such big-budget musicals. Warner Brothers, nonetheless, made $75,000,000 on the picture.

Because the studios no longer could guarantee distribution or draw an audience with their trademark—phenomena that had begun with the anti–block booking decision of 1948—each production tended to develop on its own terms. Financing was obtained on the basis of the director or the star or the producer who could put together the "package"—the assemblage of key elements, such as the script, the star, and the director. While the star system had persisted in diminishing degree through the fifties, few stars were regarded as truly safe investments. Even Clark Gable, the

Pl. 93
Marilyn Monroe's dress worn to President Kennedy's birthday celebration in Madison Square Garden in 1962.

Marilyn Monroe's whispering rendition of "Happy Birthday, President Kennedy," was the legendary highlight of JFK's 1962 birthday celebration at Madison Square Garden, but her nude marquisette gown covered in brilliants that seemed to melt away in the spotlights was the stuff of myths.

most durable of the old stars, didn't work much during the fifties. His staying power, he told David O. Selznick, was due largely to the revivals of *Gone with the Wind.* "Every time they begin to forget me, out comes GWTW again," he said.

Working on a freelance basis was even more difficult for women stars. Without important roles, superlative presentation, and the efforts of the studio publicity mills, few women seemed to be able to sustain their mystery and allure.

An exception was Elizabeth Taylor, whose career spanned the last of the major studio years and the virtual disappearance of Hollywood-made productions. Carefully groomed by MGM, Elizabeth Taylor had begun her career at the studio in 1943 at the age of eleven, after having made one movie at Universal the year before. Her violet eyes, pale skin, and dark hair, a sort of pure English beauty, quickly made her a star in some of MGM's most extravagantly sentimental confections, including Lassie movies, *Life with Father,* 1945, and *Little Women,* 1949.

In *Father of the Bride,* 1950, she grew up, or at least she was married. With that movie she became one of the major stars of the decade, zigging and zagging between the last of the MGM costume romances—*Quo Vadis,* 1951; *Ivanhoe,* 1952; *Beau Brummell,* 1954; and *Raintree County,* 1957—and contemporary dramas— *Rhapsody,* 1954; *Elephant Walk,* 1954 (in the role originally intended for Vivien Leigh); *The Last Time I Saw Paris,* 1955; *Giant,* 1956; *Cat on a Hot Tin Roof,* 1958; and *Suddenly Last Summer,* 1959.

"Name me one actress who survived all that crap at MGM," said Ava Gardner. "Maybe Lana Turner. Certainly Liz Taylor. But they all hate acting as much as I do. All except for Elizabeth. She used to come up to me on the set and say, 'If only I could learn to be good,' and, by God, she made it."

Elizabeth Taylor spent the fifties breaking away from the studio, swinging in larger and larger arcs away from the image the studio had created for her, demanding to do movies at other studios. Until 1954 and *The Last Time I Saw Paris,* with perhaps the exception of *A Place in the Sun,* 1951, Elizabeth Taylor was entirely a creature of the studio's imagination: "Up until this picture, Miss Taylor has been just about the loveliest thing seen in a fan magazine," wrote one reviewer. "The trouble was that when you went to see her in the theatre, she still looked like she *was* in a fan magazine. Her appearance was so perfect that, before every take, you could almost see the make-up men running off the set with their powderpuffs."

Her contract with Metro-Goldwyn-Mayer ran seventeen and a half years, from *Lassie Come Home* in September, 1942, to the

Butterfield 8, 1960. Elizabeth Taylor.

Elizabeth Taylor, in the days before full movie candor, often wore slips and, in this scene from Butterfield 8 *and an equally famous scene from* Cat on A Hot Tin Roof, *Helen Rose supplied her with some of the sexiest lingerie ever made for the movies.*

completion of *Butterfield 8* in the spring of 1960—about the same duration as Greta Garbo, Norma Shearer, and Joan Crawford. And when she became the highest-paid of the freelancers in 1960, she still retained a knot of MGM craftsmen in all her projects, most notably the designer Helen Rose and the hairdresser Sidney Guillaroff, for whose services MGM stars had been fighting since the thirties.

Her thinking was evident in the last big fight she had with the studio, over releasing her to play in *Cleopatra:* she didn't need the studio but she did need the look the studio gave her. To gain her freedom, she had to film *Butterfield 8*—ironically, the role that won her an Oscar. Her demands: the movie must be shot in New York, she must have Helen Rose for her wardrobe and Sidney Guillaroff to do her hair, and Eddie Fisher must have a role in the picture.

At the stormy end of her time at MGM she asked Sol Siegel, "Is this the way to end a seventeen-year relationship?" He replied, "Fortunately or unfortunately, Miss Taylor, sentiment went out of this business years ago."

Thus, in 1960, began production of the film industry's biggest-deficit movie. The series of misfortunes, blunders, and peccadilloes, ranging from terrible to colossal, that brought *Cleopatra* this distinction began with the decision to shoot it in England. This seemed a strange choice for a film set in Rome and Egypt, but both Elizabeth Taylor and Twentieth Century–Fox wanted the advantage of the tax allowance given by the British to foreign film-makers. Trouble began immediately. When Taylor asked for Guillaroff as her hairdresser, British unions threatened to strike the film. The star prevailed, but Guillaroff was not allowed to set foot in the studio. He had to comb her hair out in her hotel.

Outside London, at the Pinewood Studios, eight and a half acres of ancient Alexandria had been constructed at a cost of $600,000 under the supervision of designer John DeCuir. There was an assortment of palaces and temples using some 80,000 cubic feet of lumber, 750,000 feet of tubular steel, and 7 tons of nails and screws. Artificial lakes and ponds had also been constructed. For the star, at a fee of $24,000, Oliver Messel had designed forty costumes and headdresses that cost $40,800 to make.

A year passed, during which little shooting was done because of a series of illnesses that struck Elizabeth Taylor. A few major scenes had been shot, including Cleopatra's arrival in a rug. After "careful historical corroboration," Taylor agreed to play the scene in the nude, with the set closed to all but a minimum of technicians.

New sets had to be thrown up, including forty-seven interiors and thirty-two exteriors. Only one of those was ready when filming began in September. Thousands of costumes had to be remade when their seams were found ripped out in a mysterious act of sabotage. Other costly delays began to pile up.

One of the major problems was the filming of Cleopatra's triumphal entry into Rome. One segment had already been filmed six months earlier in London. Altogether that one sequence would cost $250,000.

Irene Sharaff, who had been called in to create new costumes to replace Messel's, which had been dropped when the production was shifted to Rome, had designed a gown for Cleopatra's impersonation of the goddess Isis which Taylor wore during the entrance to Rome and also for the last scene in the film. The $6,500 gown was made of cloth of 24-karat gold. The cast call for the dazzling invasion included: 50 archers, shooting arrows from which unfurled veils the hues of the sunrise, symbolizing the approach of Isis and Horus; 26 snake dancers to represent the Sacred Serpent of Egypt; 38 girls with gilded wings and headdresses to symbolize the Sacred Vulture; 36 trumpeters on 36 white horses; 8 charioteers driving 16 black horses; 8 bowmen on the chariots; a 20-piece Egyptian band; 28 pole dancers (female and fair); 1 old hag; 1 beautiful girl; 3 oxenmen with 6 white oxen; 16 dwarfs on 16 zebras; 7 acrobats (male); 4 acrobats (2 male, 2 female) on 2 elephants; 4 girls with gifts on elephants; 4 mahouts; 12 Watusi green-smoke dancers (male and dark); 14 yellow-smoke dancers; 18 dancers (male and dark, four of them with drums); 12 dancers (female and dark); 10 red witch dancers (male and dark); 8 pole vaulters (male and fair); 16 gold fan-bearers (male and fair); 7 gold tree-porters (male and fair); 30 elite honor guards on 30 sorrel horses; 12 slaves for the pyramid; 8 Nubians painted like marble and posed as a frieze to carry Cleopatra; 300 slaves for the Sphinx. As a part of the Roman Forum crowd: 3,000 men, 1,500 women, 20 children, 6 Egyptian dignitaries, 6 Egyptian slaves, 30 Roman Senators' wives, 20 Roman court ladies, 150 Roman Senators, 24 lictors (officers bearing the fasces, the Roman symbol of authority), 350 Praetorians, and 12 Roman trumpeters.

Hermes Pan, the choreographer, orchestrated the extras to keep all the elements moving on the ground and in the air. Chariots crisscrossed in and out of the procession, the archers shooting forth the flying streamers; the girls on the elephants tossed golden coins to the throngs; Watusi dancers moved through clouds of green and yellow smoke, the air glittering with tons of golden confetti, as they approached Caesar's throne; the pole vaulters dressed as birdmen vaulted over the Watusi and seemed to fly

Cleopatra, 1962.

Cleopatra, 1962, *was the last gasp of the old-style costume epic. Delays in production, switches in directors, and finally a move to Rome caused two complete sets of costumes to be made—the first by Oliver Messel and the second by Irene Sharaff. The costumes were expensive, but they failed to capture the magic of the two earlier versions of* Cleopatra, *starring Theda Bara and Claudette Colbert.*

right into the audience; the golden pyramid bearing the gilded girls opened at the top as it approached Caesar and two thousand doves flew out.

Pan said that the doves were shut up in the pyramid so long waiting for their cue that they fell asleep in the dark interior and a man had to be stationed with a gun firing blanks to get them off.

Last, the massive Sphinx, with the incarnations of Isis and Horus between its paws, drawn by three hundred slaves and attended by the eight Nubians, would come through the archway and up to the throne.

Elizabeth Taylor, wearing the headdress of Isis—two and a half feet high and weighing fifteen pounds—was at a height of three stories atop the sphinx. On the day of the shooting, she was uneasy not only because of the height but also because of a newspaper attack by the Vatican on her affair with Richard Burton.

In 1961 Twentieth Century–Fox ruinously heightened the financial difficulties of the film by transferring the production to Rome. Joseph Mankiewicz was brought in to direct. Within two weeks, the women in Cleopatra's entourage had gone on strike because, they said, their skimpy costumes invited untoward attentions. An "antipinch" squad was brought in at sixty-five dollars a day, according to publicity.

The script called for the extras to come running toward the Sphinx shouting, "Cleopatra! Cleopatra! Cleopatra!" As the huge contraption neared Caesar's throne, she saw the crowds break and run toward her. "My God!" she said she had thought. "Here it comes, Bessie."

Suddenly she realized that they were not shouting, "Cleopatra!" They were screaming, "Leez! Leez! Baci! Baci!" She began to cry at their call for kisses and, when the camera was stopped, used a microphone to thank them.

This scene, including Cleopatra's arrival on a barge, had cost $750,000. Altogether, the expenses of the film were staggering. The 65 costumes Irene Sharaff designed for Elizabeth Taylor cost $130,000, and she had 30 wigs and 125 separate pieces of jewelry as well. (The porter who attended to Cleopatra's wigs was paid $18 a day.) The 26,000 other costumes for the film cost $475,000.

Surprisingly, in spite of the cost of *Cleopatra,* Elizabeth Taylor continued to pull down a million dollars a picture. Her performances received mixed to poor reviews, but her personal life received so much publicity that she was still excellent box office.

Cleopatra, 1962.

The most remarkable of her roles was as Martha in *Who's Afraid of Virginia Woolf?*, 1966, its strength derived largely from the collision between her carefully tended Technicolor image and her part as a forty-five-year-old academic housewife. Her costumes, by Irene Sharaff, are determinedly lumpy and misshapen; her makeup might have been done by the English painter Francis Bacon: a blur of messy hair, a series of chins, and heavily sagging eyes. The result is a devastating revision of what had been on the screen.

Even more significant is her conscious use of parody to add another level to her characterization. Her first line—"What a dump!"—is delivered in roaring contempt, an hilarious echo of Bette Davis and a stunning entrance. Then, with a rolling walk, she moves into the vastly untidy kitchen and takes a chicken leg out of the refrigerator while she both imitates and expounds on Bette Davis in *Beyond the Forest*, 1949. (*Who's Afraid of Virginia Woolf?* was produced by Warner Brothers for seven million dollars, the highest budget ever for a black-and-white film.)

With that brilliantly delivered passage of dialogue, the movies and the experience of the movies passed into a new and highly articulated phase, both of history and of nostalgia. The accretion of time had transformed the film from fairytales, fables of appearance and reality, into modes of conduct, a shared past.

Who's Afraid of Virginia Woolf?, 1966. Elizabeth Taylor, Richard Burton. Photo: MoMA.

The assault on the image of the Star was carried even further by Elizabeth Taylor, who put on pounds and wrinkles to play Martha in Who's Afraid of Virginia Woolf?, *1966. From the opening line, delivered in the manner of Bette Davis, the movie is stunning in its sense of film culture.*

Thus, in the sixties, a variety of thinkers and writers began to approach the significance of the movies with a greatly expanded perspective. Part of that sensibility had been created by the *Cahiers du Cinéma,* started by some of the younger French film directors, but it was reflected diversely in Susan Sontag's *Against Interpretation,* particularly in her articulation of "camp"; in Roland Barthes's writings on movies as signs; in the popularity of Parker Tyler's mythic criticism and its offshoot in Gore Vidal's *Myra Breckinridge* and its sequel *Myron Breckinridge* and, of course, in Edward Albee's *Who's Afraid of Virginia Woolf?*

The Albee play and the screenplay that were taken from it were the final confession of the immense importance of the movies to the American psyche. When Elizabeth Taylor joked that Walter Wanger and Joseph Mankiewicz should have been painted into the Times Square billboard advertising *Cleopatra* with her, Richard Burton, and Rex Harrison—with Freud floating above them all—she was pointing to a Hollywood religious iconography.

The camp sensibility with its pantheon of Hollywood goddesses was yet another sign of Hollywood's rapidly receding past. At seventy-one, Colleen Griffith, the silent screen star, told a divorce judge, "I'm not Colleen Griffith. I'm just a stand-in." She was fifty-one, she said. Her about-to-be-divorced husband was forty-four. Because of television, the stars of the twenties and thirties found themselves haunted by their youthful images, mocked by what was.

The grotesque self-consciousness of *Sunset Boulevard,* 1950, gave way to the ghoulish in *Whatever Happened to Baby Jane?,* 1962, an independently produced film starring Bette Davis and Joan Crawford. With that film—about two silent movie stars, one of whom was a murderer—Hollywood began to take a darker look at its origins, to discover more pessimistic sources for the fantasies it had produced. The film is Grand Guignol, so misanthropic in its conception that its very blackness transcends the silly screenplay. It was, indicatively, turned down for distribution by every other studio until Warner Brothers agreed to take it.

More, perhaps, *Whatever Happened to Baby Jane?* is a rewriting of the Creative Myth, a corrective to the sunniness of *Singin' in the Rain* and the bitchy humanity of *All About Eve.* Such revisionism is evident in Kenneth Anger's first underground version of *Hollywood Babylon* in the sixties (tidied up in its subsequent 1975 version) and a string of other movies and TV dramas. Typical of those is *The Legend of Lylah Clare,* 1968, starring Kim Novak, in which gossip about the personal lives of Greta Garbo and Marlene Dietrich is served up as a bloody Svengali-and-Trilby story with some heavy-handed transvestism to boot.

Whatever Happened to Baby Jane?, 1962. Joan Crawford, Bette Davis. Photo: MoMA.

The disintegration of the old Hollywood was mirrored in Whatever Happened to Baby Jane?, *1962, in which Bette Davis and Joan Crawford gave up their glamour to play a couple of old horrors. Bette Davis revived the pasty-faced look of the silent movies, applying layer after layer of powder and grease-paint and heavily lining her eyes.*

Last Year at Marienbad, 1961. Delphine Seyrig. Photo: MoMA.

Last Year at Marienbad, *1961, was one of the first movies to take the Hollywood conventions and tradition seriously—with no plot, only a series of poses, it is an anatomy of the romantic movie. Chanel's costumes for Delphine Seyrig looked back to the thirties, notably to* Shanghai Express.

Blow-Up, 1966. David Hemmings.

In Blow-Up, *1966, the world of fashion became a symbol for the layers of appearance and reality that make up glamour, a sort of detective story of images. The costumes, silly and extreme, were not by a costume designer but imported from the pop world.*

On the one hand, the reinterpretation of the Hollywood goddesses who shared such unquestioning devotion for fifty years was inevitable. But that reevaluation was linked with a larger rethinking of women's roles, for which Hollywood, as a source of the myths, was particularly culpable.

With the accretion of time the movies were passing into the realm of poetry—a self-enclosed system of images whose tradition was becoming more and more remote from everyday existence. TV had given the failed and glorious dreams an afterlife.

Pl. 94
Vanessa Redgrave costume for *Camelot*, 1967, designed by John Truscott.

Adrian's last designs were for the stage production of Camelot, *1967—showy and heraldic. For the movie, John Truscott adopted a style at once lyrical and feudal, a poetic version of the rustic world in which Guinevere, Lancelot, and Arthur lived.*

Pl. 95
Gina Lollabrigida costume for an unfilmed version of *Lady L*, early sixties, designed by Orry-Kelly.

Costumes were often made for films that never went into production. One such was Lady L, *slated for Gina Lollobrigida but later made starring Sophia Loren in another version with other costumes. Orry-Kelly's unused costumes were splendid, with luxuriously worked embroidery and lace.*

Pls. 96, 97
Gina Lollabrigida costume for an unfilmed version of *Lady L*,
early sixties, designed by Orry-Kelly. With detail.

In 1964 Jack Warner made the last of the big studio movies, *My Fair Lady*, at a cost of seven million dollars. (Thirty years earlier, Busby Berkeley had begun the tradition of the movie musical at Warner Brothers on budgets of only a few hundred thousand dollars.) There were seven sound stages in use simultaneously; 1,500 technicians worked on the film at once; 33 wardrobe women worked full-time making thousands of costumes. More than a hundred were needed to work on makeup.

George Cukor was the director and Cecil Beaton was in charge of the sets and costumes—a division of duties, according to Cukor,

Pl. 98 [*opposite*]
Vanessa Redgrave costume for *Camelot*, 1967, designed by John Truscott.

Camelot, 1967, was a Never-Never land and John Truscott's designs were full of fantasy touched by realistic detail, as in the pumpkin seed embroidery that covered Guinevere's wedding veil and the fish-net-like crocheted overdress.

Pl. 99
Supporting actresses costumes for *My Fair Lady*, 1964, designed by Cecil Beaton.

Cecil Beaton so much admired his costumes for the extras in My Fair Lady *that he supervised the dressing and make-up on the sound stage himself—subsequently even photographing the star, Audrey Hepburn, in these costumes.*

263

My Fair Lady, 1964. Photo: MoMA.

Edwardian England supplied Cecil Beaton with many of the ingredients of glamour that he used in every phase of his work. Beaton's role in the production of My Fair Lady, *1964, was encyclopedic. He not only designed the costumes but instructed the actors in how to wear them—and their hats and their hairdos.*

that Beaton seemed to resent. In discussing the effects in the movie, George Cukor told Gavin Lambert, "Although we did a lot of research for the sets and the background, it was in order to *know* what we had to stylize. In England, Beaton, Gene Ellen, and I looked at actual houses to get the architectural feel. We'd go through book after book of the period and suddenly something would hit us. 'Here's a significant detail,' we'd say. 'They'd have a gong in the hall.' Little details like that bring places and habits to life, like the stuffed animals on the second floor of Professor Higgins' house and the art nouveau in his mother's house."

Cecil Beaton, a photographer and extraordinary memoirist as well as a designer, was deeply immersed in the Edwardian period— the setting of the movie and the source for his conception of luxury and elegance. For him, the generation of his parents was the epitome of high style, and he contrived to re-create a whole world, a careful synthesis of setting, furniture, clothing, and objects. His particular flair was in his specific knowledge of the color, texture, and fabric of the period. Unlike many of the historical costumes put together in Hollywood, Beaton's costumes were authentically of the period rather than tricked-up contemporary costumes. (Two other designers who work with a strong sense of the history of taste are Piero Tosi, the costume designer for many of Visconti's period films, and Shirley Russell, who designs for her husband Ken Russell's films and television programs. Tosi likes to combine antique clothes and costumes of his own design. Shirley Russell is more keenly alert to the Hollywood tradition of costume and makes a humorous use of pastiche.)

Beaton's most inspired design conception for the screen had been the earlier *Gigi,* 1958, one of the last of the original MGM musicals. His evocation of *belle époque* Paris is superb—shimmering with allusions to Toulouse-Lautrec, Helleu, and Boldini. That movie was probably to a large extent responsible for the subsequent revival of art nouveau, and perhaps indirectly for a more serious acceptance of the decorative arts. Certainly Beaton, because of his photography and journalism—notably his fashion exhibition at London's Victoria and Albert Museum, 1971—has been responsible for a heightened awareness of the cultural significance of dress.

Pl. 100
Audrey Hepburn hat for *My Fair Lady*, 1964, designed by Cecil Beaton.

Cecil Beaton lavished detail on My Fair Lady, 1964, taking as much care with the costumes of the chorus as with Audrey Hepburn's. Among the most remarkable small touches are the hats—extravagant and memorable in their millinery daring, veritable summaries of Edwardian style.

Pls. 101, 102
Audrey Hepburn costume for *My Fair Lady*, 1964, designed by Cecil Beaton. With detail.

Beaton seemed to work by accumulating detail, in both authentic and reconstructed materials. But his care went even further by reviving the styles of needlework and embroidery that had been popular at the time.

...starring
barbra streisand

Plain, shrill, but somehow gorgeous, Barbra Streisand was the first of the new breed of actresses raised on the movies to make it big in them. Before a single reel of film had been shot, Twentieth Century–Fox had put down twenty million dollars for her first three pictures— with only one, the first, Funny Girl, *making a real profit. With a wisecracking toughness Streisand redid the history of the movies: Fanny Brice in* Funny Girl, *1968; the Broadway hit in* Hello Dolly, *1969; the MGM–Vincente Minnelli musical in* On a Clear Day You Can See Forever, *1970; the sex comedy in* The Owl and the Pussycat, *1970; the thirties screwball comedy in* What's Up Doc?, *1972; the socially conscious movie in* Up the Sandbox, *1972; the forties tearjerker in* The Way We Were, *1973; the thirties in* Funny Lady, *1975. She also made a rock version of* A Star Is Born, *originally made as a comeback film by Janet Gaynor in the thirties and Judy Garland in the fifties. At one point she had announced she would play Sarah Bernhardt for Ken Russell. Her sense of fashion was equally eclectic, ranging from Cecil Beaton in* On a Clear Day, *to thrift-shop elegant. Perhaps no other movie star had experimented so openly with style or was afforded so many styles to experiment with. In the Twilight of the Goddesses Streisand took on a whole repertory of screen types, playing them not with nostalgia, but as if their power had been real and efficacious—which it was.*

Funny Girl, 1968. Barbra Streisand.

Fanny Brice became Barbra Streisand's big mythic identification, first on Broadway in Funny Girl, *1968, and then in the movie. Ray Aghayan designed the costumes with an eye to Brice's great style and her zany sense of humor.*

1970s

Instant replay

...starring
cher

Pl. 103 [*preceding page*]
Cher costume for *The Sonny and Cher Comedy Hour*, 1973–74, designed by Bob Mackie.

Bob Mackie's witty sense of costume conventions is often at play even in his most serious designs, such as this one in which the pattern of pink, red, and lavender silk—bold, even strident—becomes the excuse for a virtuoso exercise in matching sequins and beads, glossing over and further enlivening the fabric.

[*opposite*]
Photo: Richard Avedon, Condé Nast Publications.

The MGM auction in 1970 was a sign of the irreversible end of the once coherent and complexly interrelated world of the Hollywood studio and its craftsmen. What finally remained was a memory of what the studios had been: the sum total of millions of feet of film that had been made in the sixty years since the American film industry moved west. The idea of Hollywood was a persistent one—perhaps the most readily identifiable form the American imagination had yet assumed. That idea, however, was no longer uniquely American, in terms of either market or content. The style of movies, the tradition of film-making, would continue in relation to the modes of Hollywood—standards that are now clearly seen to reflect a certain moment in history.

The heirs to this tradition, the children of the movies, are much like the generations influenced by romanticism in the last century, acutely aware that they are after the fact, that the Golden Age has passed. As a result, a certain connoisseurship of the movie past has developed—perhaps too narrowly thought of as nostalgia or camp. Perhaps, for this generation, the movies have somewhat the same function as surrealism had for the previous—as an

Women in Love, 1969. Glenda Jackson, right. Photo: MoMA.

Adopting D. H. Lawrence's view of his book Women in Love *as a novel of ideas and of individuals personifying ideas, Ken Russell made everything in his movie version topical. Even the costumes are symbols of the forces that have attracted the characters to each other. Shirley Russell's designs border on caricature, but they are saved by their rightness.*

The Boyfriend, 1971. Twiggy, Christopher Gable. Photo: MoMA.

Ken Russell, the British director, sought in The Boyfriend, *1971, to capture all the conventions of the Hollywood musical and make them into a summary statement about the movies. The chief elements of his parody were the costumes by Shirley Russell, his wife.*

Death in Venice, 1971. Sylvana Mangano.

Luchino Visconti in his overblown, operatic movies, has been fascinated by the death of the old order, a sort of decadent remembrance of things past that Piero Tosi has captured in his costumes. Tosi's method is not so much to reconstruct as to revive the costumes, piecing together fragments of lace and decoration, building a dress around a set of buttons.

intellectual and spiritual analogue. Certainly, the movies were the most universally shared experience, a locus of ideas and images that is readily available on many levels. Film has become for the post-sixties what literature was for the post–World War II generation —a code of conduct.

Even more indicative of the movies' influence is the range of artists who are now consciously involved in various ways in the tradition of the Hollywood film: Woody Allen, the actor-writer, with his fiction, particularly in his sense of the philosophical dimensions of movie style; Randy Newman, the singer-composer, the scion of the movie-music Newmans, with his scenario-like lyrics and songs; Charles Ludlam, the actor-entrepreneur, with his Theatre of the Ridiculous productions, notably *Camille,* in which he impersonates Mlle. Gautier; Bette Midler, the singer, with her plagiarisms of B movies, an anatomy of the trashy "in" look and sound; Paul Morrissey, the film director-producer, with his retreading of the movie genres for Andy Warhol Productions; E. G. Doctorow, with his use of film tricks in *Ragtime;* Michaele Vollbrach with his Hollywood glamour-haunted fashion illustrations; Michael McClure, the poet, with his formulation of a movie metaphysics in *The Beard;* and Ken Russell, the director, with his exploration of the high preciosity of movie conventions.

Movie culture has also produced some remarkable connoisseurs, remarkable not just for their collections of knowledge but for their pursuit of movie style. Although it has not yet been consciously formulated as such, the movie sensibility is involved with a range of esthetic criteria, criteria implicit in the parodistic tone of directors Mel Brooks and Peter Bogdanovich, designers Yves St. Laurent and Zandra Rhodes, singer David Bowie.

The most influential of those connoisseurs are performers themselves—not always, because of the changed nature of Hollywood, movie performers. For some of the connoisseurs, the style is expressed simply by how they dress, as is the case with Bianca Jagger and with Tatum O'Neal, who at eleven already understood the rhetoric of a tux and black tie. For others, like Madeline Kahn and Woody Allen, the connoisseurship is expressed as an extravagant, comic displacement. For a few, it is a renewal of the values of glamour and romance.

Barbra Streisand helped to invent the sixties. When she began singing at the Manhattan nightclub Bon Soir early in the decade, she dressed in her fantasies from the Loew's King Theater on Flatbush Avenue in Brooklyn, where she had worked as an usherette. On her opening night, she wore a four-dollar dress salvaged from a thrift shop, white makeup with kohled eyes, a pouf of curls, and bigger-than-life shoe buckles. On the second night, her mother came to take in her act. "I wore a white lace

Funny Lady, 1975. Barbra Streisand.

Ray Aghayan and Bob Mackie continued the grand tradition of the Hollywood costume, often returning to common sources in the Ziegfeld Follies. *Streisand's costumes for* Funny Lady, *1975, were an instant replay of the grand moments of the twenties and thirties.*

combing jacket from 1890 with junk satin shoes from the twenties," Barbra Streisand said. "My mother was sure I was singing in my nightgown, but to me it was beautiful."

She was certain that her roots were at Loew's King: "I hid my face when I directed people to seats, because I knew I'd be famous one day, and I didn't want the embarrassment of having them say later: 'Oh yeah, the big star. She used to be an usherette at the local theater.'"

Barbra Streisand's look was not beautiful, but she waited until the world came round to her way of seeing things. She was a fan of Sarah Bernhardt and the stars of the thirties, so she collected the mementoes of their world, the artifacts of the universe she had dreamed of in the Loew's King. Because of her tastes, tastes that the rest of America was about to discover as well, Barbra Streisand collected art nouveau and art deco almost before anyone else.

Pls. 104, 105
Barbra Streisand costume for *Funny Lady*, 1975, designed by Ray Aghayan and Bob Mackie. With detail.

An accessory, such as this Barbra Streisand turban for one of the production numbers in Funny Lady, 1975, might take as many hours to construct and finish as the matching dress itself, an evening gown of black marquisette embroidered and fringed with steel gray beads—a seventies extravagance of a kind which was a Hollywood commonplace in the twenties and thirties.

After Broadway, she began to impose her look on the movies. She was one of the few stars since the days of the silent movies to be so much involved in the look of her movies. *Hello Dolly,* 1969, was gorgeous, but *Funny Girl,* 1968, was a digest of all the styles she'd been experimenting with since she was a girl popping quarters in subway photograph stalls—a rehearsal, it turned out, for her sittings with Richard Avedon and Cecil Beaton. Fanny Brice was almost too logical a heroine—a comic and a singer with great taste and a penchant for interior decoration. *On a Clear Day You Can See Forever,* 1970, even had historical fashion flashbacks. *The Way We Were,* 1973, was forties fantasy, the sort of women's movie that went out with hats and gloves. *Funny Lady,* 1975, gave Barbra Streisand her turn in the *Ziegfeld Follies.* With each film, with each television special, Barbra Streisand was dressing up in all the roles she'd been rehearsing in her head since Flatbush.

Her chief collaborators in those fantasies were designers Ray Aghayan and Bob Mackie, also connoisseurs of Hollywood dressup. They were thinking up costumes as well for Liza Minnelli, Ann-Margret, Raquel Welch, Carol Channing, and Diana Ross. Their biggest project was 940 costumes for a Las Vegas revue in 1974, for which they were paid $600,000. Because they work year-round and do not depend on one production or another, their studio is the only full-time costume factory left in Hollywood besides Western Costume Company, the oldtime costume rental agency that can still outfit armies.

Pls. 106, 107
Barbra Streisand costume for *Funny Lady,* 1975, designed by Ray Aghayan and Bob Mackie.

Ray Aghayan and Bob Mackie are unusual among contemporary Hollywood designers because they seldom confine their designs to what is feasible, or even possible. Most producers now press for simplified period costumes, but Aghayan and Mackie still manage to pile on the feathers and glitter.

Working for movies, television, and the stage, Aghayan and Mackie always conceive of their designs in motion. As a result, they give unusual attention to the treatment of the backs of their costumes—a glamorous surprise for the audience.

Pls. 108, 109
Cher costume for *The Sonny and Cher Comedy Hour*, 1973–74, designed by Bob Mackie. With detail.

Bob Mackie's Indian showgirl costume for Cher has close affinities with John Harkrider's design for Glorifying the American Girl, *1929 and* Whoopee, *1930, designs adapted from the Ziegfeld Follies. Like Harkrider, Mackie used sequins and feathers as major components of his look.*

Aghayan and Mackie have a way with rhinestones, sequins, and feathers, but they also have a feeling for detail and the niceties of Hollywood workmanship. As the movie studios fell apart, they picked up some of the pieces, often hiring workmen who had been phased out, thus becoming the repository of what remained of the skills associated with the Hollywood costume. More remarkably, because of Streisand, Carol Burnett, and Cher, they were able to work in the musical genre after it had expired in the studios.

In addition to his continuing collaborations with Aghayan, Mackie in his own right began to do costumes for Cher and then for the *Sonny and Cher Comedy Hour.* He made thirteen to sixteen costumes a week for the *Cher Show,* never leaving the stage during a taping. He and Cher spent about three hours a week together, going over sketches and thinking up ideas. The balance of the time, he used a Cher dummy for fittings. Most of the finished costumes cost about $1,500 each, with some costing as much as $5,000 and others as little as $600.

Bob Mackie, foreground, and Cher, rear, during CBS television rehearsal.

Most of Bob Mackie's designs for the Cher television show were designed and made up during the same week. While complicated work such as beading was farmed out, the bulk of the work, from cutting to fitting, was done in his own workroom.

Pl. 110
Cher costume for *The Sonny and Cher Comedy Hour,* 1973–74, designed by Bob Mackie.

Bob Mackie used for Cher many of the flashy flourishes that distinguished the Follies costumes —particularly the skinny, elongated silhouette and the oversize headdress.

For Cher's first nightclub act, Mackie created designs that were new even to him. "Designing for Cher was an opportunity to do things I'd never done before. I could do bias-beaded dresses. I could do interesting strap combinations, and I could cut down to where I wouldn't cut down on most people. On Cher, low-cut dresses look terrific."

Mackie said he liked to dress Cher in "clear and bright" colors. "She looks terrific in white and terrific in black. She doesn't look good, however, in grays and khakis. With Cher's long hair, I like bare shoulders, even one bared shoulder, or high, simple turtlenecks. A lot of sleeve or fancy high necklines don't go with long hair."

Pl. 111 [*opposite*]
Cher costume for *The Sonny and Cher Comedy Hour*,
1973–74, designed by Bob Mackie.

*Bob Mackie is a complex designer with flairs for
fantasy, glamour, and comedy. With Cher, Mackie
has had the chance to revive many of the movie
classics, including adding sequins to these see-
through lounging pajamas.*

Pl. 112
Barbra Streisand costume for *Funny Lady*, 1975, designed by
Ray Aghayan and Bob Mackie.

*In the past, every Hollywood workroom included
beaders who worked on nothing else. For Funny
Lady, 1975, and other projects for movies and television, Ray Aghayan and Bob Mackie, in spite of
their corps of cutters and seamstresses, farmed their
beading out, since the beaded costume has become
the glamorous exception.*

[above]
Cabaret, 1972. Liza Minnelli.

[left]
The Damned, 1969. Helmut Berger. Photo: MoMA.

[opposite]
The Blue Angel, 1930. Marlene Dietrich.

The waves of nostalgic revival—the twenties, the thirties, the forties, and fifties—were inextricably linked with the mythic images generated by the movies. None of those was more potent than Marlene Dietrich in The Blue Angel, *1930, re-created by Helmut Berger in* The Damned, *1969, and Liza Minnelli in* Cabaret, *1972.*

The team's costumes for both Barbra Streisand and Cher, their work for Las Vegas and, less flamboyantly, Mackie's designs for Carol Burnett, are directly in the tradition of the *Follies*-like costumes that Joseph Urban and John Harkrider contributed to films some fifty years before.

The showgirl costume is fascinating because it joins the western preoccupation with sex and money with the idea of the beautiful woman in which both these obsessions intersect. If the monastic

life is a reflection of the extreme form of Christian value, then the extravagance of the showgirl costume, with its emphasis on conspicuous wealth and the flash of flesh, demonstrates survival of the pagan values. That those values survived the Middle Ages and blossomed again in the Renaissance triumphs and masques is remarkable. But even more remarkable is the persistence of these forms in the film, which gathered up the visual folklore of the theater, the pageant, and the circus.

In that sense, the movies served certain crafts and certain forms of expression long after they had disappeared from the rest of society. As a result, the movies became a reservoir of reaction, conservative in the pure-impure sense of legends and fairytales. That that reservoir reflected the minds of those who made the movies is not surprising. However, because the film industry was economically marginal in its beginnings, more marginal than the theater, movies were more responsive to the popular taste and imagination during their period of dominance than any other medium—more so than newspapers, magazines, or books. To a great extent, television forced the movies into becoming art. But the change also cut down the enormous flow of dollars that had given the Hollywood movies their exuberant vitality and their extravagant character.

For almost half a century the movies were—more than politics, religion, or culture—the experience that Americans had in common. That experience shaped both the movies and the American people.

Costume in the movies was the indelible fingerprint of the psychological moment. Little of those costumes entered directly the visual life or fashions of America. Rather, the Hollywood costume remained a sacrosanct garment whose ritual value was to set the star apart—to confer divinity, to pay homage in terms of wealth and glory. The actual life of the sacred garments is relatively short. They survive by caprices—the caprices of gods who have moved on to apotheosis. Their other life, their real life on film, is now more assured. Until recently, however, the movie imagination and visual presentation have been little studied or thought about except in terms of camera work and direction. Cultural history has only now begun to digest the remnants of Hollywood in response to the pervasive interest and participation in the movies' past. For the first time there is access, at least in part, to the dreams and reflections of our parents and grandparents.

Central among the connoisseurs of the movie past, one of the movie children in actuality, is Liza Minnelli, daughter of Vincente Minnelli and Judy Garland, and wife of Jack Haley, Jr., the producer of *That's Entertainment,* 1974, a film tribute to the MGM years. Her first movie appearance was in *Easter Parade* in 1948. At every step, her career has been played off not only against her mother's

Cabaret, 1972. Liza Minnelli. Photo: MoMA.

What the novel had been for the forties and fifties, the movies became in the sixties—a pervasive and shared culture. Even movies began to refer to other movies, as in Liza Minnelli's visual impersonation of Louise Brooks in Cabaret, 1972. *Louise Brooks was the American who had become a German movie star in the twenties.*

career, but also against the heyday of the studio when her father, with whom she made *A Matter of Time,* and her godmother, Kay Thompson, were both part of the Freed Unit. Thus, her sense of movie tradition, beginning with the copies of costumes from his movies that her father had made for her, is acute. However, her derby and high-cut dance costume for *Cabaret,* 1972, her Louise Brooks hair and green nail polish are more in response to the early Hollywood days than to her father's years at MGM. And certainly that was the basis of her projected collaboration with her father on a filmed life of the modern Marchesa Casati, who wore white makeup and blacked her eyes, who walked the halls of her Venetian palace with a leopard on a leash.

Barbra Streisand remakes *A Star Is Born.* Cher perpetuates the *Ziegfeld Follies* on television. Liza Minnelli plays MGM. The past persists. Romantic, glittering, glamorous Hollywood has lost none of its power.

CAROL BURNETT'S HISTORY OF THE MOVIES —AS DESIGNED BY BOB MACKIE

Photos: *The Carol Burnett Show,* CBS

For almost ten years, Carol Burnett has regularly included spoofs of the movies as a major feature of her weekly hour on CBS-TV. Her comedy writers come up with the ideas, often sparked by the lives and careers of the guest stars, but the success of the feature hangs to a large extent on Bob Mackie, who has a remarkable, satiric eye for the foibles of movie costumes—and it is not a slur on Burnett's wonderful comic talent to say that the hilarious costuming is at the core of the feature's smashing audience response. "Carol loves what I do," Mackie said, "but she doesn't usually get to see what I'm doing until it's done. Then she begins to remember. She's quite a movie fan, too." Mackie's get-ups since 1967 have included:

1 *Sid Caesar and Carol Burnett as silent stars on the rocks*
2 *Gloria Swanson as Charlie Chaplin*
3 *Carol Burnett as Marlene Dietrich in* The Blue Angel
4 *Bernadette Peters in "We're in the Money"*
5 *Carol Burnett as Mae West*
6 *Carol Burnett as Jeanette MacDonald*
7 *Carol Burnett and Harvey Korman in* Camille
8 *Carol Burnett in* The Wizard of Oz
9 *Carol Burnett and Lyle Waggoner in a Maria Montez colossal*
10 *Carol Burnett and Steve Lawrence in "The Murderer Always Rings Twice"*
11, 12, and 13 *Carol Burnett and Vicki Lawrence in "The Doily Sisters," an hour-long parody of* The Dolly Sisters, *with Jill St. John*
14 *Carol Burnett, Mickey Rooney, and John Davidson in a take-off on the MGM musicals*
15 *Carol Burnett, Harvey Korman, and Steve Lawrence in* Sunset Boulevard
16 *Carol Burnett and Sid Caesar in a Roman epic*

*1   Sid Caesar and Carol Burnett
as silent stars on the rocks*

2   Gloria Swanson as Charlie Chaplin

3   Carol Burnett as Marlene Dietrich in The Blue Angel

293

4   Bernadette Peters in "We're in the Money"

6   Carol Burnett as <u>Jeanette MacDonald</u>

5   Carol Burnett as <u>Mae West</u>

7   Carol Burnett and Harvey Korman in Camille

8 *Carol Burnett in* The Wizard of Oz

9 *Carol Burnett and Lyle Waggoner in a Maria Montez colossal*

10 *Carol Burnett and Steve Lawrence in "The Murderer Always Rings Twice"*

11, 12, and 13   Carol Burnett and Vicki Lawrence in "The Doily Sisters," an hour-long parody of The Dolly Sisters, with Jill St. John

14   Carol Burnett, Mickey Rooney, and John Davidson in a take-off on the MGM musicals

15 *Carol Burnett, Harvey Korman, and Steve Lawrence in* Sunset Boulevard

16 *Carol Burnett and Sid Caesar in a Roman epic*

The designers

ADRIAN (Gilbert Adrian Greenburg), 1903–1960, was the principal designer at MGM from the early thirties until 1942—his career at the studio almost spanning those of Greta Garbo, Norma Shearer, and Joan Crawford, three of the stars for whom his designs are most remembered. In 1920 he entered the Parsons School of Fine and Applied Art, studying at both the Manhattan and Paris branches. In Paris, Adrian was particularly drawn to the work of Erté, and to the paintings of Rosa Bonheur, whose feeling for animals was later reflected in his own paintings. Then a Grand Prix Ball costume he made for a friend attracted the attention of Irving Berlin, who asked the eighteen-year-old student to design costumes for his series of *Music Box Revues*. Adrian worked for Berlin in New York from 1921 until 1923, and then designed for the *Greenwich Village Follies* and *George White's Scandals*. Natacha Rambova, the designer and the wife of Rudolph Valentino, signed Adrian to design Valentino's movie costumes. The costumes for *The Hooded Falcon* were made, but the film, a year in preparation, was never completed. In the meantime, he designed the costumes for Mae Murray in *The Merry Widow* and the Valentino costumes for *The Eagle* and *Cobra*. At Paramount, after Valentino's death, Adrian worked with Cecil B. De Mille on such silent productions as *The Sign of the Cross* and *The King of Kings*. Later, in his MGM years, he worked in a wide variety of styles, but he always personally supervised the making of his costumes, often putting in fifteen to eighteen hours a day when a film was in progress. His favorite costume designs, he said, were those for *The Great Ziegfeld, Idiot's Delight,* and *Marie Antoinette*. When he left MGM in 1942 he opened a private dressmaking salon in Beverly Hills, and then became a dress manufacturer—grossing two million dollars a year at the top of his career. Except for *Lovely to Look At,* 1952, an MGM movie with a fashion background, he did not design again for the movies. In 1953 he retired to his Brazilian ranch with his wife Janet Gaynor. He died suddenly in 1960, after having returned to the United States and designed the costumes for the Broadway musical *Camelot*.

Adrian

Ray Aghayan

RAY AGHAYAN, 1927–, is one of the most influential of the younger generation of Hollywood designers. Born in Teheran, the son of a major Iranian couturière, Aghayan began to work for his mother at the age of fourteen. At fifteen he designed the widow's weeds for Queen Fawsia. His parents sent him to Los Angeles to study architecture but he turned to drama instead—in the meantime pursuing his education at Los Angeles High School, Los Angeles City College, UCLA, and the Frank Wiggins Trade School. After school, his first job was with Vincente Minnelli, as an actor. Shortly thereafter he became a director and began to stage operettas, often designing costumes for the productions. From there he joined NBC television as a director and, after six years, was promoted to head designer. His credits include costume designs for over 300 productions. In 1963 he hired Bob Mackie as his assistant on *The Judy Garland Show,* and their partnership began. Aghayan and Mackie worked both individually and as partners. Aghayan has designed alone for Carol Channing and Mackie for Cher. In collaboration, the two have designed for television, movies, the stage, and nightclubs. Among the most important of their designs for the movies are those for Diana Ross in *Lady Sings the Blues* and for Barbra Streisand in *Funny Lady.* Their most ambitious project to date was the designing of 940 costumes, at a fee of $600,000, for the opening of the MGM Grand Hotel in Las Vegas in 1974. Aghayan and Mackie have also produced four ready-to-wear collections a year.

Travis Banton

HANS DREIER, 1885–1966, was the head of the art department at Paramount during the most influential years of the studio's production. He chiefly was responsible for what became known as "the Paramount look"—atmosphere derived from lighting more than expensively constructed scenery. His accomplishments may be seen in the films he made with Lubitsch, Mamoulian, von Sternberg, Raoul Walsh, Stiller, Borzage and others. Born in Bremen, Germany, Dreier received a degree in architecture from the University of Munich. Before the first World War, he was supervising architect for the German government in the Cameroons, West Africa. After 1919 he worked for various concerns connected with UFA-EFA, Paramount's German subsidiary in Berlin. In 1923, he moved to the United States, working at Paramount until his retirement in 1955. The movies he designed include: *Morocco, Shanghai Express, I'm No Angel, Duck Soup, Cleopatra, Design For Living* (considered by many the quintessential art deco movie), *The Scarlet Empress,* and, at the end of his career, *Sunset Boulevard,* a pastiche of his contributions to the look of the movies.

TRAVIS BANTON, 1894–1958, the chief designer at Paramount, was, with Adrian, one of the two most important designers of the golden years of Hollywood moviemaking. Born in Waco, Texas, Banton was taken to New York as a child and attended Columbia University, the Art Students League, and the New York School of Fine and Applied Arts. In World War I he served in the Navy aboard a submarine chaser. He became a designer after the war, working for Lucille, the most famous New York couturière of the period, and for Madame Frances—both houses specializing in careful and expensive dressmaking. In 1924 he was hired by Walter Wanger to design the costumes for Leatrice Joy and the cast of *A Dressmaker of Paris,* one of the many Hollywood fashion pictures. He stayed on, and his elegant, beautifully-worked designs became synonymous with "the Paramount look" in costumes. Banton had a particular affinity for the theatrical etchings and drawings of Marcel Durand, the French artist, whose influence was apparent in his work. His most memorable designs were for Marlene Dietrich and Mae West, and his use of the bias-cut was a trademark of Hollywood fashion design in the thirties. In 1938, when his contract was up at Paramount, he moved on to Twentieth Century-Fox and then subsequently to Universal, where he worked sporadically. Banton left Hollywood, not to return until 1956, when he opened a custom salon with Marusia, the designer with whom he collaborated on the costumes for the stage version of *Auntie Mame.*

Hans Dreier

SIR CECIL BEATON, 1904–, is one of the most ubiquitous figures of twentieth-century fashion—an artist, photographer, memoirist, and stage and costume designer. Educated at Harrow and Cambridge, he was in the vanguard of a generation of English dandies that included Evelyn Waugh and the Duke of Windsor. He first gained fame as a photographer for American *Vogue* in the early thirties, and his photographs have been widely published in slick magazines and shown in galleries and museums. His designs for ballet scenery and costumes include: *Les Pavillons, Apparitions, Les Sirenes, Marguerite et Armand, Swan Lake,* and *Picnic at Tintagel.* His designs for theatrical décor and costumes include: *Lady Windermere's Fan, The Second Mrs. Tanqueray, Quadrille, The Chalk Garden,* and *My Fair Lady;* and for the opera, *Vanessa, Turandot,* and *La Traviata,* all three for the Metropolitan Opera in New York. His films include *Gigi, The Doctor's Dilemma,* and *My Fair Lady.* His exhibition of fashions at the Victoria and Albert Museum in 1971 marked the beginning of an enlarged understanding of fashion as an art form.

ERTÉ (Romain de Tirtoff), 1893–, the designer and illustrator, was closely associated with the evolution of art deco and the modern styles of the twenties and thirties. Born in Russia, he went to Paris at nineteen, joining the studio of Paul Poiret, the revolutionary couturier whose oriental and theatrical designs greatly influenced his work. Erté designed for the Folies-Bergère and other stage extravaganzas, as well as illustrating covers for the twenties *Harper's Bazar.* In 1925, with great publicity, he was brought to Hollywood to design for MGM. He stayed for only a few months, and his contributions to Hollywood design were more in terms of the influence of his taste and his ideas than the films he designed. Among his designs for films were the costumes for the segment of *Ben Hur* completed in America, the costumes for Aileen Pringle in *The Mystic,* and those for King Vidor's *La Bohème,* except for Lillian Gish's costumes. Erté's later work was mainly for the stage, and in the 1960s his designs enjoyed a great revival, along with other artifacts of the twenties and thirties.

Sir Cecil Beaton

Erté

Cedric Gibbons

CEDRIC GIBBONS, 1895–1960, was the art director at MGM during the most powerful of the studio years. Although he often said that the settings he designed were secondary to the actors, they were among the most detailed and elaborate ever created for the movies. Born in Dublin, Ireland, he was educated privately abroad. He was art director for the Thomas A. Edison Studio in Bedford Park, New York, from 1915 to 1917. Then he was the art director for Samuel Goldwyn from 1918 to 1923, working the first year in New York and then moving to Culver City. He was the major art director at MGM from 1924 until his retirement in 1956. His discerning touch played a large part in establishing MGM's reputation for quality. Characteristic of the productions he designed were the silent films *Ben Hur*—notably the famous coliseum race track—and *The Big Parade*, and such sound productions as *A Tale of Two Cities*, *Mutiny on the Bounty*, *Camille* (in fact, all of the Garbo pictures), *Romeo and Juliet*, *The Good Earth* and *The Thin Man*.

HOWARD GREER, 1886–1964, was a major Hollywood figure starting in the twenties, when he was a costume designer, to the early sixties, when he retired as a wholesale dress designer. Born in Nebraska, he began his career in New York as a sketcher for Lucille (Lady Duff-Gordon), the authority in post-Victorian British style. He served in the army in France in World War I, staying on to work with Paris couturiers Paul Poiret and Molyneux. Returning to America in 1923, he was hired by Famous Players–Lasky, the predecessor of Paramount, to design costumes. In 1927 he was the first big-name designer to open his own custom salon in Hollywood. He had a star-packed opening that became a part of Hollywood lore. Greer left Paramount in 1930 to become one of the first West Coast designers to establish his own wholesale business. He designed wedding gowns for Shirley Temple and Gloria Vanderbilt and, at various times, both on- and off-screen, dressed Mary Pickford, Theda Bara, Pola Negri, Gloria Swanson, Joan Crawford, Ginger Rogers, Katharine Hepburn, Irene Dunne, among others. His autobiography, *Designing Male,* was full of anecdotes about early Hollywood, and contained the line, "Madame may be a dreamboat to her friends, but to her dressmaker she can be a fishwife."

Howard Greer, with Sylvia Sidney

JOHN HARKRIDER b.—?, a third generation Texan, brought the look of the *Ziegfeld Follies* to the movies. At the age of fourteen he got his start in New York playing juvenile parts in silent pictures opposite Mary Pickford, Theda Bara, and Rudolph Valentino. He later became one of the key members of Florenz Ziegfeld's production team, staging and designing, including the costumes, many of the *Follies'* most memorable ensembles and spectacles. These productions included: *Rio Rita, Showboat, Whoopee, Three Musketeers, Rosalie, Show Girl, Follies, Simple Simon, Palm Beach Nights, American Girl, Smiles* and *Hot-Cha.* He went to Hollywood in 1929, where he designed for Paramount the *Ziegfeld Follies* sequence for *Glorifying the American Girl,* the only movie that Ziegfeld himself supervised. For Samuel Goldwyn he designed *Whoopee* and *Roman Scandals.* For Metro-Goldwyn-Mayer he was the art director and designer of the spectacles in *The Great Ziegfeld,* including the hit shows sequence that is the classic of all Hollywood production numbers. He also designed productions or sequences of movies for RKO and Universal, notably the elaborate costuming for *My Man Godfrey* and *Top of the Town.* In 1940 he became a talent scout, booking agent, and entrepreneur—well-known as a casting director of models for advertising.

Edith Head, with Claudette Colbert

EDITH HEAD, 1907–, has had the longest and most prolific career of any of the Hollywood designers. Born in California, she received her BA at the University of California and her MA at Stanford. She was particularly interested in the Spanish period of California history and the influence of the Indians. After graduating, she taught Spanish at the Bishop School at La Jolla. While teaching, she studied design at night at the Otis Art Institute and Chouinard Art School, finally giving up teaching to study costume design. She started at Paramount in 1923 as a sketcher for Howard Greer, and later became his assistant. When Banton joined the studio she worked for him, designing the costumes mainly for B movies. She is one of the few Hollywood designers to have such wide experience, having worked on Westerns, monster movies, and science fiction pictures. Certainly, she is the only Hollywood designer to work on both men's and women's costumes. (In fact, when she arrived at Paramount, the two wardrobes were separate.) When Banton left the studio in 1938, Head became the chief designer. Banton, she said, was "the greatest Hollywood designer." Her designs were much more journalistic than his, originating in careful observation of detail and shot through with satire. From the forties on, she showed a remarkable flexibility in working with directors, producers, and stars. By 1976 she had received 8 Oscars for her designs and thirty-three nominations since the award for designers was begun in the late forties. Her major designs include the costumes for *The Lady Eve, The Heiress, All About Eve, Sunset Boulevard, A Place in the Sun, Roman Holiday,* and *To Catch a Thief.* She is now the chief designer at Universal.

Irene

MITCHELL LEISEN, 1898–1972, was perhaps the only Hollywood designer to become a director. Born in Michigan, he studied at the Art Institute of Chicago and later trained to be an architect at Washington University. He worked briefly in the advertising art department of the Chicago *Tribune.* In 1920 he was invited to Hollywood by the dancers Ruth St. Denis and Ted Shawn, friends of his family. There he was introduced to Cecil B. De Mille by Jeannie MacPherson, the director's scenario-writer and assistant. De Mille hired Leisen as a costume designer, and then promoted him to set designer for such films as *The Ten Commandments, The King of Kings, The Sign of the Cross* and *Madam Satan.* About his twelve years with De Mille, Leisen said, "If you learned to think as he thought, you got along all right. To him everything was in neon tubes eight feet high, in capital letters: LOVE, PASSION, REVENGE . . . There were no nuances at all." In 1933, Leisen was launched as a director at Paramount and his stylish touch was evident in movies such as: *Death Takes a Holiday, Lady in the Dark, Kitty,* and *Golden Earrings.*

IRENE (Irene Lentz Gibbons), 1907–1962, became, in 1942, the successor to Adrian as executive designer at MGM. Born in Montana, she came to California as a piano student, going to the University of Southern California, where she became interested in design. After completing the course at the Wolfe School of Design, she opened a shop on the USC campus. There her work was discovered by Dolores Del Rio, who in turn introduced her clothes to other stars. Subsequently, she opened a shop in Hollywood and then started a custom salon at Bullock's Wilshire store. During that time, she planned the wardrobes for many stars and designed costumes for various films at RKO, MGM, United Artists, and Columbia. Her entrée at MGM was Cedric Gibbons, the art director and her husband's brother. Irene was particularly noted for her use of the dressmaker suit and evening gowns with draped or gathered lines. Among the MGM stars she designed for were Greer Garson, Katharine Hepburn, Ginger Rogers, Judy Garland, and Lana Turner. One of her most successful period pictures was *The White Cliffs of Dover,* with the costumes for Irene Dunne ranging from the hobbled skirts of 1914 to the short skirts of the forties. In addition to designing for films, Irene was also the head of Irene, Inc., a dress manufacturing firm.

Mitchell Leisen

Dorothy Jeakins

CHARLES LeMAIRE, 1898–, was wardrobe director at Twentieth Century-Fox from 1943 to 1959, during the most flamboyant years of the Technicolor musical. Born in Chicago, LeMaire started out as a vaudeville actor and song plugger. In New York, after a year on the circuit, he became a shopper for the couturière Antoinette Sherri. His first major commission as a designer came for a costume sequence in the *Ziegfeld Follies* of 1919. Subsequently, from 1919 to 1925, LeMaire designed costumes for a string of Arthur Hammerstein operettas, including *Rosemarie.* Other credits from the twenties include the *George White Scandals* and the *Earl Carroll Vanities.* In addition, he was the head designer at Brooks Costume from 1924 to 1929. He worked free-lance for a while and in 1931 opened his own firm, LeMaire Studio Design, designing, among other projects, a spectacle for John Ringling North's circus. After he was discharged from the army in 1943, LeMaire began his career at Twentieth Century-Fox, specializing in the Betty Grable movies. He was the first of his colleagues to insist that costume designers be included in the Annual Awards of the Academy of Motion Picture Arts and Sciences. After he left the studio in 1959 he again worked as a free-lance designer and in the wholesale dress business.

DOROTHY JEAKINS, 1914–, was one of the most versatile and knowledgeable of the Hollywood costume designers. Born in San Diego, educated at the Otis Institute, she started out coloring-in other artists' work at the Walt Disney Studio. In 1938, she became a costume illustrator for Twentieth Century–Fox. She traveled widely and received a Guggenheim Foundation Grant to study in the Orient. From 1953 to 1963, she was the costume designer for the Los Angeles Civic Light Opera Company. She designed for both the Broadway stage, most notably for Shakespearean productions, and the movies. Her film credits include: the Ingrid Bergman *Joan of Arc, My Cousin Rachel, The Greatest Show on Earth, The Music Man* and *The Sound of Music.* In 1967, she was made the curator of the Textile and Costume Department of the Los Angeles County Museum of Art, the first such museum department on the Pacific Coast.

Charles LeMaire

Orry-Kelly

JEAN LOUIS (Louis Berthault), 1907–, was much more a Hollywood couturier than a Hollywood costume designer, although his years at Columbia produced some of the movies' most glamorous designs. Born in Paris, the son of a provisioner for Atlantic steamships, Louis left art school early to become a sketcher for a small couturier. A taxi accident provided him with a damage settlement sufficient to pay for his passage to America. He arrived in New York in 1935 speaking no English, and was hired by Hattie Carnegie. One of his first designs was purchased by Irene Dunne, thus launching his career. During his 7 years at Carnegie, he designed for the Duchess of Windsor and Gertrude Lawrence, among others, and then was hired by Columbia Pictures. As Columbia's head designer he designed for Rosalind Russell, Judy Holliday, Loretta Young, Joan Bennett, and Joan Fontaine, but his most famous designs were for Rita Hayworth in *Gilda*. After leaving the movies he opened both a custom salon and a wholesale dress business in California.

ORRY-KELLY (Walter Orry Kelly), 1897–1964, the major costume designer at Warner Brothers from 1932 to 1943, was one of the most impressive talents to work in Hollywood. Born in Kiama, Australia, Kelly migrated to New York in 1923 as an actor. Finding roles scarce, he turned to painting murals and then landed a job illustrating titles for Fox silent movies. He also designed costumes for vaudeville shows. Warner Brothers discovered Kelly when his friend, the actor Cary Grant, showed studio executives some sketches by the artist, newly arrived from New York. The studio dropped his first name and added a hyphen to make him sound more exotic as Orry-Kelly. Among his most notable designs at Warners were the costumes for *Jezebel, Dark Victory, The Little Foxes,* and *Casablanca*. Earlier, he had designed the clothes for Katharine Hepburn in *Death Takes a Holiday*. In 1943 he went to Twentieth Century-Fox, then to Universal, and then to MGM. At the time of his death he was at work on an autobiography, *Women I've Undressed*. There, he wrote, "Hell must be filled with beautiful women and no mirrors." Walter Plunkett called him "the greatest of the Hollywood designers."

WALTER PLUNKETT, 1902–, was the one Hollywood designer who specialized in historical costumes. He designed perhaps the most well-known of Hollywood costumes—those for Vivien Leigh in *Gone with the Wind*. Born in Oakland, California, Plunkett started to study pre-law at the University of California in Berkeley, but he was quickly sidetracked by the campus little theater. At graduation, his father gave him a ticket to New York, where he got small parts in two Broadway shows and did a short stint on the New York City vaudeville circuit. When he returned to California he went to Hollywood, hoping to work as an extra. His first call was as a dress extra in the Great Waltz sequence from *The Merry Widow*. He was hired to be part of the crowd dancing around Mae Murray and John Gilbert, and his partner was Irene Lentz, later the designer Irene, with whom he subsequently worked at MGM. A while after, he was hired as a designer at FBO, a studio that specialized in Westerns. FBO grew, changed its name to RKO, and Plunkett found himself the head costume designer of a major studio. He designed for all of the RKO movies, most notably the early Astaire and Rogers musicals. In 1934 he left the studio to design a retail collection in Hollywood, but returned to design the period costumes for Katharine Hepburn in *Mary of Scotland*. He free-lanced for a while and then joined MGM, where he stayed until his retirement in 1966. Some of his most important designs were for *Singin' in the Rain, Raintree County,* and *Seven Brides for Seven Brothers*.

Bob Mackie

BOB MACKIE, 1940–, is perhaps the most brilliant of the costume designers for television, designing for both Cher and Carol Burnett on a regular basis. A graduate of Chouinard Art Institute, Mackie started out working for Jean Louis and then Edith Head. He was working with little theater groups when Ray Aghayan hired him in 1963. For his subsequent career, see the entry on *Aghayan*. Of the two designers, Mackie seems the most immersed in the movies' past, often making in his designs direct allusions to the costumes he admires.

Walter Plunkett

Natacha Rambova. Photo: James Abbe

HELEN ROSE, 1918–, was one of the most admired of the Hollywood designers during the forties and fifties, particularly among the stars she dressed at MGM from 1942 to 1960. Born in Chicago, as a teenager she moved with her family to Los Angeles, where she got a job with a costumer. At sixteen she was hired by Twentieth Century–Fox and was just as quickly fired. She designed for the 1939 San Francisco Ice Follies, an assignment she had for fourteen years. Then, in 1943, she went back to Twentieth Century–Fox, "the era of Gay Nineties musicals," she described it. The next year she was given a contract at MGM, working, in general, with the younger stars who did not get Irene's personal attention. Eventually, her wedding gowns were obligatory for stars such as Elizabeth Taylor, Arlene Dahl, Ann Blyth, Jane Powell, Debbie Reynolds, Pier Angeli, and Grace Kelly. As the result of the popularity of a white chiffon dress she designed for Elizabeth Taylor in *Cat on a Hot Tin Roof,* she was launched into dress manufacturing on her own. Among her most memorable movie designs were those for *The Bad and the Beautiful* and *I'll Cry Tomorrow.*

Helen Rose

NATACHA RAMBOVA (Winifred Shaunessy), 1897–1966, even with a brief film career, was perhaps the most startlingly original of the Hollywood designers. Born in Salt Lake City, the adopted daughter of cosmetics manufacturer Richard Hudnut, she took her Russian name after studying ballet in Europe and then returning to America as the première danseuse of Theodore Kosloff's Imperial Russian Ballet. As a stage designer, she went to Hollywood to work with Alla Nazimova on her production of *Camille,* which also starred Rudolph Valentino, whom she subsequently married in 1923. Her work in the movies was strongly influenced by Léon Bakst, the designer for the Ballet Russe, Aubrey Beardsley, the English illustrator, and Erté. Her extravagance as Valentino's manager turned Valentino and his studio against her, and they were divorced in 1926, six months before his death. Rambova never returned to Hollywood. In quick succession, she studied voice, hoping for a concert career, opened a Manhattan dress shop, was briefly a crime reporter, and had a fling as an actress on Broadway. Her style as a crime reporter was almost as flamboyant as her style as a costume designer: "Through one crowded hour, yesterday," one story began, "I sat in Queens County Court House at what is generally known as the Snyder-Gray murder trial. To me it was a big business conference. I was in the Office of Crime." She then went to Majorca where she lived until the Spanish Civil War in the late thirties. Toward the end of her life she edited the four-volume *Egyptian Religious Texts and Representations* for the Bollingen Foundation, having added Egyptologist to her extraordinary list of accomplishments.

IRENE SHARAFF b.—?, was one of Hollywood's most successful importations from Broadway. Born in Boston, Sharaff started out in the theater as an assistant to Aline Bernstein, the brilliant designer with Eva LeGallienne's Civic Repertory Theatre. She was with the company for three seasons and designed the fanciful costumes after Sir John Tenniel for the LeGallienne production of *Alice in Wonderland*—costumes that anticipated by a decade Sharaff's innovations for the movie musical. From the forties on, while she worked with the Freed Unit on some of the most extravagant of the MGM musicals, Sharaff continued to design prolifically for both the theater and Hollywood. For the stage, among many other productions, she designed costumes for *The King and I* and *The Flower Drum Song.* For the ballet, she designed *Fanfare.* Among her movie designs are the costumes for *The Best Years of Our Lives, A Star Is Born, Can-Can, The King and I, West Side Story, Cleopatra, Hello Dolly, Funny Girl,* and *Justine,* as well as the magnificent suite of costumes for the ballet sequence of *An American in Paris.*

Irene Sharaff

Edward Stevenson

JOSEPH URBAN, 1872–1933, after D. W. Griffith, was the most important early design force in the movies. Born in Vienna, Urban had established a major reputation for himself in Europe before World War I, designing the new town hall in Vienna, the Czar's Bridge in St. Petersburg, and the Austrian Pavilion at the St. Louis Fair of 1904, where his design won the grand prize. He had also designed over fifty stage productions. Urban joined the Ziegfeld production team as a stage designer after a series of his own productions had failed. Much of the image we associate with the Follies was a result of his work. For his theatrical designs, Urban worked with the libretto and score, constructing a carefully detailed model. He used lighting in an unprecedented way, having the sets painted in a pointillage technique to mottle the colors. He would sometimes design the costumes as well for particular numbers, always striving to create a total stage picture. Ziegfeld also used him as an architect, having had him re-model the New Amsterdam Theater in New York for the 1913 *Follies*. During this period Urban met W. R. Hearst, who was courting one of the showgirls, Marion Davies. When Hearst began to produce movies starring his mistress, he got Urban to design them—most notably *When Knighthood Was in Flower, Enchantment,* and *Little Old New York*. Urban's interior designs became one of the status symbols of Hollywood in the twenties and he worked on many of the stars' homes. In 1926, Hearst commissioned Urban to design a new theater in New York for Ziegfeld—a building that turned out to be a landmark of between-wars design. From 1918 until his death Urban designed most of the new productions at the Metropolitan Opera.

EDWARD STEVENSON, 1906–1968, was the head designer at RKO from 1936 until 1951. Born in Pocatello, Idaho, Stevenson moved to Hollywood with his family when he was sixteen. He started out as a sketch artist for Norma Talmadge pictures at United Artists. At nineteen he worked at MGM as an assistant to Erté. When he left Hollywood High School, his graduation delayed by his work in the movies, he went to work as an assistant designer at Fox. After a year he went into the wholesale dress designing business—also for a year—and then became the head designer at First National Studios, where he stayed for two-and-a-half years. By the early thirties he had become personal designer for Joan Bennett, Barbara Stanwyck, Jean Harlow, Virginia Bruce and many others. He again went into studio work, first at Hal Roach studios and then as an assistant to Bernard Newman at RKO Radio, where Newman had taken Walter Plunkett's job. Stevenson's first major recognition came with his designs for Lily Pons in *That Girl from Paris*. In 1936, when Newman resigned, Stevenson took his place, remaining at the studio for fifteen years. Subsequently, he was a designer at Twentieth Century–Fox and then, in 1953, became one of the first movie costume designers to make a successful transition into designing for television, working on three of the Lucille Ball series until his death.

Joseph Urban. Photo: MoMA

Costumes in Plates descriptions and sources

Pl. 1
Ankle-length gown with black sequined bodice and handkerchief skirt of black silk marquisette; butterfly headdress is a reproduction of the original. By permission of Theatre and Music Collection, Museum of the City of New York.

Pl. 2
Negligée of cotton lace re-embroidered in red with silk tassels. By permission of Bob Cahlman, Exits and Entrances.

Pl. 3
Dance dress of pale grey silk marquisette and silver lamé with sleeves bordered in grey fox. This dress, originally worn by Irene Castle, was reproduced for Ginger Rogers. By permission of Costume Institute Collection.

Pl. 4
Evening gown of pale pink pleated chiffon and silver lace with pearl tasselled robe of cream lace and rose-gold lamé. By permission of Theatre and Music Collection, Museum of the City of New York.

Pl. 5
Dress of blue and green plaid linen; beige and brown wool tweed jacket and tam o'shanter of oatmeal wool. Dress and Miss Pickford's curls by permission of Los Angeles County Museum of Natural History.

Pl. 6
Patched and ragged dress of indigo and white cotton. By permission of Mary Pickford.

Pl. 7
Dress and sash of black crepe with collar and cuffs of white lace-trimmed cotton eyelet. By permission of Mary Pickford.

Pl. 8
Gown, in style of 16th century, and coif headdress of golden yellow brocade and almond green silk, embroidered with pearls. By permission of Mary Pickford.

Pl. 9
Gown, in style of 16th century, and coif headdress of golden yellow brocade and almond green silk, embroidered with pearls. By permission of Mary Pickford.

Pl. 10
Gown, in Italian Renaissance style, of apricot silk velvet with gilt sleeves and couched thread embroidery; matching ribbon cap with long veil. By permission of Theatre and Music Collection, Museum of the City of New York.

Pl. 11
Long dressing gown of black silk figured with gold roses, with cerise leaves in border at hem. By permission of Paramount Pictures Corporation.

Dinner dress, with draped scarf panel, of black silk figured with gold in leaf pattern. By permission of Joseph Simms.

Long-trained dressing gown of black silk chiffon figured with silver in Japanese floral patterns, bound in silver ribbon and black satin. By permission of Paramount Pictures Corporation.

Pl. 12
Red velvet toreador's outfit with silver-gilt braid and tassels on the jacket. By permission of Bob Cahlman, Exits and Entrances.

Pl. 13
Long cape of black silk chiffon-velvet reversing to scarlet, embroidered with silver and gold sequins and brilliants in a serpentine design. By permission of The Cecil B. De Mille Trust.

Pl. 14
Detail of Pl. 13

Pl. 15
Dance gown of black silk satin with cut-out halter neckline and one cuff of white chiffon embroidered with rhinestones. By permission of Los Angeles County Museum of Art.

Pl. 16
Dance dress of cream crêpe with cut-out back, completely embroidered with rhinestones. By permission of Los Angeles County Museum of Natural History. Boots by Beth Levine.

Pl. 17
Evening gown of cream satin, with rhinestone embroidered halter neck. By permission of Los Angeles County Museum of Natural History.

Pl. 18
Gown of taupe silk marquisette. By permission of Mr. and Mrs. Thomas S. Hartzog.

Pl. 19
Gown, in style of 16th century, of forest-green silk velvet trimmed with gold braid. By permission of Design Laboratory, Fashion Institute of Technology.

Pl. 20
Evening gown completely embroidered with red bugle beads; matching short cape trimmed with silver beads. By permission of Design Laboratory, Fashion Institute of Technology.

Pl. 21
Afternoon dress, in style of late 19th century, of pale blue-green silk damask and silk marquisette, trimmed with grey-green silk taffeta. By permission of Design Laboratory, Fashion Institute of Technology.

Pl. 22
Walking costume, in style of late 19th century, of brown silk velvet trimmed with silk braid fringe and chinchilla collar; matching fur muff. By permission of Design Laboratory, Fashion Institute of Technology. Chinchilla from the Princeton Process produced for the American Fur Industry by Brothers Christie.

Pl. 23
Long dress and sunbonnet of brown and white checked gingham; white cotton apron. By permission of Mary Pickford.

Pl. 24
Evening dress in style of early 19th century, of ivory satin embroidered with rhinestones and silver beads. By permission of Mr. and Mrs. Thomas S. Hartzog.

Pl. 25
Evening dress, matching wrap coat, and cap, in style of about 1914, of lavender-grey chiffon-velvet embroidered with silver beads, rhinestones, and multicolored stones. A copy. By permission of Barbara Matera. Boots by permission of David Evans.

Pl. 26
Detail of Pl. 30

Pl. 27
Walking costume, in style of mid-19th century, of grey-beige silk-velvet embroidered with silver soutache braid and beads, bordered with deep bands of fox. By permission of Design Laboratory, Fashion Institute of Technology. Furs by Bernard Teitelbaum.

Pl. 28
Evening coat, in style of mid-19th century, of cream silk and gold lamé embroidered with gilt thread and sequins, bordered with mink; dress of matching fabric. By permission of Design Laboratory, Fashion Institute of Technology. Furs by Kosta Furs, Ltd.

Pl. 29
Walking costume, in style of mid-19th century, of black silk velvet trimmed with scrolled ruffles of ivory silk faille and bands of white mink; wide-brimmed hat of matching faille and velvet; reticule; white mink muff. By permission of Design Laboratory, Fashion Institute of Technology. Furs by Ben Kahn.

Pl. 30
Walking costume, in style of mid-19th century, of grey-beige silk velvet embroidered with silver soutache braid and beads, with vest and matching hat trimmed with pale turquoise ostrich plume. By permission of Design Laboratory, Fashion Institute of Technology.

Pl. 31
Empire-waisted gown, trimmed with lace and a rhinestone-and-jet brooch, worn with powder-blue silk crêpe scarf with gilt fleur-de-lys embroidery. By permission of Bob Cahlman, Exits and Entrances.

Pl. 32
Court gown, in style of late 18th century, of ribbed silver lamé, trimmed with scrolls of ruffled black lace and lattices of black velvet ribbon. By permission of Bob Cahlman, Exits and Entrances.

Pl. 33
Court gown, in style of late 18th century, of forest-green silk-velvet trimmed with gold braid, sequins, and ruffles of gold lace and green net. By permission of Mr. and Mrs. Thomas S. Hartzog.

Pl. 34
Court ballgown, in style of late 18th century, of black silk velvet, trimmed with gold tinsel, lace and sequins. By permission of Design Laboratory, Fashion Institute of Technology.

Pl. 35
Dinner dress of taupe silk chiffon-velvet embroidered with gold thread, sequins, and pearls. By permission of Edith Head. Chinchilla from Princeton Process produced for the American Fur Industry by Brothers Christie.

Pl. 36
Evening gown of black silk chiffon-velvet with lower sleeves and front band of salmon faille embroidered with couched gold thread and pearls. By permission of Paramount Pictures Corporation. Royal samink produced for the American Fur Industry by I. Wasserman.

Pl. 37
Evening gown and matching scarf completely embroidered with golden yellow beads, sequins and colored stones in paisley design; fox stole. By permission of Paramount Pictures Corporation. Furs by Bernard Teitelbaum.

Pl. 38
Evening gown and matching scarf completely embroidered with golden yellow beads, sequins, and colored stones in paisley design; fox stole. By permission of Paramount Pictures Corporation. Furs by Bernard Teitelbaum.

Pl. 39
Trained robe of beige panné velvet bordered with red fox; matching fox stole. A copy. By permission of Bill Blass. Furs by Daniela of H. Klein Furs, Inc.

Pl. 40
Evening gown, in style of late 19th century, of cream satin embroidered with rhinestones and trimmed with taffeta ruffles. By permission of Paramount Pictures Corporation.

Pl. 41
Dinner gown, in style of late 19th century, of ivory crepe embroidered in leaf pattern with silver sequins and beads; matching shawl. By permission of Paramount Pictures Corporation.

Pl. 42
Evening gown, in style of late 19th century, of ivory satin embroidered in floral pattern with silver sequins and beads, with cream net ruffles. By permission of Paramount Pictures Corporation.

Pl. 43
Evening gown, in style of late 19th century, of ivory satin embroidered in floral pattern with silver sequins and beads, with cream net ruffles. By permission of Paramount Pictures Corporation.

Pl. 44
Evening dress of white crêpe worn with short cape of vertically worked white fox. By permission of Bob Cahlman, Exits and Entrances.

Pl. 45
Bias-cut evening gown of white chiffon embroidered with lines of silver-gilt sequins. By permission of Edith Head.

Pl. 46
Showgirl's Indian costume of pink jersey trimmed with self fringe and beads; pink feather bonnet. By permission of The Burbank Studios Historical Costume Collection.

Pl. 47
Gown and full train of gold lamé with collar and center band embroidered with clear green stones. By permission of Paramount Pictures Corporation.

Pls. 48, 49
Man's formal dress; white tie and tails of black broadcloth, with accessories. By permission of Fred Astaire.

Pl. 50
Gown of dark green silk taffeta, in Elizabethan style, partly quilted in gilt thread and trimmed with floral brocade. By permission of The Burbank Studios Historical Costume Collection.

Pl. 51
Gown, in style of Italian Renaissance, of black silk velvet and gold lamé trimmed with appliqué and embroidery; wreath of gilt leaves. By permission of Design Laboratory, Fashion Institute of Technology.

Pls. 52, 53
Felt coat with high rolled collar of dark grey with hot pink

leg-o'mutton sleeves, decorated with pink-and-tan striped wired bows; short pink jacket with long tails, lined with appliquéd stripes of orange and white, and bows ending in tassels attached to the sleeves. By permission of Bob Cahlman, Exits and Entrances.

Pl. 54
Princess line afternoon dress, in style of about 1870, of ivory faille with embroidered sleeves and engageantes of black pleated silk. By permission of The Helen Larson Collection.

Pl. 55
Wedding dress, in style of 1830s, of ivory silk satin garlanded with leaves of matching satin and cream lace. By permission of The David O. Selznick Collection.

Pl. 56
Peignoir, in style of early 1870s, of green silk chiffon-velvet and yellow taffeta embroidered with gold thread and sequins. By permission of The David O. Selznick Collection.

Pl. 57
Peignoir, in style of 1870s, of royal blue silk chiffon-velvet bordered in black fox. By permission of The David O. Selznick Collection.

Pl. 58
Child's riding habit, in style of early 1870s, of royal blue chiffon-velvet. By permission of The Helen Larson Collection.

Pl. 59
Visiting dress, in style of late 1860s, of moss green and chartreuse velvet, trimmed with matching silk cord and tassels; matching hat trimmed with coq feathers is a reproduction of the original. By permission of The David O. Selznick Collection.

Pl. 60
Evening gown, in style of 1870s, of wine-red silk chiffon-velvet embroidered with red stones and trimmed with matching ostrich plumes. By permission of The David O. Selznick Collection.

Pl. 61
Long cape of turquoise blue velvet lined in gold lamé and trimmed with peacock feathers and medallions of multicolored stones. By permission of The Cecil B. De Mille Trust.

Pl. 62
Long cape of turquoise-blue velvet lined in gold lamé and trimmed with peacock feathers and medallions of multicolored stones. By permission of The Cecil B. de Mille Trust.

Pl. 63
Gown with long train of silver and black tissue, trimmed with ropes and pendants of pearls. By permission of Paramount Pictures Corporation.

Pl. 64
Showgirl's costume of nude marquisette and cellophane velours with one dolman sleeve trimmed with silver sequined shooting stars. Hennin headdress is a reproduction of the original. By permission of Los Angeles County Museum of Art, gift of David Weisz.

Pl. 65
Peignoir, in style of about 1840s, of white embroidered cotton trimmed with eyelet and azure velvet ribbons. By permission of Joseph Simms.

Pl. 66
Evening gown of off-white chiffon trimmed with satin appliqué in foliate pattern; matching stole bordered with white vulture feathers. By permission of Allen Florio.

Pl. 67
Afternoon gown of cream jersey decorated with gold sequin embroidery. By permission of Design Laboratory, Fashion Institute of Technology.

Pl. 68
Swimming suit outlined in pailletes ranging in color from light to medium blue. By permission of Bob Cahlman, Exits and Entrances.

Pl. 69
Evening costume: bodice, draped skirt, and scarf of white jersey handpainted to simulate marble. By permission of Universal Studios.

Pl. 70
Summer afternoon dress, in style of about 1850's, of silver-grey organdy over peach, trimmed with ivory organdy appliqués of ribbon and birds. By permission of Mr. and Mrs. Thomas S. Hartzog.

Pl. 71
Wedding gown, in style of 1840s, of ivory satin trimmed with self-tassels and rope. By permission of Bob Cahlman, Exits and Entrances.

Pl. 72
Strapless evening dress of black satin. A copy. By permission of Jean Louis.

Pl. 73
Fanciful chorus costumes of a variety of fabrics from cotton to wool flannel, with extravagant trim and appliquéing. By permission of Bob Cahlman, Exits and Entrances.

Pl. 74
Dance costume of golden yellow cotton trimmed with lattices of gold lamé and cream silk tape. By permission of Bob Cahlman, Exits and Entrances.

Dance costume of rust colored silk with petticoat of pink damask trimmed with Irish crochet and gilt thread. By permission of Mr. and Mrs. Thomas S. Hartzog.

Pl. 75
Riding habit, in style of late 18th century, of dark turquoise silk velvet trimmed with soutache braid, with cuffs and jabot of pale pink lace and silk marquisette. By permission of Mr. and Mrs. Thomas S. Hartzog.

Pl. 76
Dance costume, in style of Middle East, formed of chains of silver metal plaques and studded with purple stones. By permission of Los Angeles County Museum of Art.

Pl. 77
Negligée and peignoir, in style of early 19th century, of ivory crinkle chiffon trimmed with lace and ruffles. By permission of Universal Studios.

Pl. 78
Left background, showgirl's costume of teal patterned velvet with net ruffles and satin bustle; left foreground, showgirl's costume with split skirt of topaz satin with matching underpants, trimmed with purple organza ruffles and a ribbon bustle; right foreground, long dress of apple-green cotton, trimmed in darker green; and rear, showgirl's costume in black velvet trimmed with jet beading. By permission of Bob Cahlman, Exits and Entrances.

Pl. 79
Dance costumes of wool tartan with the plaid outlined in bead embroidery; with leggings and shawls of matching plaid. By permission of Bob Cahlman, Exits and Entrances.

Pl. 80
Strapless waltz gown of black velvet embroidered with jet beads and sequins about the hem and train. By permission of Mr. and Mrs. Thomas S. Hartzog.

Pl. 81
Strapless gown of black wool with long floating panels of cream-beige satin. By permission of The Burbank Studios.

Pl. 82
Chorus costumes of black-and-white polka-dotted cotton with large circles of other polka-dotted fabric appliquéd at random. By permission of Bob Cahlman, Exits and Entrances.

Pl. 83
Ballgown of white satin figured with silver in floral patterns, with cowl collar embroidered with pearls and brilliants. By permission of Jane Withers.

Pl. 84
Summer afternoon dress, in style of early 20th century, of cream embroidered net and lace over pale pink, with pale pink taffeta sash and reticule and embroidered net parasol. By permission of Bob Cahlman, Exits and Entrances.

Pl. 85
Ballgown of pale pink shirred silk tulle trimmed with garlands of artificial pink flowers, lace, and silver-pink tinsel ribbon. By permission of Jane Withers.

Pl. 86
Summer afternoon gown, in style of early 20th century, of floral printed lavender cotton and lace. By permission of Mr. and Mrs. Thomas S. Hartzog.

Pl. 87
Daytime dress of gold-embroidered peach velvet with split skirt and enormous sleeves lined in salmon taffeta, worn over a quilted underskirt of beige Trapunto taffeta. By permission of Bob Cahlman, Exits and Entrances.

Pl. 88
Evening gown of white satin with tunic overdress of white chiffon, embroidered with pearls and brilliants. By permission of The Burbank Studios.

Pl. 89
Halter neck dress of white pleated crêpe. A copy. By permission of John Kloss.

Pl. 90
Showgirl costume, in style of 1890s, of lilac satin, trimmed with lilacs, pink satin bows, and pink chiffon draping. By permission of Bob Cahlman, Exits and Entrances.

Pl. 91
Lounging costume: pajamas of cream satin and quilted jacket of deeper cream satin trimmed with apricot ostrich feathers and maribou. By permission of Joseph Simms.

Pl. 92
Dance costume: bolero of dark brown velvet embroidered with jet, and full skirted dress of pleated marquisette in layers of orange, pink, yellow, coral, and white. By permission of Mr. and Mrs. Thomas S. Hartzog.

Pl. 93
Evening gown of nude marquisette completely embroidered with brilliants. By permission of Anna and Lee Strasberg.

Pl. 94
Travelling costume: hooded robe of white wool trimmed with matching tabs and bordered with white goat fur. By permission of The Burbank Studios.

Pl. 95
Wedding gown, in style of late 19th century, of ivory silk satin trimmed with pearls and Irish crochet lace. By permission of California Mart.

Pls. 96, 97
Wedding dress, in the style of late 19th century, of ivory silk satin trimmed with pearls and Irish crochet lace. By permission of California Mart.

Pl. 98
Wedding gown, in medieval style, crocheted of natural and rosy beige wool trimmed with small shells; floating panels of pleated white chiffon embroidered with pumpkin seeds; gilt metal crown. By permission of The Burbank Studios.

Pl. 99
Opera cloak of zebra skin collared in black and white fox; opera cloak of black ribbon lace patterned with flowers of apricot ribbon gauze, with black monkey-fur collar. By permission of The Burbank Studios.

Pls. 100, 101, 102
Afternoon dress of white lace, with black and white ribbon trim; large hat of white straw and black velvet trimmed with flowers, striped ribbon, black and white ostrich plumes; reticule of white embroidered net. By permission of The Burbank Studios.

Pl. 103
Evening gown of pink, red, and lavender printed silk completely embroidered with matching sequins and beads. By permission of Cher.

Pls. 104, 105
Evening costume of black marquisette and sheer silk embroidered with steel grey beads and bead fringe; turban embroidered with matching beads and jet. By permission of Columbia Pictures.

Pl. 106
Detail of Pl. 107

Pl. 107
Evening gown of dark green crêpe embroidered with lines of green-black beads, and decolleté neckline bordered by ruff of coq feathers. By permission of Columbia Pictures.

Pls. 108, 109
Showgirl's Indian costume completely embroidered with red, yellow, white, and pink sequins and beads; feather bonnet headdress. By permission of Cher.

Pl. 110
One-shoulder evening gown, completely embroidered with white beads and black sequins on opposite sides, meeting at centers in flame patterns; elaborate sequined headdress of black pheasant and coq feathers. By permission of Cher.

Pl. 111
Short blouse and long pants of black lace embroidered with purple and black sequins. By permission of Cher.

Pl. 112
Dolman-sleeved evening gown of black jersey and chiffon striped with black, chartreuse, and white sequins and beads; matching turban. By permission of Cher.

Text and pictures sources and acknowledgments

A complete bibliography of the works consulted for this book follows, but the author wishes to acknowledge his special indebtedness to the writers and publishers of the following works which are quoted in each chapter of the text, as well as the individuals who, in interviews, provided both quotations and background material:

The Ruby Slippers, The Trenchcoat, and The Lion's Suit

Surprisingly little research material is available on the production side of the economic development of Hollywood movies. Producer Sol Lesser, who has been in the film business since 1907, corroborated the author's premise that the producer and the studio have been major contributors to the esthetics of the movies. Erté, Walter Plunkett, and Sidney Guillaroff were interviewed. Works quoted are: *Memo From: David O. Selznick,* edited by Rudy Behlmer.

1910's: The Vamp and The Broken Blossom

Lillian Gish and film historian Kevin Brownlow remain the best sources on the earliest days of movie production. In *The Parade's Gone By . . . ,* Brownlow discusses set and costume design briefly. Lillian Gish in *The Movies, Mr. Griffith and Me,* written with Ann Pinchot, provides invaluable material on the production of D. W. Griffith's films. Works quoted are: Linda Arvidson, *When the Movies Were Young;* Mary Pickford, *Sunshine and Shadow;* Irene Castle, *Castles in the Air.* Publications quoted are: *Photoplay,* August, 1925.

1920's: The Flapper and The Waif

Lillian Gish, Carmel Myers, Gloria Swanson, and Allene Talmey were interviewed. Works quoted were: Erté, *Things I Remember;* Jane Ardmore, *The Self-Enchanted, Mae Murray;* Thomas Quinn Curtiss, *Von Stroheim;* Irving Shulman, *Valentino;* Pola Negri, *Memoirs of a Star.*

1930's: The Fatal Woman and The Hoofer

Joan Crawford, Edith Head, Walter Plunkett, and Sidney Guillaroff were interviewed. Works quoted are: Charles Higham, *Hollywood Cameramen;* Salka Viertel, *The Kindness of Strangers;* Bob Thomas, *Thalberg, Life and Legend; Memo From: David O. Selznick,* edited by Rudy Behlmer; Fritiof Billquist, *Garbo;* Joan Crawford, *My Way of Life;* Mae West, *Goodness Had Nothing To Do With It;* Leslie Frewin, *Dietrich;* Charles Higham, *Kate, The Life of Katharine Hepburn;* Whitney Stine, *Mother Goddam,* with a running commentary by Bette Davis.

1940's: The Pinup and The Girl Next Door

Edith Head, Jean Louis, Sheila O'Brien, and Vincente Minnelli were interviewed. Works quoted are: Vincente Minnelli, *I Remember It Well;* Charles Higham, *Ava;* Gerold Frank, *Judy.*

1950's: The Sex Goddess

Edith Head, Jean Louis, Walter Plunkett, and Grace Kelly were interviewed. Works quoted are: Donald Knox, *The Magic Factory, How MGM Made An American in Paris;* Vincente Minnelli, *I Remember It Well.*

1960's: The Twilight of the Goddesses

Works quoted are: Dick Sheppard, *Elizabeth;* Cecil Beaton, *Beaton's Fair Lady.*

1970's: Instant Replay

Ray Aghayan, Bob Mackie, Cher, and Bette Midler were interviewed.

The author expresses his thanks to the following companies, persons, and institutions in connection with the reproduction of movie stills and other publicity photographs in the book: Columbia Broadcasting System; Metro-Goldwyn-Mayer; Paramount; Twentieth Century–Fox; United Artists; Warner Brothers; The Museum of Modern Art, New York (referred to in the illustration legends as MoMA); The Museum of the City of New York; The Academy of Motion Picture Arts and Sciences, Los Angeles; The American Film Institute, Washington, D.C.; Movie Star News, New York. The author is particularly grateful to Mary Corliss of MoMA and Paula Klaw and Howard Mandelbaum of Movie Star News for their aid in the picture research.

Interviews with various members of Motion Picture Costumers Local #705 and the Costume Designers' Guild, as well as its president, Sheila O'Brien, were extremely helpful. The wardrobe departments of both Paramount and Warner Pictures were remarkably generous with their time and experience. The staff of Elizabeth Courtney and Melrose Place provided invaluable information.

The author would also like to extend his gratitude to the staff of *The Carol Burnett Show* and the Hollywood picture department of the Columbia Broadcasting System, notably Keanie Voight.

Stella Blum, Judith McGee, and Gordon Stone of the Costume Institute of the Metropolitan Museum of Art, with Ferle Bramson and Jane Reagan, were of major help in the preparations for photographing the costumes in the book. Peter Bernath assisted the photographer. Jean-Jacques Bloos, Ltd. supplied the flowers for the photographs. Lighting equipment was supplied by Jack R. Glover, lighting consultant and designer, New York City.

Bob Cahlman, Exits and Entrances, New Orleans, generously loaned costumes from his extensive collection to supplement those photographed from the Metropolitan Museum's exhibition.

The author wishes to express his thanks to the following people for the personal assistance they gave in researching this book: William Kosinar, Dale Metcalfe, Angela Loyd, Ronald Harris, Charles Unger, Judith Shea, Francesca Belanger, Reva and William Tooley, and Mary Lou and Delmer Daves.

Acknowledgment is due also to Willard VanDyke, who read the manuscript and contributed many useful comments and suggestions.

Further reading

Agate, James. *Around Cinemas.* Home and Van Thal, London, 1946.

Anger, Kenneth. *Hollywood Babylon.* Straight Arrow Books, San Francisco, California, 1975.

Ardmore, Jane. *The Self-Enchanted, Mae Murray: Image of an Era.* McGraw-Hill, New York, 1959.

Himself (Arliss, George). *George Arliss.* John Murray, London, 1940.

Arnheim, Rudolph. *Film as Art.* Faber & Faber, London, 1958.

Arvidson, Linda (Mrs. D. W. Griffith). *When the Movies Were Young.* Dutton, New York, 1925.

Astor, Mary. *My Story: an Autobiography.* Doubleday, New York, 1959.

Bainbridge, John. *Garbo.* Dell, New York, 1961.

Balazs, Bela. *Theory of the Film.* Dennis Dobson, London, 1952.

Bazin, André. *Qu'est-ce que le cinéma?* (Four volumes), Editions du Cerf, Paris, 1958, 1959, 1961, 1962.

Bazin, André. Essays selected and translated by Hugh Gray. *What Is Cinema?* Volume II, University of California Press, Berkeley, 1972.

Beaton, Cecil. *Cecil Beaton's Fair Lady.* Holt, Rinehart Winston, New York, 1964.

Black, Jonathan. *Streisand.* Leisure Books, New York, 1975.

Bluestone, George. *Novels into Film.* University of California, Berkeley, 1961.

Brownlow, Kevin. *The Parade's Gone By.* Knopf, New York, 1960; Secker & Warburg, London, 1968.

Carr, Larry. *Four Fabulous Faces, The Evolution and Metamorphosis of Garbo, Swanson, Crawford, Dietrich.* Arlington House, New Rochelle, 1970.

Castle, Irene. *Castles in the Air.* As told to Bob and Wanda Duncan. Doubleday, New York, 1958.

Chaplin, Charles. *My Autobiography.* Simon & Schuster, New York, 1964; The Bodley Head, London, 1964.

Chase, Donald. *Filmmaking, the Collaborative Art.* Little, Brown, Boston, 1975.

Cooke, Alistair. *Douglas Fairbanks: The Making of a Screen Character.* Museum of Modern Art (New York) Film Library Series No. 2, 1940.

Crawford, Joan, with Jane Kesner Ardmore. *A Portrait of Joan.* Doubleday, New York, 1962.

Croce, Arlene. *The Fred Astaire & Ginger Rogers Book.* A Sunrise Book, Dutton, New York, 1972.

Crowther, Bosley. *Hollywood Rajah: The Life and Times of Louis B. Mayer.* Holt, Rinehart & Winston, New York, 1960.

Curtiss, Thomas Quinn. *Von Stroheim.* Vintage Books, New York, 1973.

Davies, Marion. Edited by Pamela Pfau & Kenneth S. Marx. *The Times We Had: Life with William Randolph Hearst.* Bobbs-Merrill, Indianapolis/New York, 1975.

Davis, Bette. *The Lonely Life, An Autobiography.* Putnam, New York, 1962.

Debrix, Jean. *Les Fondements de l'art cinématographique.* Editions du Cerf, Paris, 1961.

De Mille, Cecil B. *The Autobiography of Cecil B. De Mille.* Prentice-Hall, Englewood Cliffs, New Jersey, 1959: W. H. Allen, London, 1961.

Eames, John Douglas. *The MGM Story, The Complete History of Fifty Roaring Years.* Crown, New York, 1975.

Edwards, Anne. *Judy Garland.* Pocket Books, New York, 1975.

Eisenstein, S. M. *The Film Sense.* Faber & Faber, London, 1948.

Erté. *Erté:* Things I Remember. Peter Owen, London, 1975.

Essoe, Gabe, and Raymond Lee. *De Mille: The Man and His Pictures.* Castle Books, New York, 1970.

Finler, Joel W. *Stroheim.* University of California, Berkeley, 1968.

Fordin, Hugh. *The World of Entertainment, Hollywood's Greatest Musicals.* Doubleday, Garden City, 1975.

Frank, Gerold. *Judy.* Harper & Row, New York, 1975.

French, Philip. *The Movie Moguls.* Weidenfeld & Nicolson, London, 1969.

Frewin, Leslie. *Dietrich, The Story of a Star.* Stein & Day, New York, 1967.

Gish, Lillian, with Ann Pinchot. *Lillian Gish, The Movies, Mr. Griffith and Me.* Prentice-Hall, Englewood Cliffs, New Jersey, 1969.

Glyn, Elinor. *Romantic Adventure.* Ivor Nicholson & Watson, London, 1930.

Goldwyn, Samuel. *Behind the Screen.* George H. Doran, New York, 1923.

Gordon, Jan, and Lora Gordon. *Star-Dust in Hollywood.* George G. Harrap, London, 1930.

Griffith, Richard. Selection, text and arrangement. *The Talkies. Articles and Illustrations from a Great Fan Magazine 1928–1940.* Dover, New York, 1971.

Griffith, Richard, and Arthur Mayer. *The Movies.* Simon & Schuster, New York, 1957.

Harris, Warren G. *Gable & Lombard.* Warner Paperback Library, New York, 1975.

Haskell, Molly. *From Reverence to Rape, The Treatment of Women in the Movies.* Penguin Books, London, 1974.

Higham, Charles. *Ava.* Delacorte Press, New York, 1974.

Higham, Charles. *Ziegfeld.* Henry Regnery, Chicago, 1972.

Higham, Charles, and Joel Greenburg. *Hollywood in the Forties.* Paperback Library, New York, 1970.

Houston, Penelope. *The Contemporary Cinema.* Penguin Books, London, 1963.

Hudson, Richard M., and Raymond Lee. *Gloria Swanson.* Castle Books, New York, 1970.

Irwin, Will. *The House that Shadows Built.* Doubleday, Doran, Garden City, New York, 1928.

Jacobs, Lewis. *The Rise of the American Film.* Harcourt, Brace, New York, 1953.

Jordan, Rene. *The Greatest Star, The Barbra Streisand Story, an Unauthorized Biography.* Putnam, New York, 1975.

Kael, Pauline. *I Lost It at the Movies.* Little, Brown, Boston, 1965; Cape, London, 1966.

Kahn, Gordon. *Hollywood on Trial.* Boni & Gaer, New York, 1948.

Keim, Jean A. *Le cinéma sonore.* Albin Michel, Paris, 1947.

Knox, Donald. *The Magic Factory, How MGM Made "An American* in Paris." Praeger, New York, 1973.

Kraucauer, Siegfried. *The Nature of Film.* Dennis Dobson, London, 1961.

Lambert, Gavin. *On Cukor.* Capricorn Books, New York, 1973.

Lawton, Richard. *Grand Illusions,* with a text by Hugo Leckey. McGraw-Hill, New York, 1973.

Lawton, Richard. *A World of Movies, 70 Years of Film History,* with captions by Hugo Leckey. Delacorte Press, New York, 1974.

Lee, Raymond. *The Films of Mary Pickford.* A. S. Barnes, New York, 1970.

Leprohon, Pierre. *Histoire du cinéma.* Editions du Cerf, Paris, 1961.

Lindgren, Ernest. *The Art of the Film.* Allen & Unwin, London, revised edition, 1963.

Loos, Anita. *A Girl Like I.* Viking Press, New York, 1966. Hamish Hamilton, London, 1967.

MacCann, Richard Dyer. *Hollywood in Transition.* Houghton-Mifflin, Boston, 1962.

Macgowan, Kenneth. *Behind the Screen.* Delacorte Press, New York, 1965.

Mailer, Norman. *Marilyn, a biography.* Grosset & Dunlap, New York, 1973.

Martin, Marcel. *Le langage cinématographique.* Editions du Cerf, Paris, 1962.

Marx. Samuel. *Mayer and Thalberg, The Make-Believe Saints.* Random House, New York, 1975.

Mast, Gerald. *A Short History of the Movies.* Bobbs-Merrill, New York, 1971.

Mayersberg, Paul, and Allen Lane. *Hollywood: The Haunted House.* Penguin Press, London, 1968.

Menjou, Adolphe. *It Took Nine Tailors.* Stephen Low, Marston, London, 1950.

Minnelli, Vincente, with Hector Arce. *I Remember It Well.* Berkley, New York, 1975.

Morin, Edgar. *The Stars.* John Calder, London, 1960.

Negri, Pola. *Memoirs of a Star.* Doubleday, New York, 1970.

Pellegrino, Vicki. *Cher!* Ballantine Books, New York, 1975.

Pickford, Mary. *Sunshine and Shadow.* Foreword by Cecil B. De Mille. Doubleday, New York, 1955.

Powdermaker, Hortense. *Hollywood the Dream Factory,* Little, Brown, Boston, 1950; Secker & Warburg, London, 1951.

Pudovkin, V. I. *Film Technique and Film Acting.* Translated by Ivor Montague. Vision/Mayflower, London, 1958.

Quigly, Isabel. *Charlie Chaplin: Early Comedies.* Studio Vista London–Dutton Pictureback, New York, 1968.

Quirk, Lawrence J. *The Great Romantic Films.* Citadel Press, Secaucus, New Jersey, 1974.

Ramsaye, Terry. *A Million and One Nights.* Frank Cass, London, 1964.

Reiss, Karel. *The Technique of Film Editing.* Focal Press, London, 1952.

Ringgold, Gene, and DeWitt Bodeen. *The Films of Cecil B. De Mille.* Citadel Press, Secaucus, New Jersey, 1974.

Robinson, David. *Hollywood in the Twenties.* Edited by Peter Cowie. Paperback Library, New York, 1970.

Ross, Lillian, and Helen Ross. *The Player.* Simon & Schuster, New York, 1962.

Rosten, Leo. *Hollywood: The Movie Colony, The Movie Makers.* Harcourt, Brace, New York, 1941.

Sadoul, Georges. *Histoire du cinéma.* Flammarion, Paris, 1962.

Scherman, David E., et al. *Life Goes to the Movies.* Time-Life Books, New York, 1975.

Selznick, David O. *Memo From: David O. Selznick.* Selected and edited by Rudy Behlmer. Avon Books, New York, 1973.

Sennett, Mack, as told to Cameron Shipp. *King of Comedy.* Doubleday, New York, 1954.

Sheppard, Dick. *Elizabeth, The Life and Career of Elizabeth Taylor.* Warner Books, New York, 1975.

Shipman, David. *The Great Movie Stars. The Golden Years.* Bonanza Books, New York, 1970.

Shulman, Irving. *Valentino.* Pocket Books, New York, 1968.

Sklar, Robert. *Movie-Made America, A Social History of American Movies.* Random House, New York, 1975.

Smith, Albert E. *Two Reels and a Crank.* Doubleday, New York, 1952.

Springer, John, and Jack Hamilton. *They Had Faces Then. Superstars, Stars and Starlets of the 1930's.* Citadel Press, Secaucus, New Jersey, 1974.

Stephenson, Ralph. *Animation in the Cinema.* Zwemmer, London, 1967.

Stephenson, Ralph, and Jean R. Debrix. *The Cinema as Art.* Penguin Books, London, 1974.

Stine, Whitney. *Mother Goddam, The Story of the Career of Bette Davis.* With a running commentary by Bette Davis. Hawthorn Books, New York, 1974.

Swindell, Larry. *Screwball, The Life of Carole Lombard.* Morrow, New York, 1975.

Talmey, Allene. *Doug and Mary and a Few Others.* New York, 1927.

Taylor, Elizabeth. *Elizabeth Taylor, An Informal Memoir.* Harper & Row, New York, 1965.

Thomas, Bob. *King Cohn.* Putnam, New York, 1967; Barrie & Rockliff, London, 1967.

Thomas, Bob. *Thalberg, Life and Legend.* Doubleday, New York, 1969.

Tuska, Jon. *The Films of Mae West.* Citadel Press, Secaucus, New Jersey, 1973.

Tyler, Parker. *The Liveliest Art.* Mentor Books, New York, 1959.

Vidor, King. *A Tree Is a Tree.* Harcourt, Brace, New York, 1953.

Viertel, Salka. *The Kindness of Strangers.* Holt, Rinehart & Winston, New York, 1969.

Wagenknecht, Edward. *The Movies in the Age of Innocence.* University of Oklahoma Press, Norman, 1962.

Walker, Alexander. *Stardom, The Hollywood Phenomenon.* Stein & Day, New York, 1970.

Warner, Jack L., with Dean Jennings. *My First Hundred Years in Hollywood,* Random House, New York, 1965.

Weinberg, Herman G. *Josef von Sternberg, A Critical Study.* Dutton, New York, 1967.

West, Mae. *Goodness Had Nothing To Do With It.* MacFadden-Bartell, New York, 1970.

Windeler, Robert. *Sweetheart, The Story of Mary Pickford.* Praeger, New York, 1974.

Wollen, Peter. *Signs and Meanings in the Cinema.* Indiana University Press, Bloomington, 1972.

Zolotow, Maurice. *Marilyn Monroe.* Harcourt, Brace, New York, 1960.

Zukor, Adolph. *The Public Is Never Wrong.* Putnam, New York, 1953.

Index

Page numbers in regular typeface refer to the text or captions. Numbers in italics refer to black-&-white illustrations and numbers in brackets refer to color plates.

315

McConathy, Dale.
　Hollywood costume—glamour! glitter! romance!
　(A Balance House book)
　Bibliography: p.
　Includes indexes.
　1. Costume.　　2. Moving-pictures—History.
I. Vreeland, Diana, joint author.　II. Title.
GT1745.U6M32　　　791.43′02′60973　　　76-12128
ISBN 0-8109-1050-0